IQ AND THE
WEALTH OF NATIONS

IQ AND THE
WEALTH OF NATIONS

RICHARD LYNN AND TATU VANHANEN

Human Evolution, Behavior, and Intelligence
Seymour W. Itzkoff, Series Editor

Westport, Connecticut
London

Library of Congress Cataloging-in-Publication Data

Lynn, Richard.
  IQ and the wealth of nations / Richard Lynn and Tatu Vanhanen.
    p. cm. — (Human evolution, behavior, and intelligence, ISSN 1063-2158)
  Includes bibliographical references and index.
  ISBN 0-275-97510-X (alk. paper)
    1. Intellect—Social aspects. 2. Intellect—Cross-cultural studies. 3. National
  characteristics. 4. Economics—Sociological aspects I. Vanhanen, Tatu. II. Title. III.
  Series.
  BF431.L96 2002
  153.9'09--dc21   2001036306

British Library Cataloguing in Publication Data is available.

Library of Congress Catalog Card Number: 2001036306
ISBN: 0-275-97510-X
ISSN: 1063-2158

First published in 2002

Praeger Publishers, 88 Post Road West, Westport, CT 06881
An imprint of Greenwood Publishing Group, Inc.
www.praeger.com

Printed in the United States of America

The paper used in this book complies with the
Permanent Paper Standard issued by the National
Information Standards Organization (Z39.48-1984).

10 9 8 7 6 5 4 3 2 1

Copyright Acknowledgments
Statistical data from Angus Maddison, *Monitoring the World Economy 1820-1992*(OECD,
1995), appearing in Appendix 2 of this volume, is reprinted by permission of OECD
Publications.

Statistical data from the World Bank's "World Development Report," 1978, 1982, 1987,
1992, 1997, and 1999/2000, appearing in Appendix 2 of this volume, is reprinted by permission of Oxford University Press, Inc.

Contents

Tables

Figures

Acknowledgments

Richard Lynn wishes to express his gratitude to the Pioneer Fund for their support.

Tatu Vanhanen wants to express his gratitude to the Association of Finnish Non-Fiction Writers for a travel grant to London where he collected material for this research project in January of 2000. He also expresses his gratitude to the colleagues that commented on and criticized his papers on the preliminary results of this research project (at the XVIII IPSA World Congress in Québec, August 1–5, 2000) who were in on panel of the Research Committee 12: Biology and Politics, convened by Albert Somit and Steven A. Peterson; at the 16th European Conference on Modern South Asian Studies in Edinburgh, September 6–9, 2000; and on the panel 31: Structural Change and Economic Development in South Asia, convened by Prabir Bhattacharya.

Introduction

In 1817, the English economist Thomas Malthus wrote in a letter to David Ricardo that "the causes of the wealth and poverty of nations is the grandest of all inquiries in Political Economy" (Keynes, 1964, p. 97). This problem had already been discussed in the eighteenth century by Montesquieu and Adam Smith. In 1748, Montesquieu addressed this question in his *De L'Esprit des Lois*, in which he noted that rich nations tend to lie in temperate latitudes and poor nations tend to lie in the tropics and semi-tropics, from which he concluded that climate must be in some way associated with economic development. Adam Smith addressed the same question in 1776 in *The Wealth of Nations*, in which he proposed that the principal factors responsible for economic development were human skills, specialization and division of labor, and the existence of markets. The problem of why some nations are rich and others poor has continued to occupy scholars up to the present day. It has been discussed by economists, sociologists, psychologists, political scientists, and historians. Numerous theories have been advanced proposing the importance of climatic, geographical, psychological, social, cultural, political, and institutional factors, but no general consensus has emerged.

In this book, we advance the hypothesis that the intelligence of the populations has been a major factor responsible for the national differences in economic growth and for the gap in per capita income between rich and poor nations. As far as we are aware, this theory has never been previously proposed (see, for example, the World Development Report, 2000–2001). Hitherto, theories attempting to explain the economic gap between rich and poor countries have assumed that the people of all nations have the same mental abilities. Generally, this assumption has been implicit and the possibility that there might be differences in intelligence between the peoples of different nations has been ignored. However, some of those who have considered this issue have explicitly rejected the possibility that the peoples of different nations might differ in intelligence. For instance, Kofi Annan, the United Nations Secretary General, asserted in April 2000 that intelligence "is one commodity equally distributed among the world's people" (Hoyos and Littlejohn, 2000). Ayittey (1999) discusses the problem that economic development has been slow in sub-Saharan Africa and explicitly rejects the possibility that low intelligence might be a factor. He writes that the "notion that Africans are intellectually inferior is offensive mythology" (pp. 2–3). Kamarck (1976) explicitly rejects the possibility that "the lag of the less developed countries is a consequence of something inferior in the character, ability, or personality of the peoples of the Third World, an inferiority that brings about their low productivity" (p. xiii).

We contend that these views are mistaken and seek to show that there are large differences in intelligence between different nations, that these differences are systematically related to economic growth, and that this relationship is causal. This book is organized into ten chapters and it may be useful to summarize how the arguments are presented. Chapter 1, "Why Are Some Countries So Rich and Others So Poor?" focuses on the theoretical background of this study and reviews the major theories that have been advanced to explain the existence of the variations in the wealth and poverty of nations. This review is intended to help readers to see what is new in this study and how the explanation proposed in this book differs from previous explanations.

In Chapter 2, "Intelligence: An Introduction to the Concept," we introduce the concept of intelligence. We also describe the intelligence quotient (IQ) and how it is measured, and we outline the economic and social correlates of intelligence. We take a first look at national differences in intelligence. The evidence for the genetic basis of intelligence and its heritability is also summarized.

Chapter 3, "Intelligence and Earnings," shows that intelligence is a determinant of earnings among individuals within societies. It also shows that intelligence is a determinant of trainability and job proficiency, and that there are different cognitive capacities at different levels of intelligence, which explains why only those at higher levels of intelligence are able to do complex tasks.

Chapter 4, "Intelligence and Further Economic and Social Phenomena," reviews further evidence of the connection between intelligence and economic and social phenomena. It shows that intelligence is a significant determinant of educational achievement, socioeconomic status, and lifetime achievement, and that low intelligence is an important component of the syndrome of social pathology known as the underclass.

Chapter 5, "The Sociology of Intelligence, Earnings, and Social Competence," focuses on the sociology of intelligence at the level of subpopulations in nations. It shows that the intelligence of various national subpopulations is related to a variety of economic, social, and cultural phenomena including average earnings, employment, educational attainment, literacy, and intellectual achievement. The populations of cities, districts within cities, regions, and ethnic groups have been used as population units in these studies.

Chapter 6, "Data on Variables and Methods of Analysis," extends the analysis from the levels of individuals and sub-populations to nations and introduces, defines, and describes the independent and dependent variables and data, which tests the hypothesis that a country's economic success depends to a significant extent on the average intelligence of the population. First, it explains how national IQs for 81 countries have been calculated on the basis of the available results of intelligence tests. The reliability and validity of the measures is evaluated. Then, the method for estimating national IQs for all the nations of the world is explained. Finally, the major measures of per capita income are introduced and described. These constitute the dependent variables of the empirical analysis.

The empirical analysis starts in Chapter 7, "National IQs and Economic Development in 81 Nations," in which we examine the relation between national intelligence and economic development in the group of 81 countries for which we have direct evidence of national IQs. We find that the national IQs are substantially correlated with measures of per capita income and economic growth. The correlation analyses, which measure the strength of the relationship, cover the period of 1820 to 1998. Regression analysis is then used to show which countries deviate most from the general relationship between national IQs and economic development. These deviations must be caused by factors other than intelligence, and in this chapter we consider what the factors responsible for these deviations are.

In Chapter 8, "National IQs and Economic Development in 185 Countries," the empirical analysis is extended to the world total of 185 countries, which includes the 81 countries analyzed in Chapter 7 and the other 104 countries for which national IQs were estimated in Chapter 6. The hypothesis is tested by correlating national IQs with five alternative measures of per capita income and economic growth rates during the period of 1820 to 1998. Regression analyses complement the results of correlation analyses and have been carried out separately for the years 1900, 1930, 1960, and 1998 in order to see to what extent the relationship between national IQs and per capita income has remained stable or changed at the level of individual countries. The additional factors responsible for economic development in the most deviant countries also are discussed. Our hypothesis does not presuppose the existence of a complete correspondence between mean national IQs and per capita income. We accept that in some countries per capita incomes are much higher than expected on the basis of the intelligence level of the population and that in some other countries it is much lower. Many factors, including differences in economic and political systems and in natural resources, may affect economic growth and development. Finally, the joint impact of economic freedom and democracy in addition to intelligence is measured by multiple correlations.

In Chapter 9, "Intelligence and Markets as the Determinants of Economic Development," we discuss the results of the analyses and try to explain why intelligence and market economies are positively related to economic development and growth. We begin with a further discussion of the role of national intelligence in the rates of economic growth and development. Then, we turn to a consideration of the effects of climate and discuss economic convergence theory, which holds that national incomes should converge over time, and we point out that the convergence theory only works for countries whose populations have high IQs. This argument is supported by an analysis of world regions, in which the regional means of national IQs and per capita income and economic growth rates are compared and correlated. The chapter concludes with discussions of the contributions of intelligence and markets in the economic development of India, China, Japan, and the nations of sub-Saharan Africa.

In Chapter 10, "The Future of the Wealth of Nations," we discuss various means for attempting to reduce the gap between rich and poor countries. First, we consider what means might be used to increase the rate of economic growth in poor countries by raising the intelligence level of their populations. Attention is paid to the nutrition of pregnant women and of children, to the harmful effects of malnutrition in underdeveloped nations, and to the effects of health, education, and dysgenic fertility. We come to the conclusion that while some of these measures might increase the intelligence levels of the populations of poor countries, they are unlikely to succeed in raising intelligence up to the levels of the rich countries. National differences in IQs are therefore likely to persist and will maintain the gap between rich and poor countries in the future. Finally, we discuss the problem of living in a world with persistent and probably increasing inequalities between nations and the need for a new international moral code based on the recognition of the existence of evolved diversity of human populations.

The text is complemented by two appendices. Appendix 1, "The Calculation of National Intelligence Levels," reports and documents data on available intelligence tests in 81 countries and explains how the national intelligence levels were calculated on the basis of these data. Appendix 2, "Data on Per Capita Income and Economic Growth in 185 Countries," provides data on the measures of per capita income and economic growth rates that is used in this study.

1

Why Are Some Countries So Rich and Others So Poor?

In this chapter the major theories that have attempted to explain the causes of the inequalities in income and wealth between nations are reviewed. These comprise the following theories. First is the climate theory, which was originally advanced by Charles de Montesquieu, who proposed that temperate climates are more favorable to economic development than tropical and semi-tropical climates. Second are the geographical theories, which attempt to explain economic development in terms of geographical location. Third are the modernization theories, which regard economic development as a process of modernization through which all nations will eventually pass. Fourth are the psychological theories of M. Weber and D. C. McClelland, which propose that the psychological values and motivations of a population are the principal factors responsible for national differences in incomes and wealth. Fifth are the theories that posit "culture" as the crucial factor. Sixth are the dependency theories, which claim that the poverty of the Third World is caused by the international capitalist system. Seventh is the neoclassical or market economy theory, which holds that free markets are the key to economic development. And finally there are the multi-causal theories, which posit that a number of these and other factors are involved.

CLIMATE THEORIES

It has long been recognized that climate is related to economic development. This was observed in the mid-eighteenth century by Montesquieu (1748) who noted that affluent nations typically lie in temperate regions and poor nations typically lie in the tropics or sub-tropics. In addition, he suggested that the climate of temperate regions is more favorable for economic development. In the twentieth century, many economists and social scientists have made the same observation and drawn the same conclusion. For instance, J. K. Galbraith (1951) has written that "If one marks off a belt a couple of thousand miles in width encircling the earth at the equator one finds within it no developing countries" (p. 693). P. Streeten (1971) has written that "Perhaps the most striking fact is that most underdeveloped countries lie in the tropical and semi-tropical zones between the Tropic of Cancer and the Tropic of Capricorn" (p. 78). In his book *The Tropics and Economic Development*, A. M. Kamarck (1976) argued that tropical environments are disadvantageous for economic development because a hot and humid climate reduces human work efficiency, tends to impair the land's productivity, and provides a favorable environment for debilitating or lethal tropical diseases. He also contends that these adverse climatic conditions provide some explanation for the poverty of tropical countries and in particular that of sub-Saharan Africa. Furthermore, he believes that research may help to overcome the obstacles to economic development posed by the tropics, and "when eventually the tropical constraints are mastered, the same characteristics that now hinder the Tropics may then give them advantages over the Temperate Zones" (p. xiii, 90; Streeten, 1976).

More recently, the climate theory of economic development has again been stated by D. S. Landes (1998). In his book *The Wealth and Poverty of Nations,* he writes that "On a map of the world in terms of product or income per head, the rich countries lie in the temperate zones, particularly in the northern hemisphere; the poor countries, in the tropics and semi-tropics" (p. 5). He attributes this difference to three factors—the enervating effects of hot climates, the prevalence of diseases, especially malaria, bilharzias, and lymphatic filariasis, which spread more quickly in hot climates, and the irregular supplies of water caused by dry and wet seasons. However, although there is undoubtedly a broad association between temperate regions and affluence and tropical and semi-tropical regions and poverty, there are some notable exceptions such as rich Singapore and poor South Africa that call into question the conclusion that there is a direct causal connection.

GEOGRAPHY

A recent exponent of geography as the major determinant of economic development is J. Diamond (1998). In his book *Guns, Germs and Steel,* Diamond begins by describing how when he was working in New Guinea a tribesman named Yali asked him, "Why is it that you white people developed so much cargo and brought it to New Guinea, but we black people had little cargo of our own?" (p. 14). "Cargo" in the lingo of New Guinea means manufactured artifacts. Diamond says that he wrote his book to answer this question. The problem he seeks to explain is why over the last 10,000 years or so civilizations developed in Europe and Asia (Eurasia) and, to some degree, in the Americas, but not in sub-Saharan Africa or Australia. He rejects biological explanations based on the assumption that there are significant differences in the innate abilities of the peoples of these different regions. He asserts that there are no significant differences in average mental abilities of peoples, although he says that his subjective impression is that New Guineans are on the average smarter than Eurasians (pp. 19–20, 408).

Diamond does not propose that climatic factors have played any part in the different levels of civilization attained by different peoples. He argues that four geographical factors have been responsible. The first consists of the continental differences in the wild plant and animal species that are available as starting materials for domestication. He asserts that nearly all useful plants that could be grown as crops, particularly wheat and barley, and also nearly all potentially domesticable animals (cow, sheep, goats, pigs, and horses) happened to be in Eurasia. All these animals were easy to domesticate. They could be used to provide agricultural surpluses, which made it possible to maintain an increasing population, and for the support of towns and complex social systems, which supported scholars who developed writing, arithmetic, and other advances of the early civilizations. The second factor favoring Eurasia has been "its east-west major axis and its relatively modest ecological and geographical barriers. . . . Diffusion was slower in Africa and especially in the Americas, because of those continents' north-south major axes and geographic and ecological barriers" (p. 407). The inventions that lead to technological, economic, and cultural growth, according to Diamond, are able to spread more rapidly along an east-west axis than along a north-south axis. So once again, Eurasia was lucky because it lies on an east-west axis.

The third geographic factor has been the ease of the diffusion of inventions between continents. Intercontinental diffusion was easiest between Europe and Asia. Diffusion was difficult between Eurasia and sub-Saharan Africa because of the barrier of the Sahara desert, and was impossible from Eurasia to the Americas, Australia, and the Pacific islands because of the oceans. The fourth factor involves continental differences in area and consequently in population size. These factors were again most favorable in Eurasia, whose large area and developed food production were able to support the largest populations. Diamond argues that a larger area and population means more potential inventors, more inventions and innovations, and more competing societies (pp. 406–408). His final answer to Yali's question is, "the striking differences between the long-term histories of peoples of the different continents have been due not to innate differences in the peoples themselves but to differences in their environments" (p. 405).

Diamond's theory has a number of obvious weaknesses. First, in sub-Saharan Africa there are wild plants that could have been domesticated such as sorghum, millet, yams and rice, and wild animals that could have been domesticated such as guinea fowl, zebras, giraffes, buffalo, and wildebeests. The reason these animals were not domesticated is because people did not put the effort into domesticating them. Second, the assertion that inventions could not spread in sub-Saharan Africa or in the Americas because of their north-south axes but could easily spread in Eurasia throughout along the east-west axis is obviously wrong. There was no easy transmission of inventions between China and the rest of Eurasia because of the barriers of the Himalayas and the Gobi desert. These barriers cut off these two regions from one another as effectively as the Atlantic ocean cut off Eurasia from the Americas, and it is the reason why civilizations developed independently in them. For instance, as Diamond himself acknowledges, writing was invented independently somewhere around 3,000 to 1,000 B.C. in Sumeria (contemporary Iraq) and in China. Later, printing was invented in China in the eighth century A.D., but it did not pass by diffusion throughout the rest of Eurasia. It was invented independently by Johannes Gutenberg in Germany in the fifteenth century.

Third, Diamond's theory encounters further difficulties because of the three civilizations that arose in Central and South America. The Aztecs and Maya located in contemporary Mexico developed on an east-west axis of about 500 miles, and the Incas of Peru developed on an east-west axis of about three hundred miles. In sub-Saharan Africa, there is an east-west axis of approximately 4,000 miles from Senegal and Guinea to Ethiopia and Somalia, yet no indigenous civilizations comparable to those of the Americas or Eurasia developed along this extensive east-west axis. Finally, Diamond's theory cannot explain the slow economic growth of much of the economically developing world in the twentieth century, during which plants and animals domesticated in Europe and Asia were introduced, and when advanced technologies became available that people in the developing world could copy. Nor does Diamond's theory explain why some peoples, such as East Asians and Europeans in Australia and North America, adopted these technologies while others, such as those in Africa, south Asia, the Pacific islands and much of Latin America failed to do so.

Diamond was awarded the Rhone-Poulenc Science Book Prize, and his book carries endorsements by several eminent scholars including Paul Ehrlich who wrote that Diamond "provides a convincing explanation for the differing developments of human societies on different continents." We take a different view and suggest that a few minutes' glance at an atlas is sufficient to show the obvious flaws in Diamond's theories.

MODERNIZATION THEORIES

Research on economic underdevelopment accelerated after the World War II when former colonies in Asia and Africa began to win independence and when it became increasingly obvious that they remained much less developed and poorer than the industrialized European and North American countries. Many social scientists believed that the poverty of underdeveloped countries was only short-term and that ultimately all countries would become rich. These theories envisioned economic development as a historical process, which occurred first in Europe and the United States, that would be followed in the remainder of the world through the process of "modernization."

In the 1950s, the most influential modernization theorists were W. A. Lewis and W. W. Rostow. According to the Lewis model, the underdeveloped economy consists of two sectors—a traditional rural subsistence sector characterized by zero marginal labor productivity and a high-productivity, modern urban industrial sector. Economic development involves the transfer of workers from subsistence agriculture to the modern urban sector. Urban wages should be at least 30 percent higher than the average rural income to induce workers to migrate from their home areas. The speed of modernization is determined by the rate of industrial investment and capital accumulation in the modern sector. M. P. Todaro (2000, p. 84) says that Lewis's "two-sector model became the general theory of the development process in surplus-labor Third World nations during most of the 1960s and the early 1970s" (see Lewis, 1954 and 1955; Fei and Ranis, 1964; Nafziger, 1997, pp. 99–103; Martinussen, 1999, pp. 61–63).

A more elaborate theory of modernization was advanced by W. W. Rostow (1961). Like Lewis, he distinguished between the traditional agricultural sector and the modern capitalist sector. He formulated a theory of five stages of economic development. According to this theory, it is possible "to identify all societies, in their economic dimensions, as lying within one of five categories: the traditional society, the preconditions for take-off, the take-off, the drive to maturity, and the age of high mass consumption" (p. 4). Traditional societies are characterized by pre-Newtonian science and technology, and by pre-Newtonian attitudes towards the physical world. They are also largely agricultural societies with a hierarchical social structure. The second stage of growth occurs in societies that are in the process of transition. The preconditions for take-off are developed either endogenously or as a consequence of external intrusion by more advanced societies. The emergence of an effective centralized national state is an important feature of these societies. The third stage of "take-off" occurs when impediments and resistance to economic growth are overcome. The proximate stimulus for take-off has usually been technological. New techniques are adopted in agriculture and industry. Rostow assumes that a long interval of a sustained and fluctuating progress follows after the take-off and leads to the fourth stage of maturity. This is the stage in which "an economy demonstrates the capacity to move beyond the original industries which powered the take-off and to absorb and to apply efficiently over a very wide range of its resources—if not the whole range— the most advanced fruits of (then) modern technology" (p. 4). The fifth and final stage of economic growth is the age of "high mass-consumption" in which economic affluence comes to be enjoyed by a majority of the population. The United States entered this stage in the 1920s and, more fully, in 1946–56. Western Europe and Japan entered this final stage in the 1950s (Rostow, 1961, pp. 4–11; see also Rostow 1971, 1998, and 2000). Rostow envisioned that all countries would go through these five stages of growth and would eventually reach the last stage of high mass-consumption. The gap between rich and poor countries is expected to disappear as the developing countries progress into the later stages of growth. Rostow assumes that all populations have similar potential for economic development because there are no significant differences in the mental abilities of the different populations. He envisioned a world in which "all can share the choices open in the stage of high mass-consumption and beyond . . . " and "billions of human beings must live in the world, if we preserve it, over the century or so until the age of high mass-consumption becomes universal" (Rostow 1961, pp. 166–67).

Modernization theories emphasize the necessity of structural changes. Modernization presupposes the shift from agricultural to industrial production, higher standards of living, the accumulation of physical and human capital, increasing education and literacy, greater consumer demands, the growth of cities and urban industries, and the decline of family size. Modernization is seen as a process that includes social, psychological, economic, cultural, and political changes. The process of modernization is assumed to lead from the poverty of traditional agricultural subsistence societies to economic growth and modern affluence in all societies (see also Nafziger, 1997, pp. 91–93; Gardner, 1998, pp. 130–31; Martinussen, 1999, pp. 63–65; Roberts and Hite, 2000, p. 9; Todaro, 2000, pp. 79–90).

PSYCHOLOGICAL THEORIES

Psychological theories of economic development propose that psychological beliefs, values, and attitudes are a major factor responsible for economic growth. The two leading exponents of this approach have been Max Weber and D. C. McClelland. Weber argued in his book *The Protestant Ethic and the Spirit of Capitalism* (1904) that the emergence of Protestantism in Northern Europe in the sixteenth century was responsible for the rapid economic development of Protestant countries, particularly the Netherlands and England. Weber contended that the predominant values of Catholicism were the virtues of poverty and withdrawal from the world into the life of prayer in the monastery and that these virtues were unfriendly to the development of capitalism. On some issues, Catholicism was actively hostile to capitalism, particularly in its failure to understand the importance of capital for capitalist enterprises and its condemnation of the lending of money with interest as the sin of usury. In contrast to these Catholic beliefs, Protestantism stressed

the religious and moral value of worldly work and maintained that the accumulation of wealth as a fruit of labor in a calling was a sign of God's bless-
ing. Weber cited Luther's teaching that we should value "the fulfilment of
duty in worldly affairs as the highest form which the moral activity of the
individual could assume" and that the "only way of living acceptably to God
was not to surpass worldly morality in monastic asceticism, but solely
through the fulfilment of the obligations imposed upon the individual by his
position in the world. That was his calling" (p. 80). Thus, Protestantism gave
moral and religious sanction to organized worldly labor and acquisition of
wealth. Calvinism taught that "God helps those who help themselves"
(p. 115) and that it was religiously virtuous to dedicate one's life to contin-
ual profitable work. Protestantism also taught that waste of time is "the first
and in principle the deadliest of sins" (p. 157). A Puritan, Richard Baxter,
preached that even "the wealthy shall not eat without working, for even
though they do not need to labour to support their own needs, there is God's
commandment which they, like the poor, must obey" (pp. 159–60). Weber
concluded: "the religious valuation of restless, continuous, systematic work
in a worldly calling, as the highest means to asceticism, and at the same time
the surest and most evident proof of rebirth and genuine faith, must have
been the most powerful conceivable lever for the expansion of that attitude
toward life which we have here called the spirit of capitalism." He continued
that when "the limitation of consumption is combined with this release of
acquisitive activity, the inevitable practical result is obvious: accumulation of
capital through ascetic compulsion to save" (p. 172).

Weber's theory has won widespread acceptance as a partial explanation for
the economic development of the West from the sixteenth century onward.
The theory has been regarded as persuasive for two main reasons. First, the
countries of Protestant Northern Europe, particularly the Netherlands,
England, northern Germany, and Switzerland, began to pull ahead of the
Catholic countries of southern Europe, particularly Italy, Spain, and
Portugal. Only Catholic France and Belgium remained as partial exceptions
to the generally more rapid economic development of the Protestant nations.
This pattern was repeated in the Americas, where the mainly Protestant
United States and Canada showed greater economic progress than Catholic
South and Central America. Second, in Catholic countries, the most enter-
prising tended to be the Protestants. In France, many of these were
Huguenots, of whom the historian H. A. L. Fisher (1936) wrote that "in
commerce and maritime adventure, as well as in all branches of industry
such as the weaving of silk, which in that age demanded a high measure of
technical skill, these Protestant Frenchmen out-distanced their Catholic fellow citizens" (p. 442). Many of the rulers of the Catholic countries relied on
Protestant bankers to finance them. In seventeenth-century France, Cardinal
Richelieu borrowed from the Calvinist bankers, the Rambouillets and the
Tallemants; in Austria, the Catholic Habsburgs were financed by the

Calvinist de Witte bankers of Antwerp; and in Spain, Philip IV was financed by Francois Grenus, a Calvinist based in Berne. The historian H. Trevor Roper (1967) has reviewed this evidence and concluded that "there is a solid . . . core of truth in Weber's thesis" (p. 35). The limitation of Weber's theory is that it is local to Europe and cannot explain, for instance, the rapid economic development of the Pacific Rim in the second half of the twentieth century.

In the second major theory of psychological values as a significant factor in national differences in economic growth, D. C. McClelland (1963) has formulated the concept of "achievement motivation." This is essentially the motivation to achieve excellence, particularly by success in entrepreneurship. He contends that the strength of this motive has varied among different societies at different historical periods, which has contributed to their economic growth and decline. He devised methods for measuring the strength of the motive and claimed to show that this motive was a major determinant of economic growth. However, it has been shown that during the second half of the twentieth century, the strength of achievement motivation has not predicted subsequent economic growth (Finison, 1986) and the validity of the theory remains in doubt.

CULTURE

A number of social scientists have concluded that "culture" is a significant or even a decisive factor in economic growth. "Culture" is defined as the values, attitudes, and motivations of a population. For instance, L. E. Harrison (1985) writes that "the creative capacity of human beings is at the heart of the development process" (p. 232) and that underdevelopment is, in fact, a state of mind. Harrison's thesis (2000) is that differences in cultural values and attitudes provide the best explanation for the gap between rich and poor countries. According to his interpretation, "the failure of governments and development institutions to take into account the power of culture to thwart or facilitate progress" is a principal reason for the shortfall of human progress since World War II in many parts of the world (p. xxxii). S. P. Huntington's argument (2000) is the same. He asks, how to explain the extraordinary difference in development between Ghana and South Korea, and he answers, "Undoubtedly, many factors played a role, but it seemed to me that culture had to be a large part of the explanation. South Koreans valued thrift, investment, hard work, education, organization, and discipline. Ghanaians had different values" (p. xiii).

A. Inkeles and D. H. Smith (1974) contend that modern attitudes produce modern behaviors, which are essential to development. They "are convinced that mental barriers and psychic factors are key obstacles to more effective economic and social development in many countries" (p. 214). To achieve economic development, the traditional man of poor countries needs to be transformed into the modern man. Herman Kahn (1979) has argued that much of the rapid economic growth of Japan, South Korea, and Taiwan can be attributed to their Confucian cultures, which "may in many ways be superior to the West in the pursuit of industrialization, affluence, and modernization" (p. 219).

Another economist who has argued that psychological characteristics are important factors in economic growth and development is P. T. Bauer (1981). He writes that some "people are gifted, hard-working, ambitious and enterprising, or had far-sighted parents, and are therefore more likely to become well-off . . . People differ in economic aptitudes as they do in artistic, intellectual, musical and athletic abilities" (p. 8, 10) and "economic differences are largely the result of people's capacities and motivations" (p.19). The same is true of the economic differences between western and third world countries. Nations may also differ in economic aptitudes and motivations. Bauer does not refer to differences in mental abilities and intelligence explicitly, but he comes near to this concept when he emphasizes the significance of people's economic capacities and motivations and when, in the case of Africa, he says that the relative lack of able and effective people is crucial (p. 195).

A recent restatement of the culture theory of economic growth comes from David Landes (1998) in his book *The Wealth and Poverty of Nations: Why Some are So Rich and Some So Poor.* His answer to this problem is "culture makes all the difference . . . witness the enterprise of expatriate minorities— the Chinese in East and Southeast Asia, Indians in East Africa, Lebanese in West Africa, Jews and Calvinists throughout much of Europe, and so on and on" (p. 516). Landes defines culture as "the inner values and attitudes that guide a population" and he endorses Weber's theory that Protestantism was an example of a set of such values that are favorable to economic growth. He argues that differences in culture explain why in recent decades Japan, Germany, South Korea, and Indonesia have succeeded economically while Turkey and Nigeria have failed. He writes that the concept of culture "frightens scholars" because it "has a sulfuric odor of race and inheritance, an air of immutability" (p. 516), but that we need not be frightened of the concept because culture can be changed. The principal weakness of culture as an explanation of national differences in economic development is that it is hard or even impossible to measure and subject to rigorous testing.

DEPENDENCY AND WORLD SYSTEM THEORIES

The dependency theories formulated by A. G. Frank and others became popular in the 1970s. A number of social scientists have argued that the capitalist world system is responsible for the poverty of underdeveloped countries. One of the leading exponents of this approach is R. Prebisch (1950), who has proposed a center-periphery model to explain the gap between rich and poor countries. The center countries are the rich, industrialized nations that have been able to use their economic strength to gain advantages from international trade and to exploit the periphery countries in Latin America, Asia, and Africa. H. W. Singer (1950) proposes a similar theory. According to Prebisch and Singer, the deteriorating terms of trade for Latin American and other less developed countries resulted in a long-term transfer of income from poor to rich countries. Their conclusion is that this decline could be combated only by efforts to protect the domestic manufacturing industries by policies of import substitution (cf. Chilcote, 1984, pp. 23–27; Nafziger, 1997, pp. 502–505; Martinussen, 1999, p. 75–76; Todaro, 2000, pp. 466–67).

The dependency theory has its historic roots in Lenin's theory of imperialist capitalism's exploitation of economically underdeveloped countries. P. A. Baran (1952, 1957, 1975) was a leading exponent of the Marxist approach in the 1950s and used Lenin's concepts of imperialism and international class conflict to explain economic growth and stagnation. According to his explanation, backward societies remained underdeveloped because their propertied and economically dominant classes had no interest in promoting industrialization and the transformation of the peripheral economies, and because the foreign and national capital owners, for their own reasons, were also opposed to it. Baran emphasizes the significance of domestic class interests, but he also takes into account the international economic system by arguing that the economic development of the backward societies was inimical to the dominant interests in the capitalist countries. He recommended extensive state interventions to promote nationally controlled industrialization for backward countries (cf. Chilcote, 1984, pp. 79–86; Martinussen, 1999, pp. 86–88).

Neo-Marxist theories of development and underdevelopment led to the formulation of new dependency theories in the 1960s and 1970s. A. G. Frank is the most prominent of these theorists. He was particularly concerned with the economic underdevelopment of Latin America. In the preface to his book, *Capitalism and Underdevelopment in Latin America* (1967, p. vii), Frank states, "I believe, with Paul Baran, that it is capitalism, both world and national, which produced underdevelopment in the past and which still generates underdevelopment in the present." Frank distinguishes between what he called the economically developed "metropoles" and the economically undeveloped "satellites" He concluded that "historial research demonstrates that contemporary underdevelopment is in large part the historical product of past and continuing economic and other relations between the satellite underdeveloped and the now developed metropolitan countries" (Frank, 1969, p. 160). In other words, the dominant capitalist countries have impoverished the underdeveloped satellite countries and caused the increasing gap between poor and rich countries. He also argues that "these metropolis-satellite relations are not limited to the imperial or international level but penetrate and structure the very economic, political, and social life of the Latin American colonies and countries." The provincial capitals, which are themselves satellites of the national metropolis, "are in turn provincial centers around which their own local satellites orbit." Each of the satellites "serves as an instrument to suck capital or economic surplus out of its own satellites and to channel part of this surplus to the world metropolis of which all are satellites." Thus, the present underdevelopment of Latin America is the result of its centuries-long participation in the process of world capitalist development (Frank, 1969, pp. 161–162). Because the contacts with metropoles caused satellization and underdevelopment, Frank concludes that underdeveloped countries should dissociate themselves from the United States and the other industrialized countries. He argued that the African, Asian, and Latin American countries least integrated into the world capitalist system tend to be the most highly developed. Thus, Frank concludes that isolation from the world market would be the best development strategy for third world countries (see also Frank, 1967, 1996; Chew and Denemark, 1996).

The dependency theories formulated by Frank and other dependency theorists became popular in the 1970s. T. dos Santos (1970), a Brazilian economist, defines dependence to mean "a situation in which the economy of certain countries is conditioned by the development and expansion of another economy to which the former is subjected" (p. 194). He emphasizes that the Marxist theory of imperialism helps us to understand the consequences of dependence, whereas its attempts "to analyze backwardness as a failure to assimilate more advanced models of production or to modernize are nothing more than ideology disguised as science" (p. 201). For poor countries, he recommends the establishment of popular revolutionary governments, which open the way to socialism.

Referring to Lenin's theory of imperialism, the Brazilian sociologist, F. H. Cardoso (1972), argues that inequality "among nations and economies resulted from imperialism's development to the extent that import of raw materials and export of manufactured goods were the bases of the imperialist-colonial relationship" (p. 171). Thus, the inequality between advanced economies and dependent economies was a by-product of the process of capitalist growth. Imperialist profit was based on unequal trade and financial exploitation. Similarly, the Egyptian economist S. Amin (1996) has argued that Europe was responsible for the underdevelopment of large parts of Africa during the colonial era. Europe produced peripheral economies that were heavily dependent on the world market. Their dependence is a result of the dominance of the center countries, which have prevented the establishment of nation-wide capital goods industries and the manufacturing of goods for mass consumption. Amin suggests that the less developed countries should break their asymmetrical relationship with the center countries and pursue a socialist development strategy. He blames not only global imperialism, but also the

African ruling classes for their failure to further industrialization. He writes, "The collusion between the African ruling classes and the strategies of global imperialism is, therefore, the ultimate cause of the impasse" (Amin, 1996, p. 210). Thus, the central thesis of dependency theorists is that the "underdevelopment in the periphery is the direct result of development in the center, and vice versa" (Roberts and Hite, 2000, p. 12; see also Chilcote, 1984). Therefore, according to these dependency theorists, third world poverty is caused by the center nations through the process of exploitation.

I. Wallerstein's world system theory (1975, 1979) represents another version of the dependency theory, although Wallerstein prefers to regard the dependency theory as a subset of his world-system perspective. According to this perspective, the modern world comprises a single capitalist world-economy, which emerged historically in the sixteenth century and still exists today. He argues that the whole global system is evolving together and that the proper entity of comparison is the world system, not the national state. This world-wide system consists of three zones—the core, the semi-periphery, and the periphery. The core extracts wealth from the periphery and causes its poverty. According to this perspective, "the gap between rich and poor ultimately will disappear, but only when the capitalist world system that has been in place since the sixteenth century itself disappears" (Seligson and Passé-Smith, 1998, p. 277).

Although the dependency theories and Wallerstein's world-system perspective are closely related to each other, there are some differences between them. A. G. Frank points out that according to his current view, the existence and development of the world system in which we live stretches back at least five thousands years, not merely to the sixteenth century. He argues that "capital accumulation neither began nor became 'ceaseless' after 1500, but rather has been the motor force of history throughout. There was no sharp break around 1500" (Frank, 1996, pp. 42–44). However, the central thesis of both perspectives is the same: the poverty of third world countries is due to the exploitation by the core countries of the world economic system.

Most economists do not accept that the economically developed West has been responsible for the poverty of third world countries. M. Chisholm (1982) concludes that domestic factors are more important than external ones. He rejects the proposition that "the core has exploited the periphery, and that the penetration of the international economy into peripheral nations has caused their present state of underdevelopment" (p. 191). He also stresses the significance of natural resources and cultural factors and argues that "prosperity is a direct function of the liberties enjoyed by individuals" (p. 160). Bauer (1981) is another economist who rejects the dependency theory. He argues that the economically developed West has not been responsible for third world poverty and that, on the contrary, "contact with the West has been the principal agent of material progress there. The materially more advanced societies and regions of the Third World are those with which the West established the most numerous, diversified and extensive contacts" (p. 70). On a similar note, Weede (1998) concludes that the "dependency approach provides no reliable and valid answer to the question: why do poor people stay poor?" (p. 373).

NEOCLASSICAL THEORIES

The 1980s saw the emergence of what has become known as the neoclassical counter-revolution in economic theory. After decades of Neo-Marxist analysis, neoclassical theory once again emphasized the importance of the market economy for economic development. This has been a revival of the ideas put forward by Adam Smith (1776) in the late eighteenth century. Neoclassical theory emphasizes the importance of private initiative, deregulation of governmental controls, and the institutions of the free market for economic growth in both developed and less developed countries. The neoclassicists blame excessive state interventions for slow economic growth and argue that "promoting competitive free markets, privatizing public enterprises, supporting exports and free international trade, liberalizing trade and exchange rates, allowing exchange rates to attain a market-clearing rate, removing barriers to foreign investment, rewarding domestic savings, reducing government spending and monetary expansion, and removing regulations and price distortions in financial, resource, and commodity markets will spur increased efficiency and economic growth" (Nafziger, 1997, p. 110).

The ideas of the neoclassical counter-revolution have been adopted by the so-called Washington consensus, supported by the United States government, the World Bank, and the International Monetary Fund. These ideas recommend export promotion and market-oriented development strategy (Nafziger, 1997, pp. 110–111; Gardner, 1998, pp. 132–133). M. P. Todaro (2000) summarizes this approach: "the central argument of the neoclassical counter-revolution is that underdevelopment results from poor resource allocation due to incorrect pricing policies and too much state intervention by overly active Third World governments" (pp. 95–99). This state intervention in economic activity retarded the pace of economic growth in many third world countries. Contrary to the claims of dependency theorists, the neoclassical theorists argue that the Third World "is underdeveloped not because of the predatory activities of the First World and the international agencies that it controls but rather because of the heavy hand of the state and the corruption, inefficiency, and lack of economic incentives that permeate the economies of developing nations." Therefore, what is needed "is not a reform of international economic system, a restructuring of dualistic developing economies, an increase in foreign aid, attempts to control population growth, or a more effective central planning system" (Todaro, 2000, p. 95). What is needed is the promotion of free markets and laissez-faire economics.

Todaro, however, notes that the reality of the institutional and political structure of many third world economies "makes the attainment of appropriate economic policies based either on markets or enlightened public intervention an exceedingly difficult endeavor" (p. 99).

The variant of neoclassical growth theory proposed by R. M. Solow (1956) and a number of others stresses the importance of savings and capital formation for economic growth. The idea is that the liberalization of national markets would draw additional domestic and foreign investment, and thus increase the rate of capital accumulation. Labor and technology are other causal factors in the Solow neoclassical growth model. It is assumed that output growth results from one or more of these factors—increases in labor quantity and quality, increases in capital, and improvements in technology. It was found, however, that this model was not able to explain the sources of long-term economic growth satisfactorily. It was especially unable to explain large differences in residuals across countries with similar technologies. To deal with this problem, a new growth theory was proposed. This theory focuses on endogenous (internal) factors of growth and attempts to explain technological change as an endogenous outcome of public and private investments in human capital and knowledge-intensive industries (Nafziger, 1997, pp. 113–117; Todaro, 2000, pp. 97–102).

Neoclassical theory attributes the poverty of third world countries largely to various errors of state policy, which consist of excessive government interference in the economy, corruption, and the failure to develop free markets (Seligson and Passé-Smith, 1998, p. 7). Weede (1996) argues that the economic development of many third world nations has been retarded by the excessive "rent-seeking" of the politically powerful. Rents are profits obtained by distortions of the market above opportunity costs, and rent-seeking societies suffer from a serious distortion of incentives. Because of distortions, there are strong incentives to engage in distributional struggles but comparatively weak incentives to engage in productive and growth-promoting activities. Rent-seeking entails monopolization, cartels, corruption, barriers to entry, and conflicts of interest between urban and rural populations. Because it is easier for urban people to organize themselves for distributional struggles than it is for scattered rural agrarian people, urban groups gain benefits. Thus, there is both the incentive and opportunity for urban exploitation of the rural population. Governments support better organized urban interests and "prefer starvation in remote villages to an urban riot in front of the presidential palace" (p. 375). There is a protracted distributional struggle in which the poorest rural groups are the losers. This urban bias, price distortion, and income disparities significantly reduce growth rates. M. Lipton (1976) also identifies an urban bias in poor countries and argues that it provides the primary explanation for the internal gap between rich and poor. His thesis is that the "most important class conflict in the poor countries of the world today is not between labour and capital. Nor is it between foreign and national interests. It is between the rural classes and the urban classes" (p. 13). This urban bias has hampered economic development in poor countries (see also Lipton, 1998).

Another neoliberal economist is M. Olson (1996). He notes the experiences of the divided nations of Germany, Korea, and China, and that the economic performances have been incomparably better in the market economies of western Germany, South Korea, Hong Kong, and Taiwan than in the command economies of eastern Germany, North Korea, and China. He concludes that "the great differences in the wealth of nations are mainly due to differences in the quality of their institutions and economic policies" (Olson, 1996, p. 19; see also Olson, 2000).

A number of economists have identified the policies pursued by political leaders of many African countries as prime examples of the adverse effects of rent seeking and corruption on economic development. For instance, G. B. N. Ayittey (1999) writes that nationalist leaders in many African countries soon after independence "turned out to be crocodile liberators, Swiss bank socialists, quack revolutionaries, and grasping kleptocrats" (p. 7). The second generation of military rulers, who assumed control in the 1970s, "were more corrupt, incompetent, and brutal than the civilian administrators they replaced. They ruined one African economy after another with brutal efficiency and looted African treasuries with military discipline" (pp. 7–8). According to this interpretation, the causes of African crisis are the failures and mistakes of political and economic leadership. He writes that "the basic problem is the mafia state–government hijacked by kleptocrats and brutal despots. Their overarching ethic is self-aggrandizement and self-perpetuation in office. All power, both political and economic, has been concentrated in their hands, which they use to extract resources from the productive masses and spend them in conspicuous consumption" (p. 301).

Thus, neoclassicists contend that the flawed policies of governments and the failure to introduce market economies are largely responsible for slow growth and domestic inequality. The neoclassical model predicts that if the governments of third world countries would introduce market economies, the per capita incomes between rich and poor countries would converge (Nafziger, 1997, p. 114). This is known as the "convergence theory," which envisions that the gap between rich and poor countries will ultimately disappear.

MULTI-CAUSAL THEORIES

Many social scientists have advanced multi-causal theories of economic development, which propose the operation of a number of factors that determine economic growth and development. A recent exponent of this approach is Landes (1998). At one point he writes that "If we learn anything from the history of economic development, it is that culture makes all the difference" (p. 516). However, elsewhere he writes that "everything depends on the quality of enterprise and the technological capability of the society" (p. 493). In other places he offers a number of further explanations for national differences in economic development including climate and institutions. He compares the recovery of Germany and Japan from the devastation of World War II and the economic successes of other east Asian nations to the lower economic growth in Latin American and Middle Eastern countries and particularly in sub-Saharan Africa. He explains these differences in terms of cultural and a variety of institutional differences: "All the ills that have hurt Latin America and the Middle East are exponentially compounded in sub-Saharan Africa: bad government, backward technology, inadequate education, bad climate, incompetent if not dishonest advice, poverty, hunger, disease, overpopulation—a plague of plagues" (p. 499). Landes fails to offer a coherent or consistent theory of economic development but from the previously quoted passage, he appears to be a multicausal theorist.

Another recent multicausal theorist of economic development is H. S. Gardner (1998). He lists a variety of environmental and cultural factors that explain poverty, especially the effects of tropical climate and institutional factors. He notes, as have many others, that most of the economically undeveloped world is located in tropical and sub-tropical regions. These regions are unfavorable for agriculture, and the tropical climate and poor sanitation foster the reproduction of insects, parasites, and pests that attack people, plants, and animals. These are formidable obstacles for development. Of the institutional factors, he cites land tenure systems, market structures and political instability. In sub-Saharan Africa, an individual family has little incentive to improve the land because the land is generally held in common with no identifiable owner or it is controlled by a village, tribe, or extended family. In Latin America, the land is held privately, but mostly it is owned by a small number of very rich people, and poor tenants have no incentive to improve it. In many poor countries, there are poor transportation and communication systems that raise the costs of trade and retard economic growth. In addition, in many developing countries price controls and state monopolies cripple the operation of markets. Political instability discourages foreign investments and economic development and encourages rulers to undertake short-sighted economic policies, such as the inflationary creation of money.

In another recent multi-causal analysis, F. Doorman (1998) begins by rejecting two explanations. He asserts that poverty does not have a cultural cause, and that it cannot be explained by the lack of resources. He then argues that poverty is "a question of distribution rather than production. Resources and wealth are distributed unequally, both between and within countries" (pp. 37–38). An important factor responsible for national differences in the wealth and poverty of nations is the great differences in technical and managerial skills. Protectionism by rich nations is another factor that perpetuates poverty. So also is the high level of debt of many third world countries, which Doorman regards as the single biggest cause of continuing poverty in the developing countries. Furthermore, he believes that the rich countries are to a considerable extent responsible for the poverty in the poor countries, but he also finds domestic causes of poverty. He blames bad governments: "The ruling cliques of most poor countries have been singularly successful in increasing their own wealth at the cost of their fellow citizens. Favored means are graft, kickbacks, abuse of monopolies, and many other forms of corruption, including the downright plundering of national treasuries. Some of the gathered wealth is consumed or invested locally; much is transferred to Swiss bank accounts or other safe havens in the rich nations" (p. 42). Doorman estimates that the damage done by political leaders plundering their countries' treasuries and national resources runs into the hundreds of billions of dollars.

Although the gap between rich and poor countries is statistically described in each issue of the *World Development Report*, and the problems of economic development and poverty have been discussed extensively, it is generally difficult to find any theoretical explanation for the gap between rich and poor countries from these reports. However, the 1999/2000 issue of the report includes a review of development thinking and experience of fifty years. It concludes that there are four critical lessons—macroeconomic stability is an essential prerequisite for achieving the growth needed for development; growth does not trickle down automatically; no one policy will trigger development, a comprehensive approach is needed; and institutions matter (World Development Report 1999/2000, p. 1). These lessons do not include any reference to the possible role of group differences in mental abilities.

Several multi-causal social scientists have argued that the quality of political leaders has been a significant determinant of economic development. For example, L. Doe (1997) compares economic growth in francophone Africa and in the Republic of Korea. In 1960, Korea was nearly as underdeveloped as the African countries, but in 1993 the average income of Koreans had increased from 150 dollars to 7,660 dollars, whereas in most African countries it had only increased to around 500 dollars. Doe explains the emergence of this income gap by political factors, especially by differences in political will and leadership. He argues that the Korean leadership was much more competent than the leadership of the francophone African countries. He concludes that "economic development is, first and foremost, a matter of political will, that is essentially the determination of the executive power to change the course of history of the population." He thinks that sub-Saharan Africa "can duplicate the Korean success if its leaders so choose" (p. 115).

Other multi-causal social scientists have argued that "human capital" is a significant factor in economic development. Human capital means the quality of the population and includes its education, literacy, skills, and health. R. Jolly (1999) notes that the gap between rich and poor nations is now at its highest level ever, but he thinks that it is possible to reduce global inequality. He argues that international transfers have a role "but the primary long-run solution must be accelerated rates of growth by developing countries themselves." Large-scale investment in primary education and basic health care would be especially important. J. Temple (1999) also emphasizes the positive effect of human capital investment on growth. So also do P. Hess and C. Ross (1997), who argue that human capital formation is both a cause and a consequence of economic development. They say that human capital formation "reflected in improvements in nutrition and health and gains in knowledge and skills, not only translates into increased productivity, but directly enhances the quality of life" (p. 219).

In recent textbooks, Nafziger (1997), Gardner (1998), Martinussen (1999), Roberts and Hite (2000) and Todaro (2000) discuss the various theories of economic development, the problem of world poverty, and the gap between rich and poor countries. The list of explanatory factors includes culture, historical factors, psychological factors, attitudes, motivations, values, dependence, world-system, terms of trade, imperialist capitalism, colonialism, external factors, geographical and climatic conditions, savings and capital formation, the role of the state, differences in economic systems, institutional factors, errors of state policy, population growth, urban bias, technological factors, technical and managerial skills, human capital, and political will. It is possible that all of the factors mentioned in these studies are relevant, at least in some contexts, but we believe that they are not sufficient to explain the problem of the disparities in economic development between nations.

SUMMARY

The problem of why countries differ in economic development and why some countries are rich while others are poor has been discussed for the last two and a half centuries. The major theories that have been advanced to explain this problem have been reviewed in this chapter. These theories propose that climate, geography, modernization processes, psychological attitudes, culture, dependency of poor nations in the capitalist world system, and market economies are the significant or decisive determinants of economic development. We believe that while some of these theories may provide partial explanations for the disparities between countries in economic development, there is another factor that has not been considered hitherto. This is the intelligence of the populations.

2

Intelligence:
An Introduction to the Concept

In this chapter we present a definition of intelligence as a single unitary construct that determines the efficiency of performance of all cognitive tasks. We describe the intelligence quotient (IQ) and how it is measured, and we outline the economic and social correlates of intelligence. We take a first look at national differences in intelligence and their relation to economic growth and development. We conclude by summarizing the evidence for the genetic basis and heritability of intelligence.

DEFINITION OF INTELLIGENCE

We begin by defining intelligence. In contemporary psychology, intelligence is conceptualized as primarily a unitary construct that determines the efficiency of problem solving, learning, remembering, and the performance of all tasks ranging from complex mathematical and logical problems to simple reaction times involving the speed of pressing a button on a keyboard when a light comes on. A useful definition of intelligence has been provided by a committee set up by the American Psychological Association in 1995 under the chairmanship of Ulrich Neisser and consisting of eleven American psychologists whose mandate was to produce a consensus view of what is generally known and accepted about intelligence. The definition of intelligence proposed by this task force was that intelligence is the ability "to understand complex ideas, to adapt effectively to the environment, to learn from experience, to engage in various forms of reasoning, to overcome obstacles by taking thought" (Neisser, 1996, p. 1.) This definition is generally acceptable for our present purposes, except for the component of effective adaptation to the environment. In economically developed nations, the underclass, which consists of the long-term unemployed and welfare-dependent single mothers, is well adapted to its environment in so far as it is able to live on welfare and reproduce. It is not, however, intelligent in any reasonable sense of the word or as measured by intelligence tests (see Chapter 4, "Intelligence and Further Economic and Social Phenomena"). If other species are considered, all living species are well adapted to their environments or they would not be alive, but many living species such as reptiles, fish, and birds cannot be regarded as intelligent.

A definition that avoids this misconception was proposed by L. S. Gottfredson and was endorsed by 52 leading experts and published in the *Wall Street Journal* in 1994: "Intelligence is a very general mental capacity which, among other things, involves the ability to reason, plan, solve problems, think abstractly, comprehend complex ideas, learn quickly and learn from experience. It is not merely book learning, a narrow academic skill, or test-taking smarts. Rather, it reflects a broader and deeper capability for comprehending our surroundings—'catching on', 'making sense' of thing, or 'figuring out' what to do" (Gottfredson, 1997a, p. 13).

Intelligence conceptualized as a single entity can be measured by intelligence tests and quantified by the intelligence quotient (IQ). The theory of intelligence as largely a single entity was first formulated in the first decade of the 20th century by Charles Spearman (1904), who showed that all cognitive abilities are positively intercorrelated, such that people who do well on some tasks tend to do well on all the others. Spearman invented the statistical method of factor analysis to show that the efficiency of performance on all cognitive tasks is partly determined by a common factor. He designated this common factor, g, for "general intelligence." To explain the existence of the common factor, Spearman proposed that there must be some general mental power that determines the performance on all cognitive tasks and is responsible for the positive inter-correlation of these abilities.

THE HIERARCHICAL MODEL OF INTELLIGENCE

Spearman also proposed that in addition to g, there are a number of specific abilities that determine the performance on particular kinds of tasks, over and above the effect of g. Subsequent theorists have proposed that there are also "second order" or "group" factors, which are aggregates of the specifics. In the leading contemporary formulation of this model by J. B. Carroll (1994), there are eight of these second order factors, consisting of verbal comprehension, reasoning, memory, spatial, perceptual, mathematical abilities, cultural knowledge, and cognitive speed. This is called the "hierarchical model" of intelligence because it can be envisaged as a hierarchical pyramid with numerous narrow, specific abilities at the base, eight second order or group factors in the middle, and a single general factor—g—at the apex. This model is widely accepted among contemporary experts such as the American Task Force (Neisser, 1996; Jensen, 1998; Mackintosh, 1998; Carroll, 1994; Deary, 2000; and many others).

The most recent extensive exposition of *g* and its heritability, biology, and correlates has been presented by A. R. Jensen (1998) in his book, *The g Factor*. He conceptualizes *g* as a factor and writes that "A factor is a hypothetical variable that 'underlies' an observed or measured variable" (p. 88). It is not possible to measure *g* directly, but the scores that are obtained from intelligence tests and are expressed as IQs are approximate measures of *g*.

THE IQ

Intelligence is measured by intelligence tests. These tests typically consist of a number of different kinds of tests of verbal reasoning, non-verbal reasoning (which entails the solution of reasoning problems in design or pictorial format), mental arithmetic, vocabulary, verbal comprehension, and perceptual, spatial, and memory abilities. Tests of all these abilities are substantially intercorrelated, normally at a magnitude of around 0.6 to 0.7. The reason for these high intercorrelations is that all these tests are largely measures of *g*.

The scores obtained on intelligence tests are expressed in a metric in which the mean IQ of a representative sample of a national population is set at 100 and the standard deviation is set at 15. Thus, approximately 96 percent of the population have IQs in the range of 70 to 130. Approximately 2 percent of the population have IQs below 70 and are regarded as mentally retarded. Another 2 percent have IQs above 130 and are regarded as gifted. The maximum IQs that have ever been recorded are around 200.

The first intelligence test was constructed in France by Alfred Binet in 1905. In the early tests, the IQ was measured by using of the concept of mental age. Mental age was defined as the ability level of an average child of any particular chronological age. Thus, a mental age of eight was defined as the tests that were passed by the average 8 year old. The IQ was then calculated by the formula Mental Age divided by Chronological Age multiplied by 100 equals IQ. Thus, a child with a chronological age of 4 years who could pass the tests of the average 8 year old would therefore have a mental age of 8 years and would have an IQ of 200. An adolescent with a chronological age of 16 who functioned at the same mental level as an average 8 year old would have an IQ of 50. This formula for the calculation of IQs is not used in more recent tests, which simply transform the scores obtained on tests using only the IQ metric with the mean set at 100 and the standard deviation at 15. However, it remains a useful and approximate method for estimating IQs and for understanding what they mean. IQs obtained from intelligence tests are almost entirely measures of *g* (Jensen, 1998).

ECONOMIC AND SOCIAL CORRELATES OF INTELLIGENCE

Numerous research studies conducted over a period of almost a century have shown that intelligence is an important correlate and determinant of a wide range of economic and social phenomena including educational attainment, socioeconomic status, earnings, and lifetime achievement. Low intelligence is a significant determinant of unemployment, poverty, welfare dependency, single motherhood, mortality, and crime (Brand, 1987; Herrnstein and Murray, 1994). The advantages of having a high IQ are greatest when dealing with complex tasks such as those involved in professional and managerial occupations. A high IQ is less advantageous for dealing with routine tasks in semi-skilled and unskilled work, but even in these types of work a high IQ confers some advantage. We review the evidence on these points in detail in Chapter 3, "Intelligence and Earnings," and Chapter 4, "Intelligence and Further Economic and Social Phenomena."

When intelligence is conceptualized as general ability, g, and a number of group factors and specific abilities, it has been found that g is by far the most important determinant of task performance. Group and specific abilities make virtually no contribution to the efficiency of performance over and above the effect of g. For instance, in a study carried out for the U.S. Air Force, 78,049 trainees were given the Armed Services Vocational Aptitude Battery, a test with ten components consisting of arithmetic reasoning, numerical operations, verbal comprehension of paragraphs, vocabulary, perceptual speed (a coding test), general science, mathematics knowledge, electronics information, mechanical information, and automotive shop information. The g extracted from this battery of tests correlated .76 with attainment on job training courses. The remaining non-g portion of the test variance had a correlation of an additional .02 (Ree and Earles, 1994). Thus, for practical purposes, g is the only useful predictor of attainment on the training program. For particular areas of expertise, g is a more important predictor of performance than a test of ability in that area. For instance, performance on a test of mechanical aptitude is more strongly determined by g than by mechanical ability (Ree and Earles, 1994).

NATIONAL DIFFERENCES IN INTELLIGENCE

Most intelligence tests have been constructed in the United States and Britain. From the 1920s onward, these American and British tests have been used in many other countries, largely for educational selection and also for research purposes. In the course of this work, the tests have been administered to representative samples of the population and local norms have been obtained. It has therefore become possible to compare the mean IQs in a number of countries with those in the United States and Britain. These studies have produced a consistent pattern of results. First, in relation to American and British mean IQs of 100, the Japanese, Chinese, and other Oriental peoples have mean IQs of around 105. This has been found in Japan, Taiwan, Hong Kong, Singapore, South Korea, and China. It has also been found for ethnic Chinese living in the United States. Second, European peoples in continental Europe, Canada, Australia, New Zealand, Latin America, and South Africa have mean IQs of around 100. Third, the peoples of south and southwest Asia from Turkey through the Near East to India have mean IQs in the range between 78 and 90. Fourth, the peoples of Latin America have a range of mean IQs from 96 in Argentina and Uruguay whose populations are very largely European to around 80 in countries like Guatemala and Ecuador whose populations are largely indigenous Native American and Mestizos. Fifth, the nations of sub-Saharan Africa have IQs in the range of 65 and 75 and average around 70. A detailed review of these studies is given in Appendix 1 "The Calculation of National Intelligence Levels."

There are two noteworthy features of this general pattern of results. First, the widespread assumption of economists and political scientists who have been concerned with the problem of national differences in economic development, that the peoples of all nations have the same average level of intelligence, is seriously incorrect. On the contrary, there are huge differences in the average intelligence levels of the peoples of different countries.

Second, because intelligence is a significant determinant of attainment and achievement in all areas of life including earnings, these national differences in intelligence are bound to have some effect on national economic development and rates of economic growth. The impact of national levels of intelligence is confirmed impressionistically by the contrast between the rapid economic development in the second half of the twentieth century of the nations of east Asia, with their high average IQs, and the poorer economic performance of the nations of south and southwest Asia, Latin America, and sub-Saharan Africa. The extreme case is the nations of sub-Saharan Africa. The populations of sub-Saharan Africa possessing limited mental abilities must inevitably be unable to compete economically with European and Oriental nations whose peoples have far greater mental capacities. This thesis is worked out in Chapter 6, "Data on Variables and Methods of Analysis."

THE HERITABILITY OF INTELLIGENCE

Studies of the extent to which intelligence is determined by genetic and environmental factors have been made since the 1930s. By the last two decades of the twentieth century, a consensus had emerged that genetic factors are a significant determinant of intelligence. The magnitude of the contribution of genetic factors is measured by the heritability, which consists of the proportion of phenotypic (measured) variance that can be accounted for by the genetic differences among individuals. Heritability is measured on a scale from 0 to 1.0, and is also expressed as percentages. In the statement drawn up by Gottfredson and endorsed by 52 experts, it is stated that "Heritability estimates range from .4 to .8, most indicating that genetics plays a bigger role than environment in creating IQ differences among individuals" (1997a, p. 14).

There are three principal types of evidence that lead to the conclusion that intelligence is substantially genetically determined and from which its heritability can be calculated. The first of these consists of studies of monozygotic (identical) twins who are reared apart. Five studies have been made of these twin types from 1937 to the 1990s. They have all found that these twin pairs have highly similar IQs, despite having been reared in different environments. T. J. Bouchard (1998) has calculated the weighted average of the correlation between twin pairs as .75. This correlation is a direct measure of heritability and, therefore, indicates that the heritability is .75 or 75 percent. This figure needs to be corrected for the unreliability of test measurement. Assuming that the test has a reliability of .9 as concluded by Bouchard (1993), the corrected correlation between the twin pairs is .83.

The second method consists of comparing the degree of similarity between identical twins and same-sex, non-identical twins brought up in the same families. Identical twins are genetically identical, whereas non-identical twins have (on average) only half their genes in common. Hence, if genetic factors are operating, identical twins should be more alike than non-identicals. The simplest method for quantifying the genetic effect was proposed by Falconer (1960) and consists of doubling the difference between the correlations of identical and same-sex non-identicals. Studies of the intelligence of adult twin pairs have been summarized by Bouchard (1993, p. 58). He finds a correlation of .88 for identical twins and .51 for same-sex, non-identical twins. The difference between the two correlations is .37, and doubling this difference gives a heritability of .74. This figure needs to be corrected for the imperfect reliability of the tests. Using a reliability coefficient of .9, the corrected correlation become .98 for identicals and .56 for same-sex, non-identical twins. The difference between the two correlations is .42 and doubling this difference gives a heritability of .84. This is close to the heritability of .83 derived from the first method. This is why many experts on this issue estimate the heritability of intelligence among adults as approximately .80 or 80 percent (Eysenck, 1979, p. 102, 1998, p. 40; Jensen, 1998, p. 78). The heritability of intelligence among children is somewhat lower, probably because there are environmental effects largely from parents acting on children that wear off during adolescence. It is by including the lower heritability estimates derived from children with the estimates of around .80 for adults that some writers put the heritability of intelligence at around .70.

The third principal method for estimating the heritability of intelligence is to examine the correlation between the IQs of unrelated children who are adopted and reared in the same families. The magnitude of the environmental impact is expressed in the correlation between the twin pairs. The summary of the research literature by Bouchard (1998) concludes that among children the correlation is 0.22. This is a measure of the environmental contribution, indicating a heritability of .78. Among adults the correlation is 0.04, indicating a heritability of .96.

The conclusion that intelligence has a high heritability implies that there are genes that determine intelligence. The first of these genes in normal populations was discovered in the late 1990s by Chorley *et al.* (1998). It lies on Chromosome 6 and possession of the gene or, more strictly, the allele (alleles are alternative forms of a gene), confers about four IQ points to an individual's intelligence.

We have seen in this section that the three methods for estimating the heritability of intelligence yield closely similar conclusions and that the figure is around .80 or 80 percent. The precise magnitude of the heritability of intelligence does not matter for the purposes of the arguments advanced in this book. The significance of the high heritability of intelligence is that it implies that the differences in intelligence between the peoples of different nations are likely to have a genetic basis. This has important implications for the problem of how the underdeveloped nations, whose peoples have low levels of intelligence, could be helped to raise the intelligence levels of their populations.

SUMMARY

Intelligence is conceptualized in contemporary psychology as largely a single entity that affects the efficiency of learning, problem solving, and the performance of a very wide range of tasks. Intelligence is an important determinant of educational attainment, intellectual achievement, earnings, and socioeconomic status. Low intelligence is an important determinant of unemployment, welfare dependency, and crime. All of these phenomena are likely to have an impact on national economic growth and development. There are considerable national differences in intelligence such that the average IQs are highest among the Oriental peoples of east Asia, followed in descending order by the European peoples of Europe, North America, and Australasia; the peoples of south and southwest Asia and Latin America; and finally by the peoples of sub-Saharan Africa. There appears to be a prima facie case that these national differences in intelligence play some part in determining the national differences in rates of economic growth and development. This is the thesis which we are now ready to examine in more detail.

3

Intelligence and Earnings

In this chapter we show that intelligence is a determinant of earnings among individuals. This is the foundation of our thesis that the intelligence of national populations is a major determinant of national per capita incomes and rates of economic growth. In addition, we show also that intelligence is a determinant of trainability and job proficiency; and that there are different cognitive capacities at different levels of intelligence which explain why only those with high levels of intelligence are able to do complex tasks.

INTELLIGENCE AND EARNINGS

Because we are concerned with the relationship between IQs and earnings among nations, the most important of the studies of the explanatory power of *g* concern the relation of IQ to earnings among individuals. There have been a number of studies showing that there is a positive association between intelligence and earnings. Some of these studies have measured intelligence in childhood or adolescence and related this to earnings in adulthood, while others have measured intelligence in adulthood at the same time as earnings. Several studies have shown that intelligence assessed in childhood from the age of about eight years and above is fairly stable over the life span and is correlated at about .7 to .8 with intelligence in adulthood (McCall, 1977; Li, 1975). The longest span of time over which a high stability of IQ has been demonstrated is 66 years. This was shown in a study by Deary *et al.* (2000), in which 101 children who were tested for intelligence in 1932 at the age of eleven were tested again in 1998 at the age of 77. The correlation between the two scores was .77. Therefore, it does not make much difference for studies of the relation between intelligence and earnings whether the IQs are assessed in childhood or adolescence and are shown to predict future earnings, or whether the IQs and earnings are assessed simultaneously among adults. Because intelligence is fairly stable from around the age of eight, both methodologies imply that intelligence predicts the earnings obtained in adulthood.

The results of the major studies of the relationship between intelligence and earnings are summarized in Table 3.1. The first study shown in the table (Duncan, 1968) presents data on a sample of white males aged 24–35 from the 1964 Current Population Survey, which was carried out by the National Opinion Research Center (NORC). The second entry from Jencks (1972) is derived from a synthesis of the American research literature up to 1970. The third and fourth entries (Brown and Reynolds, 1975) are derived from a study of the relation between the IQ of males measured in early adulthood and earnings measured approximately 12 years later for samples of 24,819 whites and 4,008 blacks, for whom the study reported correlations of .327 and .126, respectively. The fifth entry (Murray, 1998) is derived from the National Longitudinal Study of Youth's nationally representative American sample of 12,686, which found a correlation of .37 between the IQ of males measured in adolescence and income approximately twelve years later, assessed in the late twenties to mid-thirties. In these studies, it is apparent that the four results for whites are closely similar, all lying in the range between .31 and .37 and averaging .34. The one correlation for blacks of .13 is substantially lower but nevertheless is statistically significant. The main reason for the lower correlation among blacks is possibly due to a greater numbers of intelligent blacks being born into poverty who do not obtain the educational credentials that are generally required to secure average to high earnings.

Table 3.1
Correlations between IQs and Earnings

Correlation	Reference
.31	Duncan, 1968
.35	Jencks, 1972
.33	Brown and Reynolds, 1975
.13	Brown and Reynolds, 1975
.37	Murray, 1998

Most students have concluded that IQ is a cause of income because IQs are established quite early in childhood, and they predict the incomes that are achieved in adulthood (for examples, see Duncan, 1968; Duncan,

Featherman, and Duncan, 1972; Jencks, 1972; Jensen, 1998). Although it might be argued that the socioeconomic status of the family is the common cause of the intelligence and subsequent earnings of children, it is shown by Duncan, Featherman, and Duncan (1972) and by Jencks (1979) that the positive relation between a childhood IQ and an adult's income is present when parental socioeconomic status is controlled.

The effect of a correlation of approximately .34 between intelligence and earnings is to produce quite considerable differences in the earnings of high and low IQ groups. As Jencks (1972, p. 222) has noted, men inducted in the Korean War who had been tested and scored above the 80th percentile for intelligence, representing IQs of 110 and over, had personal incomes of 34 percent above the national average when they returned to civilian life. Conversely, the military inductees who scored below the 20th percentile on intelligence, representing IQs of below 90, had personal incomes of approximately 34 percent below the national average when they returned to civilian life.

While these correlations show that intelligence is a significant determinant of earnings, it is not, of course, the only determinant. In psychology, it is generally considered that the other principal determinants are the strength of motivation for achievement and opportunity. These determinants have been expressed in the formula IQ × Motivation × Opportunity = Achievement (Jensen, 1980). The algebraic terms indicate that if any of the three variables is low or zero, the achievement output will also be low or zero. Thus, an individual with a high IQ and strong motivation who is reared in an environment lacking in opportunity will not achieve much. The same is true for an individual with a high intelligence reared in an environment with high opportunity who is deficient in motivation. The same is also true for a strongly motivated individual reared in an environment with high opportunity who has low intelligence.

TRAINABILITY

The explanation for the positive association between IQ and incomes is that people with high IQs can be trained to acquire more complex skills and that they work more proficiently than those with low IQs. This makes them more productive and enables them to earn higher incomes. In this section, we deal with the relation between IQ and trainability. An early study showing the positive effect of IQ on trainability was made during World War Two in the training of pilots for the American Air Force. Initially, the Air Force admitted those of all ability levels to its pilot training program but found there was a high failure rate of those who proved to be untrainable. The Air Force then examined the effect of intelligence for success in the training program. They found that 95 percent of those in the top 10 percent of intelligence successfully completed the training, while only 20 percent of those in the bottom 10 percent were able to complete the training (Matarazzo, 1972). Further work by the American military has confirmed that it is difficult and often impossible to train inductees with low IQs. A series of reports on the experience of the military on this issue has been summarized by Gottfredson (1997b, p. 91): "All agree that these men were very costly and difficult to train, could not learn certain specialties, and performed at a lower average level once on a job. Many such men had to be sent to newly created special units for remedial training or recycled one or more times through basic or technical training." As a result of this experience, the U.S. military no longer accepts recruits with IQs below 80.

There have been two major reviews of studies examining the relation between IQs and trainability for the acquisition of skills. The first consists of a meta-analysis by Hunter and Hunter (1984) of 425 studies that have used the General Aptitude Test Battery (GATB), a test of general intelligence, for the prediction of training success. They classified jobs into the two categories of general and industrial. Their conclusion was that for all occupations, IQ predicts job training success at a correlation of .45. When jobs are classified according to their complexity, IQ correlates more highly at .50 to .65, than it does for jobs of low complexity, for which the correlations are between .25 and .40. The details of the correlations are shown in Table 3.2.

Table 3.2
Correlations between IQs and Training Success

Job Complexity	Training
High—general	.50
High—industrial	.65
Medium—general	.40
Low—general	.25

The second major review of the relation between intelligence and training success consists of data collected from the American military training schools. All recruits to the American military are given an intelligence test, the Armed Forces Qualification Test (AFQT). These recruits are also sent to training schools. At the end of training, they are assessed for how well they have done on the course by tests assessing job performance, knowledge, and skills. The results are based on a sample of 472,539 military personnel and have been analyzed by Hunter (1985), who presents the correlations between the IQ and training success for five types of training: Mechanical, Clerical, Electronic, General Technical, and Combat. These correlations are shown in

Table 3.3. It will be seen that all of these correlations are substantial and lie between .45 and .67. The magnitude of the correlations depends on the cognitive complexity of the skills assessed. The highest correlation is for Electronics, which is the most cognitively demanding skill. The lowest is for Combat, which is the least cognitively demanding skill where success is heavily dependent on the recruit's physical skills. However, even for this skill the correlation of .45 is appreciable.

Table 3.3

Correlations between IQs and Training Success in the U.S. Military

Job Type	Training Success
Mechanical	.62
Clerical	.58
Electronic	.67
General Technical	.62
Combat	.45

JOB PROFICIENCY

There have been three major reviews of studies examining the relation between IQs and job proficiency. The first was carried out by Ghiselli (1966) who reviewed all of the research literature on the validity of intelligence tests for the prediction of ratings of job proficiency. Ghiselli's conclusions were that virtually all the studies found some positive correlation and that the magnitude of the correlation depended on the complexity of the job. For the least complex jobs, such as sales, service occupations, machinery workers, packers, and wrappers, the correlations between intelligence and job proficiency lay in the range between .10 and .19. For jobs of intermediate complexity, such as supervisors, clerks, and assemblers, the correlations lay in the range between .20 and .34. For the most complex jobs, such as electrical workers and managerial and professional occupations, the correlations lay in the range between .35 and .47. This conclusion that the magnitude of the correlation between intelligence and job proficiency is higher for more complex jobs has been confirmed in later studies.

The second major review consists of the meta-analysis by Hunter and Hunter (1984) of 425 studies, which used the General Aptitude Test Battery (GATB), a test of general intelligence, for the prediction of job proficiency. Hunter and Hunter classified jobs into the two categories of general and industrial. Their conclusion was that when jobs are classified according to their complexity, IQ correlates more highly for complex jobs at ranges between .56 to .58, than it does for jobs of low complexity, for which the correlations range between .23 and .40. The details of the correlations are shown in Table 3.4.

Table 3.4

Correlations between IQs and Job Proficiency

Job Complexity	Proficiency
High—general	.58
High—industrial	.56
Medium—general	.51
Low—general	.40
Low—industrial	.23

The third major review of the relation between intelligence and job proficiency has been carried out by Schmidt and Hunter (1998) and evaluates the results of research on this issue from World War I to the last few years of the twentieth century. They conclude that "The validity of different personnel measures can be determined with the aid of 85 years of research. The most well known conclusion from this research is that for hiring employees without previous experience in the job the most valid predictor of future performance is general mental ability." They estimate the overall "predictive validity coefficient" (correlation) between general intelligence and job performance at .51.

COGNITIVE CAPACITIES AT DIFFERENT LEVELS OF INTELLIGENCE

A detailed analysis of the importance of intelligence for handling the problems of work and everyday living has been made by Gottfredson (1997b). She summarizes the research evidence of the cognitive capacities and social and economic competence of those in the same five intelligence categories used by Herrnstein and Murray, consisting of those with IQs below 76 and of those with IQs in the ranges of 76–90, 91–110, 111–125, and 125 and above. Her conclusions are as follows:

IQs below 76 (the bottom 5 percent of the population).   These individuals are at high risk of failing in school and becoming elementary school dropouts, have difficulty in carrying out apparently simple tasks such as reading a letter, filling in forms, understanding doctors' instructions, and as one social anthropologist has put it, "consistently fail to understand certain important aspects of the world in which they live, and so regularly find themselves unable to cope with some demands of this world" (Edgerton, 1993, p. 222).

IQs ranging between 76–90 (the next 20 percent of the population). These individuals in this IQ band are trainable only for semi-skilled work. Some examples of such are machine operators, welders, custodians, and food service workers.

IQs ranging between 91–110 (the middle 50 percent). These individuals are trainable for skilled and lower white collar jobs, such as the skilled trades of electrician, plumber and the like, and clerks, secretaries, and insurance sales representatives. According to Carroll (1987) they are able to read and comprehend material in simple magazines, newspapers, and popular novels.

IQs ranging between 111–125 (the next 20 percent). These individuals can learn complex material fairly easily and most of them can qualify for management and the professions. Carroll (1987) concludes that only those in this IQ band and above can follow and understand serious articles in quality newspapers and magazines or serious fiction.

IQs ranging between 126 and above (the top 5 percent). Only these individuals are able to do well in cognitively demanding occupations such as law, medicine, science, university research, engineering, and senior management.

Gottfredson (1997b) concludes her review by writing that "There are many other valued human traits beside *g*, but none seems to affect individuals' life chances so systematically and powerfully in modern life as does *g*" (p. 120).

A MATHEMATICAL MODEL OF IQ, EARNINGS, AND OCCUPATION

Two economists, Brown and Reynolds (1975), have formulated a mathematical model of the relation between IQ, earnings, and occupation. It states:

$$Yij = aj + bj\,(IQi - tj) + eij$$

where tj is the required minimum or threshold IQ in occupation j; aj is a parameter equal to average income when IQ is tj in occupation j; bj is a parameter > 0; and eij is a random disturbance uncorrelated with IQ, with an expected value of zero, and a constant variance equal to d squared ej.

The model assumes a hierarchy of occupations such that IQ thresholds and income coefficients increase with occupation. It also assumes a normal distribution of IQs in the population and random assignment to occupations.

Individuals are randomly drawn from the population and are randomly assigned to an occupation, with all occupational assignments being equally probable. If an individual's IQ is below the relevant threshold, that person is not admitted to the occupation, but is returned to the population for possible reassignment. If an individual's IQ is equal to or greater than the threshold of their randomly assigned occupation, that person is employed in that occupation and their earnings are determined by the previous equation.

The model generates a number of predictions:

Mean IQs in higher occupations are greater than those in lower occupations.

Variation in IQs is greater in lower occupations.

Mean earnings are greater in higher occupations.

There is a negative correlation between mean IQ and IQ variance across occupations. This was previously implied.

Variation in earnings is greater in higher occupations.

In the two subpopulations, A and B, where the mean IQ of A is less than the mean IQ of B and the groups have the same IQ variance, if the population ratio of A to B is R, the relative frequency of A will increasingly fall further below R at each higher level of the occupational hierarchy.

Assuming that all individuals with the same IQ earn the same incomes (on average), the average earnings of A will be lower than those of B within all occupations.

If the mean IQ of subpopulation A is less than the mean IQ of subpopulation B, then within occupations subpopulation A will have a smaller range and variance in both IQ and income.

Within a given occupation, the correlation between earned income and IQ will be lower for subpopulation A than for subpopulation B, and the slope of the regression of earnings on IQ will be lower for A than for B.

Brown and Reynolds show that these predictions from the model accord with the empirical findings.

THE LAW OF SUPPLY AND DEMAND

Hitherto we have surveyed a variety of evidence showing that intelligence is positively related to earnings. The major reason for this association lies in the operation of the law of supply and demand. This fundamental law of economics states that the price of goods and services is determined by the balance of supply and demand. If the supply is abundant relative to demand, the price of goods and services will be low. Such is the case with unskilled work in the contemporary world, for which a pool of unemployed is always available providing an excess of supply over demand. Conversely, if the supply is limited relative to demand, the price of goods and services will be high. People with high IQs can acquire complex skills that cannot be acquired by those with low IQs. As a result, people with high IQs are in short supply relative to the demand for the goods and services they can produce. They are therefore able to command high earnings.

SUMMARY

In this chapter it is shown that intelligence conceptualized as a single ability is a significant determinant of earnings among individuals. In the United States, the correlation between IQs and earnings is approximately .35. This association should be regarded as a causal effect of IQ on earnings because IQs are stable from around the age of five years and predict earnings obtained in adulthood. Intelligence determines earnings because more intelligent people learn more quickly, solve problems more effectively, can be trained to acquire more complex skills, and work more productively and efficiently. In terms of economic theory, the explanation for the positive association between intelligence and earnings lies in the operation of the law of supply and demand. People with high intelligence are in short supply and are able to perform complex tasks for which is high demand. As a result, these individuals can command a high price for their skills.

4

Intelligence and Further Economic and Social Phenomena

Because intelligence is a general learning and problem solving ability, it is a determinant not only of earnings, as we saw in the last chapter, but also of a number of other important economic and social phenomena. These phenomena include educational attainment, socioeconomic status, and lifetime achievement. Low intelligence is a significant determinant of the syndrome of the social pathology known as the underclass. All of these social phenomena are likely to have an impact on economic development. The evidence for these effects of intelligence is reviewed in this chapter.

EDUCATIONAL ATTAINMENT

The general format of studies of the effect of intelligence on educational attainment has been to measure intelligence at one point in time and educational attainment later. The results of a number of major and typical studies are summarized in Table 4.1. In this table, the first column gives the stage of life at which intelligence was measured, and the second column provides the correlation between intelligence and subsequent educational attainment. In these studies, educational attainment is measured either by years of education, the highest level of education reached (such as college graduate, high school graduate, and so forth), or by performance in examinations.

The first entry in the table (Benson, 1942) presents the results of an early study in which the IQs of 1,989 school children in Minneapolis were obtained in 1923. This sample was followed up a number of years later and the number of the individuals' years of education were recorded. The correlation between the two was .57. The second entry (Duncan, 1968) presents

Table 4.1

Correlations between Intelligence and Educational Attainment

Intelligence	Correlation	Reference
High school	.57	Benson, 1942
Young adult	.59	Duncan, 1968
11 years of age	.58	Jencks, 1972
High school	.59	Haller and Portes, 1973
5 years of age	.61	Yule et al., 1982
5 years of age	.72	Yule et al., 1982
15 years of age	.65	Lynn et al., 1984

data for the IQs obtained by military conscripts and education data obtained from the 1964 Current Population Survey carried out by the National Opinion Research Center (NORC) for a sample of white males aged 24–35. The third entry (Jencks, 1972) is derived from a synthesis of the American research literature up to 1970. The fourth entry (Haller and Portes, 1973) comes from a sample of one third of Wisconsin high school seniors from whom IQs were obtained in 1957 and from whom educational attainment was obtained in 1965. The fifth entry (Yule *et al.*, 1982) comes from a British study in which IQs were obtained for 85 children at the age of 5 years and related to the grades obtained in the public examinations in reading (.61) and mathematics (.72) taken at the age of 16 years. The sixth entry (Lynn, Hampson, and Magee, 1984) gives the results of a study from Northern Ireland in which IQs were obtained from a sample of 701 15 year olds and related to performance in the public GCE/GCSE (General Certificate of Education/General Certificate of Secondary Education) examinations taken approximately eight months later.

It will be seen that all the correlations between intelligence and educational attainment lie in the quite narrow range between .57 and .72. It seems to make little difference whether intelligence is measured early in childhood or among young adults. Indeed, the highest correlation of .72 is between intelligence measured at the age of 5 years and educational attainment in mathematics at the age of 16 years. The reason for this range is that intelligence is a stable characteristic from about the age of five, as noted in Chapter 2, "Intelligence: An Introduction to the Concept."

It has sometimes been argued that the correlation between intelligence and educational attainment is not a causal one but that it arises through the common effects of the socioeconomic status of the family on both intelligence and educational attainment. Thus, middle class families produce children with high intelligence, either through genetic transmission or by providing environmental advantages, and they also ensure that their children have a good education. However, this explanation cannot be correct because the correlation between the parental socioeconomic status and their children's educational attainment obtained from a meta-analysis of almost 200 studies is only .22 (White, 1982). Such a low correlation could not account for much of the considerably higher association between children's IQs and their educational attainment. In addition, it has been found that among pairs of brothers reared in the same family, there is a correlation of approximately .3 between their IQ and educational attainment (Jencks, 1972). This shows that the correlation between IQ and educational attainment remains, although it is reduced, even when family effects are controlled. The only reasonable explanation of the correlations shown in Table 4.1 is that intelligence has a direct, causal effect on educational attainment. It has this effect because IQ determines the efficiency of learning and comprehension of all cognitive tasks.

INTELLIGENCE AND SOCIOECONOMIC STATUS

Measures of socioeconomic status are typically a composite of occupation, social status, education, and earnings. The results of four major studies of the relation between intelligence and earnings are shown in Table 4.2. The first three studies come from the United States and the fourth is from Britain. The first of the American studies (Johnson, 1948) was derived from the intelligence testing of military personnel in World War I; the second was derived from a similar program of testing of military personnel in World War II; and the third was derived from the American standardization sample of the Wechsler Adult Intelligence Scale (Revised). These IQs are based on a population mean of 100 and a standard deviation of 15. Thus, the IQ gap between Socioeconomic Status 1 (professional) and socioeconomic status 5 (unskilled workers) lies between 1.5 and almost 2 standard deviations. It will be seen that in the first two studies, the average IQs of the professional class, 1, were higher than in the later third study. The explanation for this is probably that in the earlier studies the professional class was a smaller elite than at the time of the third study. The IQs of the lowest class, 5, were also higher in the two earlier studies than in the later study. The explanation for this is probably that the lowest socioeconomic status class has declined in size, and those with higher IQs have moved out of it, thus leaving behind a smaller class with lower IQs.

The fourth study comes from Britain and is based on a representative sample of 5,565 men who were born in 1958 and intelligence tested at the age of 11 years (Saunders, 1996). Their socioeconomic status was assessed in

Table 4.2

**Mean IQs in Relation to Five Socioeconomic
Status Categories**

Socioeconomic Status							
Date	N	1	2	3	4	5	Reference
1918	28,597	123	119	104	98	96	Johnson, 1948
1943	18,782	120	113	106	96	95	Johnson, 1948
1981	1,880	111	104	99	93	89	Reynolds *et al.*, 1987
1991	5,565	—	106	97	91	—	Saunders, 1996

terms of three categories at the age of 33 years. The IQs of the three categories have been calculated from the report and show a similar gradient to those found in the United States.

Several studies have presented correlations between intelligence measured in childhood, adolescence, or early adulthood, and socioeconomic status achieved later in adulthood. The results of the major studies are given in Table 4.3. The first entry shows the results of a study by Bajema (1968) in which a sample of 979 white children from schools in Kalamazoo, Michigan, were intelligence tested during the 1916 and 1917 school year at the age of 11 years. These individuals were tested again in 1951 when they were aged 45 and 46 and their socioeconomic status was ascertained. The correlation between their childhood IQs and the socioeconomic status in their mid-forties was .46. The second entry presents the results of a study by Waller (1971) of a representative sample of 173 white adolescents with a mean age of 13 years in Minnesota. These adolescents were intelligence tested then and followed up in adulthood, at which time their socioeconomic status was ascertained. The correlation between their childhood IQ and adult socioeconomic status was .52.

Table 4.3

Correlations between IQs and Socioeconomic Status

Intelligence	Correlation	Reference
11 years	.46	Bajema, 1968
Childhood	.52	Waller, 1971
Young adults	.52	Jencks, 1972
11 years	.43	Bond & Saunders, 1999

The third entry shows the correlation of .52 given by Jencks (1972) for a sample of native, white, non-farm military inductees who were intelligence tested in early adulthood by the American military and whose occupational status was ascertained some years later when they had returned to civilian life.

The fourth entry is taken from a British study carried out by Bond and Saunders (1999) in which a nationally representative sample of 4,293 boys were given intelligence tests at the age of 11 years and were followed up to the age of 33 years, when their occupational status was ascertained. The correlation between childhood IQ and adult occupational status was .43.

The average of the four correlations in Table 4.3 is .48. Thus, this is about 50 percent higher than the average correlation between intelligence and earnings which is .34, as shown in Chapter 3, "Intelligence and Earnings." It appears, therefore, that intelligence is a stronger predictor of socioeconomic status than of earnings.

Intelligence is a determinant of socioeconomic status because more intelligent children do better in school and in college, and they are able to acquire the vocational and professional skills that qualify them for entry to the higher socioeconomic status occupations. It has been shown by J. H. Waller (1971) that this process is present within families in a study in which the IQs of fathers and sons were examined in relation to their socioeconomic status. It was found that when sons had higher IQs than their fathers, they tended to rise in the social hierarchy into higher socioeconomic status jobs. Conversely, when sons had lower IQs than their fathers, they tended to fall in the social hierarchy into lower socioeconomic status jobs. Father-son differences in intelligence were correlated at .29 with father-son differences in socioeconomic status, such that when there was a large difference in IQ, there tended to be a correspondingly large difference in socioeconomic status.

LIFETIME ACHIEVEMENT

Intelligence is an important determinant of lifetime achievement. The classical study demonstrating this association was carried out by Lewis Terman and his colleagues. The study began around 1920 by intelligence testing a large number of children in California. From this sample, they selected 1,528 (857 boys and 671 girls) with IQs of 135 and above. The minimum IQ of 135 represents approximately the top one percent of the population. The average IQ of the total sample was 151 (Terman, 1925).

These children were followed up thirty-five years after their initial identification when they were in their early forties. By this time, the authors of the follow up concluded that "the superior child, with few exceptions, becomes the able adult, superior in nearly every respect to the generality" (Terman and Oden, 1959, p. 143).

Terman and his associates found that 70 percent of their sample had graduated from college; two fifths of the men and three fifths of the women had gone through graduate school. Of the men, 86 percent were in the two highest socioeconomic categories of professions and management. None of these individuals were in the lowest socioeconomic category of unskilled workers, as compared with 13 percent of the male population at that time. Seventy of the men were listed in *American Men of Science,* and three had been elected to the National Academy of Sciences. Thirty-one were listed in *Who's Who in America*. Between them, they had produced nearly 2000 scientific papers, some 60 books in the sciences, 230 patents, and 33 novels. Fourteen percent of the men did not fulfill the promise of their high IQs and failed to obtain socioeconomic class one or two occupations. These men were almost all impaired by psychiatric problems or lack of motivation.

Among the women, most of them became housewives and mothers and consequently did not have such visible achievements. Nevertheless, seven women were listed in *American Men of Science* and two in *Who's Who in America*. Between them, they had produced 32 scholarly books, 5 novels, more than 200 scientific papers, and 5 patents.

A smaller scale study, which confirms that high lifetime achievement is associated with high intelligence, has been published by Roe (1953). He intelligence tested 23 successful and highly regarded research scientists and found that their IQs ranged from 121 to 171, with a median of 154.

GENIUS

Intelligence is also an important determinant of outstanding achievement and what in the creative sciences and arts is called genius. The classical study to demonstrate this was made in the 1920s by Catherine Cox (1926). In her study, she compiled a list of 301 historical men who had had outstanding careers as statesmen and soldiers or who had produced creative works of such quality that they could be designated as geniuses. The sample was confined to those for whom there were sufficiently good records of their intellectual development in childhood and adolescence for it to be possible to estimate their IQs. From these records she had their IQs assessed by psychologists experienced in the assessment of intelligence. She had at least two psychologists make these assessments. From this she was able to check the reliability of the assessments, which in general was high. Her method for estimating the IQs of the geniuses was to use the formula for the calculation of IQ that was devised by Stern, which consists of assessing the "mental age" of a child, dividing it by the child's chronological age, and multiplying by 100. A "mental age" is the level of cognitive ability of the average child of that chronological age. Thus, for example, if a child of 6 has the "mental age" 12—that is, this child has the abilities of the average 12-year-old—this child will have an IQ of 200 ($12 \div 6 \times 100 = 200$).

An example illustrating Cox's method is the assessment of the IQ of the French mathematician and scientist Blaise Pascal (1623–1662). From the historical record, it is known that at the age of 11 Pascal noticed that when he struck a plate with a knife it made a loud noise, but if he put his hand against the plate, the noise stopped. This led him to make a number of experiments on sound, from the results of which he wrote a treatise that he completed during his eleventh year of age. In his early teens, he developed an interest in geometry. His father was convinced that he was attempting to understand problems for which he was not sufficiently ready and prevented him from studying Euclid's geometrical theorems. Nevertheless, the young Pascal worked out a number of these for himself and at the age of 16, he wrote a treatise on the geometry of conic sections. At the age of 19, he invented a calculating machine, and at 25 he worked out the theory of atmospheric pressure by a barometric experiment. Cox's psychologists estimated Pascal's IQ at 185.

Another case of early intellectual precocity documented by Cahterine Cox is the English political theorist John Stuart Mill. It is recorded that at the age of five, he had a conversation with Lady Spencer on the comparative strengths as generals of Marlborough and Wellington. When he was six, he wrote a history of Rome using such expressions as "established a kingdom," and "the country had not been entered by any foreign invader." At the age of eleven, he was doing mathematics at present day college level. Using the Stern formula (mental age ÷ chronological age × 100 = IQ), it was estimated that the young J.S. Mill was generally performing at about the level of those twice his chronological age. His IQ was estimated at 190.

When Cox had obtained estimates of the IQs of all her geniuses, she sorted them into eight categories according to the fields in which they made their achievements. The average IQs for the categories are shown in Table 4.4. The average IQ for the entire sample is 158. In a discussion of Cox's work, Eysenck has written that "I think that she has demonstrated beyond any doubt that geniuses in many different lines of endeavor have uniformly high IQs well above the average; indeed, as all the different occupations which led to their achievements obviously needed considerable mental powers any

Table 4.4

Mean IQs of Historical Geniuses Estimated by Catherine Cox (1926)

Category	Mean IQ	Category	Mean IQ
Artists	150	Scientists	155
Musicians	164	Soldiers	132
Philosophers	175	Statesmen	162
Religious leaders	160	Writers	164

other result would have been unbelievable" (1995, p. 59). We think this is indisputable and that the conclusion to be drawn from this research is that geniuses have very high IQs.

The numbers of geniuses produced by a population depends on the population's mean IQ. For a population with a mean IQ of 100, an IQ of 158 is present in approximately one individual out of 30,000. In a population with a mean IQ of 115, there would be approximately one individual per 1,000 people with an IQ over 158, a thirty-fold increase. Thus, differences in the mean IQs of national populations will have large multiplier effects on the numbers of geniuses produced. These effects are likely to contribute both directly and indirectly to economic development.

We should note that, as with other kinds of achievement, high intelligence is not sufficient for genius. To produce a work of such outstanding quality that it can be described as a work of genius requires the personality qualities of dedication, application, persistence, and creativity. There are certainly people who have the requisite IQ to be geniuses, but who lack these personality qualities. Nevertheless, the average intelligence level in a society must be an important determinant of the numbers of geniuses.

THE BELL CURVE

An extensive analysis of the importance of intelligence as a determinant of a wide range of social phenomena was produced in 1994 by Herrnstein and Murray (1994) in their book *The Bell Curve*. The main body of the book consists of an analysis of the data contained in the National Longitudinal Study of Youth, an American study of a nationally representative sample of approximately 12,000 young people. In their analysis of this study, Herrnstein and Murray confirmed the previous research showing that intelligence is a significant determinant of educational attainment, employment, earnings, and social status, and that low intelligence is a determinant of crime. In addition, they also broke new ground by demonstrating that low intelligence is related to poverty, health, single motherhood, and welfare dependency. Most of their analyses were based on whites only, thus making it free of possible contamination by racial differences. Their principal results are summarized in Table 4.5. To display the data, they divided the sample into five intelligence bands consisting of those with IQs of 126 and above, and of those with IQs between 111–125, 90–110, 75–89, and 74 and below. They gave the percentages of a number of social phenomena for each intelligence band. It can be seen that there are large disparities between the IQ bands in the percentage incidence of these social phenomena. Thus, 75 percent of those with IQs of 126 and above gain college degrees, while none of those with IQs below 74 do so. As shown in Table 4.5, it will be seen that intelligence levels are systematically related to the proportion below the poverty line, unemployed, work impaired by poor health, high school drop outs, single motherhood, welfare dependency, and criminal records. The last row in the table shows that only 1 percent of the most intelligent group had a child with an IQ below 80, compared with 30 percent of the least intelligent group, thus showing how intelligence is transmitted in families from generation to generation.

Table 4.5
Incidence of Various Social Phenomena (percentages) in Five IQ Bands

Social Phenomena	126 +	111–125	90–110	75–89	–74
College Graduate	75	38	8	1	0
Below poverty line	1	4	7	14	26
Unemployed one month in last year (males)	4	6	8	11	14
Work impaired by poor health (males)	13	21	37	45	62
High school dropout	0	1	6	26	64
Single mother	4	8	14	22	34
Long-term welfare mother	0	2	8	17	31
Long-term welfare recipient	7	10	14	20	28
Served time in prison	0	1	3	6	13
Child with IQ below 80	1	3	6	16	30

Source: Herrnstein and Murray, 1994.

THE UNDERCLASS

It is apparent from Table 4.5 that low intelligence is a significant component of the sector of society that has become known as the underclass. First coined by Gunnar Myrdal (1962), this concept came into wide circulation in the early 1980s following the publication of the book, *The Underclass* by K. Auletta (1982). The underclass is a subculture that is typically located in impoverished inner city districts and characterized by poor educational attainment, high levels of long-term unemployment, high rates of crime, drug addiction, welfare dependency, and single motherhood. As shown in Table 4.5, all these social pathologies are particularly prevalent in the lowest intelligence group of those with IQs below 75.

In addition to *The Bell Curve*, a number of other studies have shown that low intelligence is associated with delinquency, crime, and unemployment. The leading studies of the average IQs of delinquents, criminals, and the unemployed are shown in Table 4.6. The first seven entries are taken from literature reviews and show a consensus that the average IQs of delinquents and criminals is around 92. The remaining three entries are from the original studies. The study of conduct disorders consisting of persistent anti-social behavior and disobedience in young children is included because this is typically a precursor of later delinquency.

Table 4.6

Mean IQs of Delinquents, Criminals, Children with Conduct Disorders, and the Unemployed

Criterion Group	Mean IQ	Reference
Delinquents	89	Jensen, 1980
Criminals	92	Hirschi and Hindelung, 1977
Criminals	92	Wilson and Herrnstein, 1985
Criminals	92	Quay, 1987
Criminals	92	Eysenck and Gudjonsson, 1989
Criminals	92	Raine, 1993
Criminals	92	Lykken, 1995
Conduct disorders	83	Moffit, 1993
Unemployed	81	Toppen, 1971
Unemployed	92	Lynn, Hampson, and Magee, 1984

An alternative way of expressing the relationship between crime and intelligence is in terms of the correlation coefficient. Four studies, of which the first three are based on literature reviews, expressing the relationship as correlations are shown in Table 4.7.

The explanation for the relationship between low intelligence and crime proposed by Wilson and Herrnstein (1985) is that those with low IQs have a greater need for immediate gratification, weaker impulse control, a poorer understanding of the consequences of punishment, and a more poorly developed moral sense. In addition, adolescents with low IQs tend to do poorly at school and fail to obtain vocational skills, As a result, they are only able to get badly paid jobs, or they find it impossible to obtain any kind of employment. This makes them disaffected; they become alienated from society; and as a result, many of them turn to crime.

Table 4.7

Correlations of Delinquency and Crime with IQ

Variable	Correlation/IQ	Reference
Delinquency	−.45	Jensen, 1980
Crime	−.19	Moffit *et al.*, 1981
Crime	−.25	Eysenck and Gudjonsson, 1989
Crime	− .25	Gordon, 1997

SUMMARY

In this chapter we have seen that intelligence is a significant determinant of educational attainment, socioeconomic status, and lifetime achievement. Low intelligence is a significant determinant of a number of social pathologies including crime, unemployment, welfare dependency, and single motherhood. Nations whose populations have high levels of intelligence are likely to have high levels of educational attainment and relatively large numbers of individuals who make significant contributions to national life. Not all of these contributions can be expected to have a direct economic impact, but many of them will contribute to an economic and social infrastructure conducive to economic development. These nations will also have low levels of crime, unemployment, and welfare dependency. Conversely, nations with low levels of intelligence can be expected to have low levels of educational attainment and relatively few individuals who make significant positive contributions to social well being. These nations are likely to have a large underclass with high rates of crime and unemployment. All of these impose costs on society and will act as a drag on economic growth and development.

5

The Sociology of Intelligence, Earnings, and Social Competence

The sociology of intelligence is concerned with the intelligence levels of sub-populations within nations and their relation to a variety of economic, social, and cultural phenomena including average earnings, employment, educational attainment, literacy, intellectual achievement, and the like. In studies of this kind, the population units have been the populations of cities, districts within cities, regions, and ethnic groups. We have seen in Chapters 3, "Intelligence and Earnings," and 4, "Intelligence and Further Economic and Social Phenomena," that intelligence among individuals is positively related to their earnings, educational attainment, efficiency of job performance, socioeconomic status, and intellectual achievement, and is negatively related to their unemployment, welfare dependency, poverty, single motherhood, and crime. If we regard these populations as aggregates of individuals, we can infer that the same relationships would be present among populations, and that populations with high average intelligence levels would be characterized by higher rates of the desirable social characteristics and lower rates of the undesirable ones. In this chapter, we review the leading studies showing that this is the case.

NEW YORK CITY, 1930–32

The first study of the sociology of intelligence was carried out by J. B. Maller (1933a, 1933b) between 1930 to1932 in New York City. He took as his population units the 310 administrative districts into which the city was divided. The average intelligence levels of the children in these districts were calculated from tests that were administered to approximately 100,000 ten-year-old children. He noted that there was a wide variation in the mean IQs between the districts ranging from 74 to 120. Maller also collected data on per capita incomes, educational attainment, welfare dependency, juvenile delinquency, mortality, and infant mortality. Although he did not publish the complete correlation matrix, it is evident from the correlations he did publish that the intelligence levels found in the districts were positively correlated with educational attainments and were negatively correlated with earnings, welfare dependency, delinquency, death rates, and infant mortality. Table 5.1 shows these published correlations, all of which are statistically significant.

Table 5.1

Sociology of Intelligence in New York City, 1930–32

Variable	IQ	Educational Attainment
IQ	—	.70
Educational attainment	.70	—
Per capita income	—	.53
Welfare dependency	—	−.50
Delinquency	−.57	−.43
Mortality	−.43	−.34
Infant mortality	−.51	−.46

It will be seen that the mean level of intelligence in these districts was highly correlated at .70 with the mean level of educational attainment. The magnitude of this correlation is toward the high end of the range of correlations between IQs and educational attainment among individuals presented in Table 4.1. The IQs show a high negative correlation with delinquency (−.57), as they do among individuals shown in Table 4.5. In addition, the IQs also show appreciable negative correlations with mortality (−.43) and infant mortality (−.51). Although the correlations of IQs with income and welfare dependency were not published, it is evident that they must have been substantial from the high correlations between these and educational attainment and between educational attainment and IQ. Maller did not publish the missing correlations because his principal objective was to ascertain how far educational attainment in the districts was predictable from the economic and social variables.

LONDON, 1937

The second major study of the sociology of intelligence was carried out by C. L. Burt (1937) in London later in the 1930s. As his population units, he used the 29 city boroughs. For each borough, he obtained a measure of the average intelligence level from tests administered to ten year olds. He calculated the correlations between the average IQs and a variety of economic and social phenomena. The results were closely similar to those obtained by Maller in New York City. The intelligence level of children in the London boroughs was positively related to their level of educational attainment, indexed by the proportion of children obtaining scholarships to selective grammar schools, and it was negatively correlated with the prevalence of poverty, unemployment, juvenile delinquency, mortality, and infant mortality. Burt's correlations, all of which are statistically significant, are shown in Table 5.2.

Table 5.2

Correlations of the Intelligence Levels in London Districts with Educational Attainment and Economic and Social Phenomena

Variable	Correlation
Educational attainment	.87
Poverty	−.73
Unemployment	−.67
Delinquency	−.69
Mortality	−.87
Infant mortality	−.93

AMERICAN CITIES, 1939

The next study of the sociology of intelligence was published by E. L. Thorndike (1939) in his book, *Your City,* and was supplemented by E. L. Thorndike and E. Woodyard (1942). *Your City* presented data for 37 economic, social, and epidemiological variables, including average incomes, material possessions (ownership of automobiles, telephones, and so forth), health (mortality and infant mortality), and literacy. The cities were scored for these variables and these scores were summed to give a single measure designated Goodness. The highest score was obtained by Pasadena, followed by Montclair and Cleveland Heights, and the lowest scores were obtained by Augusta, Meridian, High Point, and Charleston.

In a supplementary paper, Thorndike and Woodyard (1942) presented data for the average IQs of 12-year-olds in 30 American cities. The correlation between the cities' average IQs and their Goodness score was 0.86, showing that intelligence is a very powerful determinant of what may be called the economic and social quality of a city.

AMERICAN STATES

The first investigation of this kind to use American states as population units was carried out by K. S. Davenport and H. H. Remmers (1950). In this study, they obtained intelligence data for over 300,000 young men who took tests for training programs in the armed services in 1943. Using these tests, they calculated the average IQ for each of the American states. They found that the average IQs were correlated at .81 with average state incomes and at 0.67 with the proportion of adults in the state appearing in *Who's Who in America*. This was a further demonstration of the strong association between the population's IQ and earnings and the first empirical demonstration that a high level of intelligence in a population produces a large number of intellectually outstanding individuals.

THE BRITISH ISLES

In the late 1970s, a study of the sociology of intelligence in the British Isles was made by one of the authors (Lynn, 1979). In this study, the British Isles were divided into 13 regions and data were collected for mean IQs and for a variety of educational, social, economic, and health phenomena. Educational attainment was measured for the British Isles by using the numbers of first class degrees that were awarded by universities as a proportion of the numbers of young people. Intellectual achievement was measured by the proportions of the population born in the respective regions who became Fellows of the Royal Society. The correlations of the average IQs with these economic and social phenomena are shown in Table 5.3. All the correlations are statistically significant. It will be seen that, as shown in previous studies, the intelligence levels of the populations are positively associated with educational attainment, intellectual achievement, and earnings, and are negatively associated with unemployment and infant mortality.

FRANCE AND SPAIN

Studies similar to those of the British Isles have been made for France and Spain (Lynn, 1980, 1981). In the case of France, intelligence test data were collected from military conscripts for the 90 administrative departments into which the country is divided. Intellectual achievement was measured by the proportions of the populations born in these departments who were members of the Institut de France in 1975. (The Institut de France consists of five academies for language, science, social science, literature, and fine arts, and its members are considered the intellectual elite of France. In 1975, it had 250 members.) Data were also obtained for their average earnings, the percentage of the labor force unemployed, and infant mortality. The correlations between the IQs and these economic and social phenomena are shown in Table 5.4.

In the case of Spain, mean IQs for regions were calculated from military conscript data for the 48 administrative districts into which the country is divided. In addition, data were also obtained for earnings and infant mortality. It was not possible to find data for intellectual achievement or unemployment. The

Table 5.3

Correlations between Intelligence Levels and Economic and Social Phenomena in the Regions of the British Isles

Variable	Correlation
Educational attainment	.60
Intellectual attainment	.94
Earnings	.73
Unemployment	−.82
Infant mortality	−.78

Table 5.4

Correlations between Intelligence Levels and Economic and Social Phenomena in the Regions of France and Spain

Variable	France	Spain
Intellectual achievement	.26[*]	.11
Earnings	.61[*]	.65[*]
Unemployment	—	−.20
Infant mortality	−.30[*]	.54[*]

[*] Denotes statistical significance at p < .05.

correlations between the IQs in the regions and earnings and infant mortality are shown in Table 5.4, together with the corresponding correlations for France. It will be seen that these results confirm the previous studies, showing that the intelligence levels of populations are positively associated with earnings and negatively associated with infant mortality.

INTELLIGENCE AND MORTALITY

In all the studies reviewed in this chapter, we have seen that the intelligence levels of populations are negatively associated with mortality and infant mortality. The explanation for this is that intelligence is a determinant of all abilities, and this includes the abilities entailed in keeping adults and babies alive. Intelligent individuals are better able to avoid accidents, to look after their health by exercising, eating sensibly, and not taking drugs, and are more likely to seek medical attention when they are ill. Thus, they are more likely to stay alive than the unintelligent. Direct evidence for the relation between intelligence and mortality has been provided by B. I. O'Toole and L. Stankov (1992) in a study in which they examined mortality in a sample of military conscripts in Australia. The men in this sample were conscripted into the army at the age of 18 and were intelligence tested. A sample of 2,309 men was followed up approximately seventeen years later and divided into 1,786 men who survived into their mid-thirties and 523 who died before they reached their mid-thirties. It was found that those who had died were significantly less intelligent than those who survived. The single most common cause of death was motor vehicle accidents. In regard to infant mortality, it has been shown that the incidence of infant deaths is greater among those born to parents with low intelligence (Savage, 1946). The explanation for this is likely to be that less intelligent parents are less competent at looking after their babies, so that these babies have a higher mortality from accidents and from failures to obtain medical attention.

SELECTIVE MIGRATION AND POPULATION IQ DIFFERENCES

The most straightforward explanation for the differences in intelligence between the populations of the districts of the cities of New York and London, between American cities, and between the regions of the British Isles, France, and Spain, is that these differences have arisen as a result of geographical segregation by intelligence over the course of several generations. What has taken place is that those with higher IQs have done well economically and have moved into more affluent districts, while those with lower IQs have done poorly and have moved into impoverished districts. This geographical segregation has occurred in parallel with the segregation by intelligence of the socioeconomic classes (as noted in Chapter 4). There is also a considerable overlap between the two processes because the districts and regions whose populations have higher average IQs are also those whose populations have higher socioeconomic status. Once the differences in intelligence between the districts and regions have become established, they tend to stabilize for generations, partly through the transmission of intelligence from parents to children and partly through social and geographical mobility. This ensures that in each generation the more intelligent move geographically into more affluent districts and regions, while the less intelligent move into the less affluent districts and regions. The stability of the differences in affluence between the districts of cities is well illustrated by the city of London. In Burt's study (1937) carried out in the 1930s, the most affluent districts were Hampstead, Westminster, and Chelsea, and the most impoverished were the east-end districts of Stepney, Shoreditch, and Bethnel Green. These differences are still present seventy years later.

In the regions of the British Isles and France, selective migration by intelligence has led to a concentration of the highest level of intelligence in the capital cities of London and Paris, as shown in Lynn (1980). What has evidently occurred is that over the course of centuries, individuals with high intelligence attracted by the opportunities for acquiring fame and fortune, have migrated to these capital cities. Once they have settled in the capital cities, they have left descendants who have inherited their high IQs, leading to a higher average level of intelligence in the capital cities than in the remainder of the country.

The impact of selective migration on the intelligence of populations is well illustrated by the experience of Scotland in relation to the rest of Great Britain and analysed in Lynn (1977c). Evidence that emigration from Scotland has been selective for intelligence is provided by the study of a representative sample of 1,000 Scottish 11-year-old children who were intelligence tested in 1947. These children were followed up when they were in their early thirties, and it was found that 17.2 percent had emigrated and that the mean IQ of this group was 108.1 (Maxwell, 1969). This shows the presence of selective emigration by intelligence. The effect would be to reduce the mean IQ of those remaining in Scotland to 98.3. Allowing for regression effects, the mean IQ of the children of this group would be approximately 99. Thus, selective migration reduced the mean IQ in Scotland by one IQ point in one generation. Continued over the course of several generations, this process can comfortably account for the mean IQ of 97.3 found in Scotland in the middle decades of the twentieth century. The presence of selective emigration from Scotland is corroborated by further studies. For instance, Clement and Robertson (1961) have shown that from the eighteenth century, approximately half of Scotland's most outstanding scientists and engineers emigrated from Scotland. It has also been shown that from the mid-nineteenth century, around half of the graduates of the University of Aberdeen left Scotland (MacKay, 1969).

The conclusion to be drawn from this analysis is that selective migration between districts in cities and regions of countries has led to genetic segregation by intelligence. This has brought about the intelligence differences in the populations of these districts and regions and has been responsible for the differences in earnings, intellectual attainment and achievement, unemployment, and mortality.

POSITIVE FEEDBACK EFFECTS

In the case of the positive association between intelligence and earnings among individuals, reviewed in Chapter 3, the causal effect is clearly that intelligence is the determinant of earnings because IQs are approximately stable from the age of five years. Earnings obtained in adulthood cannot therefore have any effect on intelligence, and the causal sequence can only be from intelligence to earnings. In the case of the sociological associations between the intelligence of groups and the average earnings and other economic and social phenomena reviewed in this chapter, the causal sequence is not so straightforward. While the general thrust of our argument is that the intelligence level of groups is the determinant of earnings and the other economic and social phenomena, it may be argued that the causal sequence is in the other direction and that the per capita incomes of groups are a determinant of the intelligence of the children born into and reared in these groups. It might be argued that groups with high per capita incomes provide a better environment for the nurturance of their children's intelligence by the provision of good quality nutrition, health care, and education, all of which are known to have an effect on the development of intelligence in children. We accept that a process of this kind is almost certainly present and that it operates in conjunction with a causal impact of group intelligence on earnings and other economic and social phenomena. The process should be regarded as one of positive feedback in which the intelligence level of the group is a determinant of its per capita income, and the per capita income of the group has an impact on the intelligence level of the children born and reared in the group.

THE GENETIC COMPONENT IN SUB-POPULATION DIFFERENCES

Because intelligence is determined by both genetic and environmental factors, those individuals with high intelligence who have migrated into the more affluent districts of the cities and regions of countries will have possessed both the genetic and environmental components of intelligence. This will have led to a geographical and genetic segregation of the sub-populations by intelligence of a similar kind to the socioeconomic and genetic segregation that we discuss in Chapter 4. Once the sub-populations of the districts of cities and the regions of nations have become segregated by intelligence, environmental factors will reinforce the genetic differences between the sub-populations in so far as the sub-populations with high intelligence will provide their children with the environmental and developmental advantages of intelligence through the process of positive feedback described in the preceding section.

In genetics, such positive feedback effects are well recognized and are described as a genotype-environment correlation. The general principle has been described by R. Plomin, J. C. DeFries and G. E. McClearn (1980, p. 360) as follows: "Genotype-environment correlation refers to the differential exposure of genotypes to environments. In other words, GE correlation is a function of the frequency with which certain genotypes and certain environments occur together. For example, if talented children are exposed to a special training that enhances their talent, there is a positive correlation between genetic differences in talent and environmental differences." This is the process that is taking place at a group level in the positive association between the intelligence of groups and the provision of favorable or unfavorable environments for the development of intelligence in children who are born and reared in these groups.

The principle of genotype-environment correlation implies that both genetic and environmental factors are involved in individual and group differences in intelligence. Thus, the conclusion to be drawn from this analysis is that selective migration between the districts in cities and regions of countries has led to genetic segregation by intelligence. This segregation has created intelligence differences in the populations of districts and regions that cause the differences in earnings, intellectual attainment and achievement, unemployment, and mortality.

SUMMARY

In this chapter, a number of examples have been presented showing that the average intelligence levels of the sub-populations in the districts of cities and the regions of countries is positively associated with group earnings, educational attainment and intellectual achievement, and is negatively associated with group unemployment, crime, and mortality. These differences in the intelligence of sub-populations have come about through selective migration of the more intelligent into the more affluent districts of cities and regions of countries over a period of several generations, thus leading to genetic differences between the populations. These genetic differences are reinforced by the environmental advantages, which more intelligent populations are able to give their children through the process of genotype-environment correlation. The evidence presented in this chapter is an extension of the data on individuals reviewed in Chapters 3 and 4 and shows that the intelligence levels of groups are important determinants of per capita group earnings and other economic and social phenomena.

6

Data on Variables and Methods of Analysis

We have seen in Chapter 3, "Intelligence and Earnings," that intelligence is a determinant of incomes among individuals, and in Chapter 5, "The Sociology of Intelligence, Earnings, and Social Competence," that intelligence is a determinant of earnings among sub-populations of nations, consisting of the districts of cities and geographical regions. We now extend this analysis to include nations. In addition, we will consider whether there are national differences in intelligence that may contribute to rates of economic growth and development and may provide an explanation for the gap between rich and poor countries. In this chapter, we introduce the empirical variables and data by which we intend to test the hypothesis that a country's economic success depends to a significant extent on the average intelligence of the population. This hypothesis is testable and can be falsified. It can be tested by examining data on national IQs and on the economic success of countries. We consider that per capita rates of economic growth and per capita national income are best suited to measure differences in the economic success of countries and the gap between rich and poor countries. In the last sections of this chapter, we introduce the methods of statistical analysis that will be used to test the hypothesis.

CALCULATION OF NATIONAL IQs IN 81 COUNTRIES

Most intelligence tests have been constructed in Britain and the United States, and these tests have subsequently been administered to samples of the populations in many other countries throughout the world. From these studies, we have calculated the mean IQs of the populations of 81 nations. In making these calculations, the mean IQ in Britain is set at 100 with a standard deviation of 15, and the mean IQs of other nations have been calculated in relation to this standard. The technical details of how these calculations have been made are given in Appendix 1, "The Calculation of National Intelligence Levels."

These 81 countries constitute the first group of countries analyzed in this study. However, because these 81 countries do not represent a random sample of the total population of the countries and because we want to apply the hypothesis to all countries of the world, we have estimated the national IQs for 104 other countries whose population is more than 50,000 inhabitants. However, Bosnia and Herzegovina has been excluded from our study because this country was without an effective national government for the most part of the 1990s. All of the 185 countries in this study are independent countries, except Hong Kong and Puerto Rico and also Taiwan, which is a Chinese province controlled by the government of the Republic of China, whose authority since 1949 has been limited to the island of Taiwan (see Banks et al., 1997, p. 171).

The results of the calculations of national IQs for the 81 countries for which we have measurements have been grouped into seven geographical regions and are shown in Table 6.1. Shown first are the IQs for 25 European nations. These IQs fall in the range between 90 in Croatia and 102 in Austria, Germany, Italy, and the Netherlands. The median IQ for this group of nations is 98. The IQ for Ireland is a little lower than that given in Table 5.4 because it is based on more recent data. The depressed IQ in Ireland is attributable to a long history of selective emigration and to the low standard of living that was present until the mid-1990s. Apart from Ireland, there is a trend for IQs to be higher in northern and western Europe, where the IQs are around 100, than in southern and eastern Europe, where the IQs fall as low as 90 in Croatia and are in the low 90s in Greece (92), Bulgaria (93), and Romania (94).

Table 6.1
IQs in 81 Nations

Country	IQ	Country	IQ	Country	IQ
		Europe			
Austria	102	Denmark	98	Ireland	93
Belgium	100	Finland	97	Italy	102
Britain	100	France	98	Netherlands	102
Bulgaria	93	Germany	102	Norway	98
Croatia	90	Greece	92	Poland	99
Czech. Republic	97	Hungary	99	Portugal	95

Country	IQ	Country	IQ	Country	IQ
		Europe (cont.)			
Romania	94	Slovenia	95	Switzerland	101
Russia	96	Spain	97		
Slovakia	96	Sweden	101		
		North America and Australasia			
Australia	98	New Zealand	100	United States	98
Canada	97				
		East Asia			
China	100	Japan	105	Taiwan	104
Hong Kong	107	South Korea	106		
		South and Southwest Asia			
India	81	Lebanon	86	Singapore	103
Iran	84	Malaysia	92	Thailand	91
Iraq	87	Nepal	78	Turkey	90
Israel	94	Qatar	78		
		Southeast Asia and Pacific Islands			
Fiji	84	Marshall Islands	84	Samoa	87
Indonesia	89	Philippines	86	Tonga	87
		Latin America and the Caribbean			
Argentina	96	Ecuador	80	Puerto Rico	84
Barbados	78	Guatemala	79	Suriname	89
Brazil	87	Jamaica	72	Uruguay	96
Colombia	89	Mexico	87		
Cuba	85	Peru	90		

Table 6.1   continued

Country	IQ	Country	IQ	Country	IQ
		Africa			
Congo (Brazzaville)	73	Guinea	66	Sudan	72
Congo (Zaire)	65	Kenya	72	Tanzania	72
Egypt	83	Morocco	85	Uganda	73
Equatorial Guinea	59	Nigeria	67	Zambia	77
Ethiopia	63	Sierra Leone	64	Zimbabwe	66
Ghana	71	South Africa	72		

Shown second in Table 6.1 are the IQs for North America and Australasia. These populations are of mainly northern and western European origin and have the same IQs as those of their parent populations in Europe. The IQ of 98 in the United States is slightly depressed because of the substantial numbers in the population of Blacks and Hispanics, whose mean IQs are approximately 85 and 92, respectively (Herrnstein and Murray, 1994). The mean IQ of the Whites in the United States is 100, the same as that in Britain (Jensen and Reynolds, 1982).

Shown third in the table are the IQs of the five East Asian countries that are populated by Oriental peoples. In Hong Kong, Japan, South Korea, and Singapore, the mean IQs lie in the range of 104 (in Taiwan) to 107 (in Hong Kong), which are significantly higher than the IQs found in Europe. The IQ of 100 found in the People's Republic of China is depressed due to the economically backward state of the country and the low living standards, which have impaired the development of intelligence to its full potential. If the rapid economic growth of the 1990s continues, it can be anticipated that the IQ in China will rise to about 105, the same level as the other Oriental peoples.

Shown fourth in the table are the IQs of the 11 nations of South and Southwest Asia, which run from Turkey through the Middle East to Southeast Asia. These IQs lie in the range between 78 in Nepal and Qatar and 103 in Singapore. The high IQ in Singapore is anomalous and is due to the predominantly ethnic Chinese population whose mean IQ is 107, which is closely similar to the IQ of the Chinese in Hong Kong and Taiwan. The IQ of Singapore is reduced by the 14 percent of Malays whose mean IQ is 92, which is the same as the IQ in Malaysia, and the 7 percent of Indians whose IQ is assumed to be 81, the same as that in India.

The IQ of 94 in Israel is higher than the IQs in the remainder of this group of nations. The explanation for this is that Israel is an ethnically diverse nation with about equal numbers of Western (European) and Eastern (Asian) Jews. Western Jews have an IQ 12 points higher than Eastern Jews (Lieblich, Ninio, and Kugelmass, 1972; Zeidner, 1987). The IQ of Eastern Jews in Israel is approximately 88 and is closely similar to the IQs of the neighboring South Asian populations like Turkey (90), Lebanon (86), Iraq (87), and Iran (84). The IQ of Western Jews in Israel is approximately 100, which is about the same as that of other Northern and Western European populations, although Jews in the United States and Britain have substantially higher IQs averaging around 110 or even 115 (Herrnstein and Murray, 1994; MacDonald, 1994). Most western Jews migrated to Israel during the second half of the twentieth century and have raised the intelligence level above those of other south Asian populations.

Shown fifth in the table are the IQs found in six nations of Southeast Asia and the Pacific Islands. These IQs fall in the narrow band ranging between 84 and 89.

Shown sixth in the table are the IQs found in thirteen Latin American and Caribbean countries. The range of IQs is considerable from 72 in Jamaica to 96 in Argentina and Uruguay. These IQs appear to be determined by the racial and ethnic make-up of the populations. In Argentina and Uruguay, the populations are very largely European at 85 percent for Argentina and 86 percent for Uruguay (*Philip's World Atlas*, 1996). The IQs of 96 are typical of Europeans. The countries with lower proportions of Europeans and greater proportions of Native Americans, Blacks, and Mestizos have lower IQs. This applies to Brazil with its IQ of 87 (53 percent European, 22 percent Mulatto, 12 percent Mestizo, and 11 percent Black); Colombia with its IQ of 89 (20 percent Europeans, 68 percent Mestizos, 7 percent Native American Indian, and 5 percent Black); Mexico with its IQ of 87 (9 percent European, 60 percent Mestizos, and 30 percent Native American Indian); and Peru with its IQ of 90 (12 percent white, 47 percent Native American Indian, and 32 percent Mestizos). Countries with very low percentages of Europeans have even lower IQs. This applies to Guatemala with its IQ of 79 (3 percent White, 55 percent Native American Indian, and 42 percent Mestizos); Barbados with its IQ of 78 (4 percent European, 80 percent Black, and 16 percent Mulatto); and Jamaica with its IQ of 72 (3 percent European, 3 percent East Indian, 80 percent Black, and 15 percent Mulatto).

Shown last in the table are the IQs in seventeen African countries. The two countries in North Africa, Egypt and Morocco, have higher mean IQs at 83 and 85, respectively, than any of the countries of sub-Saharan Africa. The explanation for this is that their populations are Caucasian and they are genetically part of the Caucasian family of peoples of Europe and South and Southwest Asia rather than of the African peoples south of the Sahara (Cavalli-Sforza, Menozzi, and Piazza, 1996, p. 78).

The IQ in South Africa is 72. The country contains four racial groups of Whites, Blacks, Indians, and Coloreds (mainly of mixed black-white ancestry). There have been a number of studies of the intelligence of these groups. Their average IQs are Whites: 94; Blacks: 66; Coloreds: 82; Indians: 83 (see Appendix 1, "The Calculation of National Intelligence Levels"). The percentages of the four groups in the population are Whites: 14 percent; Blacks: 75 percent; Coloreds: 9 percent; Indians: 2 percent (Ramsay, 2000). Weighting the IQs of the four groups by their percentages in the population gives an IQ of 72 for South Africa. The remaining fourteen countries in the last section of Table 6.1 have racially homogeneous black populations. Their IQs fall in the range between 59 and 77 with a median of 69.

We conclude this section by noting that although the 81 nations for which national IQs have been calculated are not a random sample, they are nevertheless a representative sample of the world's nations in so far as they include nations from all continents and from all levels of economic development. The sample includes the "first world" of the economically developed market economies, the "second world" of the former communist economies of the Soviet Union, Eastern Europe, and China, and the "third world" of the economically developing and undeveloped economies of South and Southwest Asia, the Pacific Islands, Latin America, the Caribbean, and Africa.

RELIABILITY OF NATIONAL IQs

The national IQs presented in Table 6.1 are subject to sampling and measurement errors. The degree to which these measures are true is known as their reliability. It is quantified by the correlation between two measures taken from a number of countries. In the sample of 81 nations, there are 45 for which there are two or more measures of the IQ. There are also 15 countries for which there are more than two measures and for these we have used the two extreme values. The correlation between the two measures of national IQ is .939. This high correlation establishes that the measure of national IQ has high reliability.

VALIDITY OF NATIONAL IQs

It has sometimes been argued that no valid comparisons can be made between IQs obtained from different nations. This is the problem of the "validity" of the national IQs presented in Table 6.1. One variant of this argument is that intelligence tests are biased in favor of the white Americans and Europeans who construct the tests because they measure the cognitive skills taught or acquired incidentally in western cultures, but do not equally test the complex cognitive skills possessed by peoples of other cultures. For instance, it has been asserted by Kagan (1971, p. 92) that "the IQ test is a seriously biased instrument that almost guarantees middle class white children higher scores than almost any other group of children." The strong version of this thesis that white Americans and Europeans "almost" inevitably perform better on these tests than other peoples has been shown to be incorrect by the accumulating evidence showing that the Japanese, Chinese, and Koreans perform better on the tests than Americans and Europeans. In addition, it is not only in their own countries that these peoples achieve higher IQs than whites. Ethnic East Asians in the United States have a mean IQ of 104.4 in relation to the white IQ of 100 (Lynn, 1996).

Another variant of the position that intelligence tests do not provide valid measures of the mental abilities of different peoples has been advanced by J. Diamond (1998, p. 20). He contends that the stone age peoples of New Guinea are more intelligent than westerners even though they do not perform so well on intelligence tests: "New Guineans impressed me as being on the average more intelligent, more alert, more expressive, more interested in things and people around them than the average European or American. Of course New Guineans tend to perform poorly at tasks that westerners have been trained to perform since childhood and that New Guineans have not." What Diamond is contending is that intelligence tests do not provide valid measures of the intelligence of peoples who are outside the economically developed western societies.

Another assertion that no valid comparisons can be made between IQs obtained in different societies has been made on the grounds that intelligence has different meanings in different cultures. This view has been advanced by S. H. Irvine and J. W. Berry (1988, p. 6) who write that "Our mature judgment is that most attempts to use test scores as operational measures of the mental status of groups or populations have little claim to scientific validity". Contrary to this view, it has been shown by H. Reuning (1988) that even among such a primitive group as the Bushmen hunter-gatherers of the Kalahari desert, ability tests are positively intercorrelated and have a general factor similar to the g found in western studies. Reuning also shows that the Bushmen have an understanding that some people are bright and others dull, corresponding to similar notions in economically developed countries, and that these concepts correlate well with scores on intelligence tests. It has also been shown in numerous other studies of peoples from a variety of different cultures that cognitive abilities have the same pattern of positive intercorrelation and a general factor identifiable as g as has been found in the populations of economically developed nations. This has been shown to be true in Turkey (Kagitcibasi and Savasir, 1988), for Ugandans, Eskimos, and Native American Indians (Hakstian and Vandenberg, 1979), and for Blacks as well as Whites in South Africa (Kendall, Verster, and von Mollendorf, 1988).

For further evidence that national IQs are meaningful and valid constructs, we present evidence in the next two sections that they are positively associated with reaction times and educational attainment.

NATIONAL IQs AND REACTION TIMES

Intelligence can be measured by reaction times, which consist of the speed of reaction to a visual or auditory stimulus. The explanation generally adopted for the correlation between reaction times and intelligence is that reaction times measure the neurophysiological efficiency of the brain's capacity to process information accurately and that the same ability is measured by intelligence tests (Jensen, 1998; Deary, 2000). Children are not trained to perform well on reaction time tasks so the advantage of the more intelligent on these tasks cannot arise from practice, familiarity, education, or training. To examine whether the national differences in intelligence measured by intelligence tests are valid measures of mental capacities, we can examine whether the same differences are present in reaction times.

The simplest procedure usually employed for the measurement of reaction times is that a light comes on and the participant in the experiment has to react by moving a finger. In one of the most frequently used procedures, the participant has his or her finger on a button and has to lift and move their finger to the light when it comes on, thus causing it to be switched off. This procedure is known as simple reaction time and the time taken to react by moving the finger is known as the decision time. There are two other slightly more complex procedures that have commonly been employed. The first of these is known as choice reaction time and consists of the illumination of one of several lights. In this procedure, the participant has to move the finger to the illuminated light. The second procedure is known as the odd man out procedure, in which three lights come on simultaneously and the participant has to move the finger to the light that is furthest from the other two. Normally, some twenty to thirty trials are given and the speed of reaction is averaged. Averaging makes it possible to obtain a measure of the variability of reaction times.

All three reaction time procedures and the variability of reaction times are correlated with intelligence, such that more intelligent individuals have faster reaction times and less variability. For any single measure the correlations normally lie between 0.2 and 0.4. A review of several studies concludes that when the measures are combined, they produce a multiple correlation of 0.67 (Vernon, 1987). This is about the same size of correlation as found between two conventional intelligence tests of, say, reasoning ability and vocabulary.

It is possible to use reaction time tasks to ascertain whether the national differences in intelligence are a function of some neurophysiological differences in the efficiency of the brain, in which case the differences will also be present in reaction times. Alternatively, the national differences in intelligence may simply reflect differences in the ability to do the tests devised by psychologists in economically developed western societies and not be measures of real differences in mental abilities between populations, as argued by Diamond and by Irvine and Berry. A series of studies of the reaction times of nine-year-old children in Japan, Hong Kong, Britain, and Ireland and of Blacks in South Africa enabled us to distinguish between these two theories. In these studies, the children were given the Progressive Matrices as a non-verbal test of intelligence, and the simple choice and odd-man-out reaction times tasks. Their reaction times and variabilities were measured by computer and hence were not subject to any human error in recording. The results have been described in detail for Japan by Shigehisa and Lynn (1991), for Hong Kong and Britain by Chan and Lynn(1989), for Ireland by Lynn (1991a), and for South Africa by Lynn and Holmshaw (1990). The results of the IQs and the reaction times for the five countries are summarized in Table 6.2. It will be seen that the highest IQs are obtained by the children in Hong Kong and Japan, and are followed in descending order by the children in Britain, Ireland, and the Black children in South Africa. The first row gives the numbers of children from each country. The second row gives their mean IQs. The next three rows give the median reaction times and follow the same descending order as the IQs. The second set of three measures are the variabilities and show the same general descending trend, although for these measures the relationship with IQ is not linear. The column headed SD contains the standard deviations for the total sample. The final column on the right gives the correlations between IQs and the reaction times, from which it will be seen that all the correlations are high and that five of the six are statistically significant.

Table 6.2

IQs and Reaction Times (in milliseconds) in Five Countries

	Hong Kong	Japan	Britain	Ireland	South Africa	SD	r
Number	118	110	239	317	350	—	—
I.Q.	113	110	100	89	67	—	—
Simple RT	361	348	371	388	398	64	.94**
Choice RT	423	433	480	485	489	67	.89*
OMO RT	787	818	898	902	924	187	.96**
Simple RT-V	99	103	90	121	139	32	.83*
Choice RT-V	114	138	110	141	155	30	.73
OMO-RT	269	298	282	328	332	95	.85*

* and ** = statistically significant at p < .05 and p < .01, respectively.

NATIONAL IQs AND EDUCATIONAL ATTAINMENT

For a further examination of the validity of the national IQs, we have examined their relation with measures of national educational attainment. This follows the long established methodology of the validation of intelligence tests among individuals by showing that they are positively correlated with measures of educational attainment. What these studies show is that intelligence tests measure something important. They do not simply measure the ability to perform well on the puzzles devised by psychologists.

The measures of national levels of education attainment are taken from the second and third international studies of educational achievement in mathematics and science. These data are shown in Table 6.3 for the countries for which we have IQ measures. The correlations between educational attainment and IQ are shown in the bottom two rows of the table. It will be seen that five of the six correlations are statistically significant and establish the validity of the measures of national IQ.

Table 6.3
National Attainments in Math and Science

Country	Math	Math	Math	Science	Science	Science
Australia	—	546	530	12.9	262	545
Belgium	20.0	546	511	—	—	—
Britain	15.2	513	506	11.7	551	552
Canada	18.4	532	527	13.7	549	531
Czech. Republic	—	567	564	—	557	574
Denmark	—	502	478	—	—	—
Finland	14.1	—	—	15.3	—	—
France	15.2	538	498	—	—	—
Germany	—	509	531	—	—	—
Hong Kong	16.3	587	588	11.2	533	522
Iran	—	429	428	—	415	470
Ireland	—	550	527	—	539	538
Israel	18.3	531	522	—	505	524
Italy	13.4	—	—	—	—	—
Japan	23.8	597	605	15.4	574	571

Country	Math	Math	Math	Science	Science	Science
Korea	—	611	607	15.4	597	565
Netherlands	21.1	577	541	—	557	560
New Zealand	14.1	499	508	—	531	525
Nigeria	9.3	—	—	—	—	—
Philippines	9.5	—	—	—	—	—
Poland	11.9	—	—	—	—	—
Portugal	—	475	454	—	480	480
Romania	—	482	486	—	—	—
Russia	—	538	538	—	—	—
Singapore	—	625	643	11.2	547	607
Slovak Republic	—	547	544	—	—	—
Slovenia	—	552	541	—	546	560
South Africa	—	354	326	—	—	—
Spain	—	487	517	—	—	—
Switzerland	—	545	522	—	—	—
Thailand	13.1	490	522	—	473	525
USA	15.1	545	500	13.2	565	534
Correlation with IQ	.676	.768	.766	.477	.839	.698
Significance	.01	.001	.001	.1	.001	.001

Source: Column 1: Study of 13-year-olds, Second International Study of Mathematical Achievement, 1982 (Baker and Jones, 1993). Column 2: Study of 10-year-olds, Third International Mathematics and Science Study, 1994–5 (Mullis, 1997). Column 3: Study of 14-year-olds, Third International Mathematics and Science Study, 1994–5, (Beaton *et al.*, 1996a). Column 4: Study of 10-year-olds, Second International Study of Science Achievement, 1985 (IEA, 1988). Column 5: Study of 10-year-olds, Third International Mathematics and Science Study, 1994–5 (Martin, 1997). Column 6: Study of 14-year-olds, Third International Mathematics and Science Study, 1994–5 (Beaton *et al.*, 1996b).

The results of the 1999 International Mathematics and Science Study for 38 countries are shown in Table 6.4.

Table 6.4

Mathematics and Science Achievement Scale Scores in 1999

Country	Mathematics	Science
Australia	525	540
Belgium (Flemish)	558	535
Bulgaria	511	518
Canada	531	533
Chile	392	420
Chinese Taipei (Taiwan)	585	569
Cyprus	476	460
Czech Republic	520	539
England (United Kingdom)	496	538
Finland	520	535
Hong Kong	582	530
Hungary	532	552
Indonesia	403	435
Iran	422	448
Israel	466	468
Italy	479	493
Japan	579	550
Jordan	428	450
Korea (Republic of)	587	549
Latvia	505	503
Lithuania	482	488
Macedonia	447	458
Malaysia	519	492
Moldova	469	459
Morocco	337	323
Netherlands	540	545

Country	Mathematics	Science
New Zealand	491	510
Philippines	345	345
Romania	472	472
Russia	526	529
Singapore	604	568
Slovakia	534	535
Slovenia	530	533
South Africa	275	243
Thailand	467	482
Tunisia	448	430
Turkey	429	433
United States	502	515

Source: Mullis *et al.*, 2000; Martin *et al.*, 2000.

The correlation between national IQs and mathematics achievement scores is .881 ($N = 38$) and between national IQs and science achievement scores .868 ($N = 38$). Figure 6.1 illustrates the correspondence between national IQs and mathematics achievement scores. All countries are relatively close to the regression line, which indicates a very strong correspondence between national IQs and national differences in school achievements.

ESTIMATION OF MISSING NATIONAL IQs

We want to further extend the analysis to the 104 countries with populations of more than 50,000 for which we have not been able to find IQ data. For these 104 countries, we have estimated the IQs. Two principles have been adopted for making the estimates of national IQs for those countries for which data are lacking. First, it is assumed that the national IQs, which are unknown, will be closely similar to those in neighboring countries whose IQs are known. It can be seen from the results set out in Table 6.1 that neighboring countries normally have closely similar IQs. For instance, the IQ in both Germany and the Netherlands is 102; the IQ in Japan is 105 and the IQ in South Korea is 106; the IQ in Argentina and in Uruguay is 96; the IQ in Uganda is 73 and in Kenya 72; and so forth. Therefore, it is assumed that where the national IQs are unknown, they will be closely similar to

Figure 6.1

The Results of the Regression Analysis of TIMSS Mathematics Scores 1999 on National IQ for 38 Countries

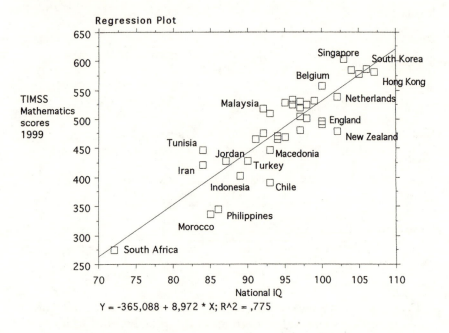

Y = -365,088 + 8,972 * X; R^2 = ,775

those in neighboring countries. We have consequently taken the most appropriate neighboring countries and used their IQs to assign IQs to those countries with unknown IQs. Where there are two or more appropriate neighboring countries, the IQs of these countries are averaged to obtain an estimated IQ for the country whose IQ is unknown. For example, to estimate an IQ for Afghanistan, we average the IQs of neighboring India (81) and Iran (84), which gives an IQ of 83. Averages with decimal points have been rounded toward 100.

A second principle for the estimation of national IQs has been used for several countries that are racially mixed and for which there is no similar neighboring country. In these cases, we have assigned IQs to the racial groups on the basis of the known IQs of these groups in neighboring countries. For example, Cape Verde, the archipelago off the coast of Senegal, has a population that is 1 percent White, 28 percent Black, and 71 percent mixed Black-White (*Philip's World Atlas*, 1996). On the basis of the IQs of these groups in South Africa, it is assumed that the Whites have an IQ of 94, the Blacks of 66, and the mixed of 82, the IQ of South African coloreds (see Appendix 1, "The Calculation of the National Intelligence Levels"). Weighting these figures by the percentages in the population gives an IQ of 72.

The racially mixed population of the Comoros consists of African (Black), Arab, and Malagasy elements. It is not possible to separate these different racial groups. Because the racial composition of the population is similar to Madagascar's population, we estimate its national IQ to be 79, the same as in Madagascar. The Malayo-Polynesians and Negroids constitute the principal elements of the racially mixed population of Madagascar. The contribution of each of them is assumed to be approximately equal. Therefore, the IQ for Madagascar has been estimated from that of the Philippines (86) and Tanzania (72), which gives an IQ of 79 for Madagascar. For Mauritius, the population consists of 68 percent Indians, 27 percent Creole (mix of Black-White), 3 percent Chinese, and 1 percent Whites. It is assumed that the IQs are 81 for the Indians (as in India), 82 for the Creoles (as for South African coloreds), 100 for the Chinese (as in China), and 94 for the Whites (as for the Whites in South Africa). Weighting these figures by the percentages in the population gives an IQ of 81.

Table 6.5 shows the estimated IQs and the comparison countries on which they are based, together with measured IQs.

Table 6.5

National IQs Based on the Results of Intelligence Tests and Estimated National IQs Based on the IQs of Neighboring or Other Comparable Countries

Country	National IQ based on arithmetic means	Comparison countries
1 Afghanistan	83*	Iran 84, India 81
2 Albania	90*	Croatia 90, Turkey 90
3 Algeria	84*	Morocco 85, Egypt 83
4 Angola	69*	Zambia 77, Zimbabwe 66, Congo (Zaire) 65
5 Antigua and Barbuda	75*	Barbados 78, Jamaica 72
6 Argentina	96	
7 Armenia	93*	Turkey 90, Russia 96
8 Australia	98	
9 Austria	102	
10 Azerbaijan	87*	Turkey 90, Iran 84

Table 6.5   continued

Country	National IQ based on arithmetic means	Comparison countries
11 Bahamas	78*	Barbados 78
12 Bahrain	83*	Iraq 87, Qatar 78
13 Bangladesh	81*	India 81
14 Barbados	78	
15 Belarus	96*	Russia 96
16 Belgium	100	
17 Belize	83*	Guatemala 79, Mexico 87
18 Benin	69*	Ghana 71, Nigeria 67
19 Bhutan	78*	Nepal 78
20 Bolivia	85*	Ecuador 80, Peru 90
21 Botswana	72*	Zambia 77, Zimbabwe 66
22 Brazil	87	
23 Brunei	92*	Malaysia 92
24 Bulgaria	93	
25 Burkina Faso	67*	Guinea 66, Sierra Leone 64, Ghana 71
26 Burma (Myanmar)	86*	India 81, Thailand 91
27 Burundi	70*	Congo (Zaire) 65, Tanzania 72, Uganda 73
28 Cambodia	89*	Thailand 91, Philippines 86
29 Cameroon	70*	Nigeria 67, Congo (Brazzaville) 73
30 Canada	97	
31 Cape Verde	78*	Mixed population—see text
32 Central African Republic	68*	Congo (Brazzaville) 73, Congo (Zaire) 65, Nigeria 67
33 Chad	72*	Sudan 72
34 Chile	93*	Argentina 96, Peru 90
35 China	100	
36 Colombia	89	

	Country	National IQ based on arithmetic means	Comparison countries
37	Comoros	79*	Mixed Negroid—Arab-Malay population— see text
38	Congo (Brazzaville)	73	
39	Congo (Zaire)	65	
40	Costa Rica	91*	Argentina 96, Uruguay 96, Colombia 89, Puerto Rico 84
41	Côte d'Ivoire	71*	Ghana 71
42	Croatia	90	
43	Cuba	85	
44	Cyprus	92*	Greece 92
45	Czech. Republic	97	
46	Denmark	98	
47	Djibouti	68*	Sudan 72, Ethiopia 63
48	Dominica	75*	Barbados 78, Jamaica 72
49	Dominican Republic	84*	Mixed population, Puerto Rico 84
50	Ecuador	80	
51	Egypt	83	
52	El Salvador	84*	Guatemala 79, Colombia 89
53	Equatorial Guinea	59	
54	Eritrea	68*	Sudan 72, Ethiopia 63
55	Estonia	97*	Finland 97, Russia 96
56	Ethiopia	63	
57	Fiji	84	
58	Finland	97	
59	France	98	
60	Gabon	66*	Congo (Brazzaville) 73, Equatorial Guinea 59
61	Gambia	65*	Sierra Leone 64, Guinea 66
62	Georgia	93*	Russia 96, Turkey 90

Table 6.5   continued

Country	National IQ based on arithmetic means	Comparison countries
63 Germany	102	
64 Ghana	71	
65 Greece	92	
66 Grenada	75*	Barbados 78, Jamaica 72
67 Guatemala	79	
68 Guinea	66	
69 Guinea-Bissau	66*	Guinea 66
70 Guyana	84*	Suriname 89, Barbados 78
71 Haiti	72*	Jamaica 72
72 Honduras	84*	Guatemala 79, Colombia 89
73 Hong Kong	107	
74 Hungary	99	
75 Iceland	98*	Norway 98
76 India	81	
77 Indonesia	89	
78 Iran	84	
79 Iraq	87	
80 Ireland	93	
81 Israel	94	
82 Italy	102	
83 Jamaica	72	
84 Japan	105	
85 Jordan	87*	Iraq 87, Lebanon 86
86 Kazakhstan	93*	Russia 96, Turkey 90
87 Kenya	72	
88 Kiribati	84*	Marshall Islands 84, Fiji 84
89 Korea, North	104*	South Korea 106, Japan 105, China 100

	Country	National IQ based on arithmetic means	Comparison countries
90	Korea, South	106	
91	Kuwait	83*	Iraq 87, Qatar 78
92	Kyrgyzstan	87*	Turkey 90, Iran 84
93	Laos	89*	Thailand 91, Philippines 86
94	Latvia	97*	Russia 96, Finland 97
95	Lebanon	86	
96	Lesotho	72*	Zambia 77, Zimbabwe 66
97	Liberia	65*	Sierra Leone 64, Guinea 66
98	Libya	84*	Morocco 85, Egypt 83
99	Lithuania	97*	Russia 96, Finland 97
100	Luxembourg	101*	Netherlands 102, Belgium 100
101	Macedonia	93*	Bulgaria 93, Greece 92
102	Madagascar	79*	Mixed Malay-Negroid population—see text
103	Malawi	71*	Congo (Zaire) 65, Tanzania 72, Zambia 77
104	Malaysia	92	
105	Maldives	81*	India 81
106	Mali	69*	Guinea 66, Sudan 72
107	Malta	95*	Italy 102, Spain 97, Morocco 85
108	Marshall Islands	84	
109	Mauritania	74*	Guinea 66, Morocco 85, Sudan 72
110	Mauritius	81*	Mixed population—see text
111	Mexico	87	
112	Micronesia	84*	Marshall Islands 84
113	Moldova	95*	Romania 94, Russia 96
114	Mongolia	98*	Russia 96, China 100
115	Morocco	85	
116	Mozambique	72*	Tanzania 72, Zimbabwe 66, Zambia 77
117	Namibia	72*	Zambia 77, Zimbabwe 66

Table 6.5   continued

Country	National IQ based on arithmetic means	Comparison countries
118 Nepal	78	
119 Netherlands	102	
120 New Zealand	100	
121 Nicaragua	84*	Guatemala 79, Colombia 89
122 Niger	67*	Nigeria 67
123 Nigeria	67	
124 Norway	98	
125 Oman	83*	Iraq 87, Qatar 78
126 Pakistan	81*	India 81
127 Panama	85*	Colombia 89, Ecuador 80
128 Papua New Guinea	84*	Marshall Islands 84, Fiji 84
129 Paraguay	85*	Ecuador 80, Peru 90
130 Peru	90	
131 Philippines	86	
132 Poland	99	
133 Portugal	95	
134 Puerto Rico	84	
135 Qatar	78	
136 Romania	94	
137 Russia	96	
138 Rwanda	70*	Congo (Z) 65, Tanzania 72, Uganda 73
139 Samoa (Western)	87	
140 Sao Tome/Principe	59*	Equatorial Guinea 59
141 Saudi Arabia	83*	Iraq 87, Qatar 78
142 Senegal	65*	Sierra Leone 64, Guinea 66
143 Seychelles	81*	Mixed population, India 81
144 Sierra Leone	64	

Country	National IQ based on arithmetic means	Comparison countries
145 Singapore	103	
146 Slovakia	96	
147 Slovenia	95	
148 Solomon Islands	84*	Marshall Islands 84, Fiji 84
149 Somalia	68*	Ethiopia 63, Kenya 72
150 South Africa	72	See text
151 Spain	97	
152 Sri Lanka	81*	India 81
153 St. Kitts and Nevis	75*	Barbados 78, Jamaica 72
154 St. Lucia	75*	Barbados 78, Jamaica 72
155 St. Vincent/Grenadines	75*	Barbados 78, Jamaica 72
156 Sudan	72	
157 Suriname	89	
158 Swaziland	72*	Zambia 77, Zimbabwe 66
159 Sweden	101	
160 Switzerland	101	
161 Syria	87*	Iraq 87, Lebanon 86
162 Taiwan	104	
163 Tajikistan	87*	Turkey 90, Iran 84
164 Tanzania	72	
165 Thailand	91	
166 Togo	69*	Ghana 71, Nigeria 67
167 Tonga	87	
168 Trinidad and Tobago	80*	Suriname 89, Barbados 78, Jamaica 72
169 Tunisia	84*	Morocco 85, Egypt 83
170 Turkey	90	
171 Turkmenistan	87*	Turkey 90, Iran 84
172 Uganda	73	

Table 6.5   continued

Country	National IQ based on arithmetic means	Comparison countries
173 Ukraine	96*	Russia 96
174 United Arab Emirates	83*	Iraq 87, Qatar 78
175 United Kingdom	100	
176 United States	98	
177 Uruguay	96	
178 Uzbekistan	87*	Turkey 90, Iran 84
179 Vanuatu	84*	Marshall Islands 84, Fiji 84
180 Venezuela	89*	Colombia 89
181 Vietnam	96*	China 100, Thailand 91
182 Yemen	83*	Iraq 87, Qatar 78
183 Yugoslavia	93*	Croatia 90, Slovenia 95
184 Zambia	77	
185 Zimbabwe	66	

The estimated national IQs are marked by an asterisk (*).

DATA FOR ECONOMIC GROWTH AND DEVELOPMENT

National differences in economic growth and development are most frequently measured by per capita income. There are several different ways in which this can be measured. We have adopted five alternative data sets. These are 1) Gross Domestic Product (GDP) per capita (1820–1992) compiled by A. Maddison (1995); 2) Gross National Product (GNP) per capita (1976–98); 3) GNP per capita measured at Purchasing Power Parity (PPP) (1995–98); 4) real GDP per capita (PPP) (1987–98); and 5) GDP per capita (1983–96). Note that the time periods of these data sets are partly overlapping. Each data set is based on one particular source. All sources of these data are documented in Appendix 2, "Data on Per Capita Income and Economic Growth in 185 Countries."

The basic difference between Gross Domestic Product (GDP) and Gross National Product (GNP) is that GDP comprises the total output of goods and services for final use produced by an economy by both residents and non-residents within the geographical boundaries of a nation, whereas GNP comprises GDP plus income from abroad, which is the income residents receive from abroad, less similar payments made to non-residents who contribute to the domestic economy. Thus, GDP can be defined to be the annual market value of final goods and services produced within the geographic boundaries of a nation, whereas GNP represents the annual market value of all final goods and services produced by the nation both within the country and abroad. The difference between GDP and GNP is relatively small for most countries, but there are exceptions. It should be noted that GNP and GDP include only the value of goods and services that are produced legally and sold on open markets. For this reason GNP and GDP measurements exclude most of the goods and services produced by families for their own consumption because these items are never sold on an open market. Non-market activities, such as subsistence agriculture and unpaid work by family members, are relatively more important in poor countries (Gardner, 1998, pp. 22–26; *Human Development Report* 1999, p. 254; *World Development Report 1999/2000*, p. 274).

The longest time series for national incomes has been constructed by Maddison (1983, 1995, 1998) who has estimated GDP per capita and economic growth rates for 56 countries from 1820 to 1992. These countries account for 93 percent of the world's output and 87 percent of world's population. Maddison's *Monitoring the World Economy 1820–1992* (1995) includes a historical compilation of data on GDP per capita during the period 1820–1992. His sample of countries covers 12 West European countries, 4 Western Offshoots, 5 South European countries, 7 East European countries, 7 Latin American countries, 11 Asian countries, and 10 African countries. His data on GDP per capita are provided in 1990 Geary-Khamis dollars for the period 1820–1992. Geary-Khamis dollars are estimated by converting currencies into a common unit. They are based on the twin concepts of purchasing power parity of currencies and international average prices of commodities (for more details, see Maddison, 1995, pp. 162–169). In addition, Maddison presents estimates of GDP per capita for 143 countries in 1950 and 1990. His compilation includes not only independent states, but also numerous dependent territories. Appendix 2 provides Maddison's estimates of per capita GDP for the years 1820, 1850, 1870, 1890, 1900, 1910, 1920, 1930, 1940, 1950, 1960, 1970, 1980, 1990 and 1992.

Our data on GNP per capita are principally from the World Bank's *World Development Reports*. These reports cover the period 1976–1998. Nafziger (1997, pp. 21–24) discusses the problems with using GNP to make comparisons over time and in comparing developed and developing countries. One problem is that GNP per capita overstates real income differences between developed and developing countries because many economic activities in developing countries are not taken into account in GNP. For example, in developing countries, a greater proportion of their goods and services are produced within the home by family members for their own use, rather than for sale in the marketplace (as in developed countries). Similarly, much of the productive activity of subsistence agriculture is considered an integral part of family and village life, not an economic transaction. The same concerns the work of the housewife who grinds the flour, bakes the bread, and makes and mends the clothes in poor countries. These activities are not taken into account in GNP, but the same services when purchased are included in a rich country's GNP. For the same reasons, GNP overstates the income differences between the United States in the nineteenth and twentieth centuries. The real difference is much smaller than the GNP indicates. Another problem is that the exchange rate used to convert the GNP in local currency units into U.S. dollars is usually based on the relative prices of internationally traded goods, not on purchasing power. The GNP is understated for developing countries "because many of their cheap, labor-intensive, unstandardized goods and services have no impact on the exchange rate, since they are not traded" (Nafziger, 1997, pp. 23–24). In addition, national income estimates exclude the value of goods and services produced in the unofficial or shadow economy (Gardner, 1998, p. 26). It includes production that is hidden from governmental authorities to escape taxation, regulation, and prosecution for criminal activities. In many African and Latin American countries, this informal sector employs between 40 to 50 percent of the non-agricultural labor force.

Data on GNP per capita measured at PPP cover the period from 1995 to 1998 and are also from the World Bank's *World Development Reports*. As noted in the previous paragraph, GNP tends to underestimate the value of goods and services in developing countries. Attempts to overcome this problem have been made by measuring countries' purchasing powers relative to all other countries rather than using the exchange rate (Nafziger, 1997, p. 26). The Purchasing Power Parity (PPP) exchange rate tries to take into account the currency's real domestic purchasing power. This method reduces the gap between rich and poor countries considerably. The GNP per capita measured at PPP is for most poor countries two to five times higher than the GNP per capita, while it is somewhat lower than the GNP per capita for most developed countries (Ray, 1998, pp. 12–16). The *World Development Report 1999/2000* (p. 274) notes that because "nominal exchange rates do not always reflect international differences in relative prices, table 1 also shows GNP converted into international dollars using PPP exchange rates." However, World Development Reports have published these data only from 1995 onwards.

Our data on real GDP per capita (PPP) cover the period 1987 to 1998 and are from the United Nations Development Program's (UNDP) *Human Development Reports*, in which real GDP per capita is used as a component of the Human Development Index (HDI). The *Human Development Report 2000* (p. 144–145) notes that their "GDP per capita (PPP US $) data used in the Report are provided by the World Bank and are based on the latest

International Comparison Program (ICP) surveys." It emphasizes that data are not strictly comparable across regions, because the regional data are expressed in different currencies and may be based on different classification schemes or aggregation formulas. For countries not covered by the World Bank, estimates provided by Alan Heston and Robert Summers of the University of Pennsylvania are used. It is reasonable to assume that the real GDP per capita data (and the GNP per capita measured at PPP) measure the differences in per capita income more reliably than data on GNP per capita.

Finally, our data on GDP per capita cover the period 1983 to 1996 and are from the United Nations' *Statistical Yearbooks*. These per capita data are in U.S. dollars at current prices. For many countries, these data seem to be highly unreliable measures of per capita income because they may vary considerably from year to year as a consequence of changes in exchange rates. It is noted in the *Statistical Yearbook 1996* (United Nations, 1999, p. 164) that there are practical constraints in the use of market exchange rates for conversion purposes, "particularly in the case of countries with multiple exchange rates, those coping with inordinate levels of inflation or experiencing misalignments caused by market fluctuations, the use of which may result in excessive fluctuations or distortions in the dollar income levels of a number of countries. Caution is therefore urged when making inter-country comparisons of incomes as expressed in US dollars."

The above review of our five alternative data sets indicates that these are not perfect variables to measure the differences in per capita income between countries, but they are the best data that we have found for the purposes of our study. The use of the five alternative data sets increases the reliability of results. Data on the national per capita incomes for the second half of the twentieth century are available from many sources. The most extensive data collections are provided in the World Bank's *World Development Reports* and *Social Indicators of Development*, in UNDP's *Human Development Reports*, and in the United Nations' *Statistical Yearbooks*. *World Development Reports* have provided data on GNP per capita (in U.S. dollars) since the first issue in 1978 (first year 1976) and data on GNP measured at PPP since the 1997 issue (first year 1995). *Social Indicators of Development* also includes estimates of GNP per capita from more than 100 countries. *Human Development Reports* have provided data on real GDP per capita (PPP $) and on GNP per capita since the first issue in 1990 (first year 1987). The United Nations' *Statistical Yearbooks* have reported some data on GDP per capita at current prices since the 1950s, but because the earlier data vary greatly, we restrict our attention to the data collected since 1983.

Comparable data and estimates of GNP per capita and GDP per capita are available also from several other yearbooks and international compilations of data. *The Europa World Year Book* and its regional volumes include data and estimates of GNP per capita from all countries of the world. Most of their data and estimates are based on the publications of the World Bank. Annual

reference supplements of *Keesing's Record of World Events* report data and estimates of GNP per capita from all countries of the world. *The World Factbook*
(1992, 2000) published by the Central Intelligence Agency (in the United
States) also provides data and estimates of GDP per capita from all countries
of the world. *Philip's Encyclopedic World Atlas Country by Country* (Second
edition, 1993) reports estimates of the annual income per person in U.S.
dollars. The *Encyclopedia of the Third World* edited by G. T. Kurian provides
data on GNP per capita, GDP per capita, and annual growth rates of GNP
and GDP for nearly all developing countries. It also provides data on income
distributions and on the percentages of population in absolute poverty. *The
World Guide 1999/2000: A View from the South* (1999) provides data and
estimates of GNP per capita in U.S. dollars and annual growth of GNP from
most of countries in the world.

We have focused on data on the GDP per capita, the GNP per capita, the
GNP per capita measured at PPP, and the real GDP per capita (PPP $), and
have tried to get these data for periods as long as possible (for further discussion and definition of these statistical terms, see Nafziger 1997, pp. 23–27;
Gardner 1998, pp. 22–28; the *Human Development Report* 1999, pp.
254–255; the *World Development Report* 1999/2000, pp. 274; and Todaro
2000, pp. 43–44). These variables will be used alternatively as the dependent
variable to measure the extent of the income gap between the rich and poor
countries. Data on these variables for individual countries are provided in
Appendix 2.

The available data on GDP per capita cover a much longer period than the
data on GNP per capita. As noted, Maddison's (1995) compilation of data on
GDP per capita extends from 1820 to 1992. Data on GNP per capita given in
the *World Development Reports* start in 1976. All years of the period of 1976 to
1998, except 1996 for which data are not available, are taken into account in
correlation analyses, although Appendix 2 reports these data only for the years
of 1976, 1980, 1985, 1990, 1995, and 1998. The *World Development Reports*
provide data for nearly all countries included in our study. In the cases of
Puerto Rico and Taiwan, the data provided in Appendix 2 are derived from
other sources. Because the data provided in the *World Development Reports* do
not cover all countries, these data for 1998 are complemented by data from
other sources and by estimates for missing countries. Estimates are usually
made on the basis of neighboring countries. Data on the GNP per capita measured at PPP provided in the *World Development Reports* since 1995 constitute
an alternative data set. Appendix 2 provides these data for the years of 1995
and 1998. The data do not cover all countries of our study.

Data on the real GDP per capita (PPP) provided in the *Human Development
Reports* are available since 1987. The study covers the years of 1987 to 1998,
except 1996 for which data are not available. In Appendix 2, these data are
given for the years of 1987, 1990, 1995, and 1998. As in the case of GNP per
capita, these data for 1998 are complemented by data from other sources and

by estimates for missing countries. Finally, data on GDP per capita provided in the United Nations' *Statistical Yearbooks* have been used for the years 1983 through 1996. In Appendix 2, these data are provided for the years 1983, 1990, 1993, and 1996. They cover nearly all countries.

In addition, data on economic growth rates are used to measure differences in the economic success of countries. Long-term economic growth rates are higher for rich countries than for poor countries, but there is no clear difference in short-term economic growth rates. This is because per capita income is already many times higher in rich countries than in poor countries and because growth rates may fluctuate significantly from year to year. We test this assumption by examining per capita income growth rates for Maddison's GDP per capita data over the periods 1820–1992 and 1950–1990, GNP per capita over the period 1976–1998, GNP per capita measured at PPP over the period 1995–98, real GDP per capita (PPP) over the period 1987–1998, and GDP per capita over the period 1983–1996. The economic growth rates for these periods are provided in Appendix 2. The economic growth rates calculated for this study are based on the difference in per capita income between the first and last year of comparison. The difference is calculated as the percentage changes from the per capita income in the first year of comparison to the last year. The statistical data given in Appendix 2 on the gap between rich and poor countries indicate that the gap between rich and poor countries is wide and that it increased after the World War II despite the efforts to promote equality within and between countries.

METHODS OF ANALYSIS

Data on national IQs and per capita income are measured by interval scales. Correlation analysis is best suited to measure the strength of the linear relationship between national IQs and alternative measures of per capita income and long-term economic growth rates. Correlations should be clearly positive and relatively strong. Weak or negative correlations would falsify the hypothesis that national IQs are a significant determinant of rates of economic growth and per capita income.

We use the Pearson correlation coefficient (r) to measure the strength of relationship between national IQs and measures of economic growth and development. A weakness of the Pearson correlation coefficient is that it is highly affected by a few extreme values of either variable. The Spearman rank correlation coefficient is an alternative correlation coefficient. It calculates a correlation coefficient based on the rank-orders of the values of two variables. Because it is based on the ranks of the data and not the data itself, it is resistant to outliers. Consequently, rank correlations tend to be somewhat higher than Pearson correlations. In this study, we use both correlation coefficients, but the Pearson correlation coefficient will be the principal measure because it is based on the values of the variables.

Correlation analysis indicates the average relationship between national IQs and measures of economic growth and per capita income, but it does not tell anything about the position of individual countries in this relationship. For some countries, the level of per capita income may be approximately what is expected on the basis of the average relationship between national IQs and per capita income, but some other countries may deviate greatly from the average relationship. Regression analysis will be used to disclose the position of individual countries in this relationship. In the regression analyses, national IQ is used as the independent variable and per capita income as the dependent variable because we assume that there is a causal relationship between national differences in intelligence and the level of per capita income and that national IQ is the causal factor in this relationship rather than per capita income. The results of regression analysis indicate which countries are consistent with the general relationship between national IQs and economic development and which are deviant and to some degree anomalous. Deviant countries shown by regression analysis may also help to identify other systematic factors affecting the wealth and poverty of nations and make predictions on the prospects of economic development in different countries.

The 81 countries for which we have direct evidence of national IQs and the total group of 185 countries constitute the two principal groups of countries in this study. They are analyzed separately. Data on national IQs are more reliable for the 81 countries for which we have direct evidence than for the other 104 countries for which we have estimated national IQs on the basis of neighboring or other comparable countries. For this reason, we examine first the group of 81 countries. However, this group of 81 countries does not constitute a random sample from the total population of countries. Therefore, it is questionable whether it would be justifiable to generalize the results from the group of 81 countries to the total population of countries. We solve this problem by testing the hypothesis for the 185 countries, which include practically all the countries of the world with populations greater than 50,000.

SUMMARY

This chapter is concerned with the methodology of the study. It begins with an explanation of the calculation of national IQs in 81 nations and considers the reliability and validity of these measures. It then describes the method for estimating national IQs for all of the nations in the world. Finally, the chapter ends by describing the measures of economic growth and per capita income that we seek to explain in terms of national IQs.

7

National IQs and Economic Development in 81 Nations

In this chapter we examine the relation between population intelligence and economic development for the 81 countries for which we have direct evidence of national IQs. We consider first the correlations found between national IQs and per capita incomes from 1820 up to 1998. Second, we turn to the correlations found between national IQs and rates of economic growth. Next, we report the results of regression analyses designed to show which countries deviate from the general relationship found between national IQs and economic development, and we then consider the factors responsible for these deviations.

CORRELATIONS OF NATIONAL IQs AND PER CAPITA INCOME

We examine first the relation between national IQs and per capita income. There are data on per capita income (GDP per capita) for a number of countries from 1820 onward; it is therefore possible to see whether a relationship between national IQs and per capita income existed as early as 1820 and whether it has remained approximately the same or possibly become stronger as a consequence of technological development occurring during the last 180 years. Although we do not have direct evidence for national IQs for the nineteenth century or for the first half of the twentieth century, we assume that national differences in intelligence have been approximately the same throughout the period.

We have calculated correlations between national IQs and per capita incomes using both Pearson product-moment and Spearman rank correlation coefficients. The results for the Pearson correlation coefficients are presented in Table 7.1 and are presented for the Spearman coefficients in Table 7.2.

Table 7.1

Pearson Product-Moment Correlations between National IQs and GDP Per Capita, GNP Per Capita, GNP Per Capita Measured at PPP, Real GDP Per Capita (PPP), and GDP Per Capita during the Period 1820 to 1998 in 81 Countries

Year	GDP N	r	GNP N	r	GNP-PPP N	r	Real GDP N	r	GDP N	r
1820	24	.535	—	—	—	—	—	—	—	—
1850	19	.669	—	—	—	—	—	—	—	—
1870	30	.481	—	—	—	—	—	—	—	—
1890	28	.489	—	—	—	—	—	—	—	—
1900	37	.505	—	—	—	—	—	—	—	—
1910	41	.478	—	—	—	—	—	—	—	—
1920	30	.423	—	—	—	—	—	—	—	—
1930	40	.486	—	—	—	—	—	—	—	—
1940	39	.527	—	—	—	—	—	—	—	—
1950	78	.257	—	—	—	—	—	—	—	—
1960	49	.609	—	—	—	—	—	—	—	—
1970	48	.651	—	—	—	—	—	—	—	—
1976	—	—	74	.540	—	—	—	—	—	—
1977	—	—	74	.553	—	—	—	—	—	—
1978	—	—	72	.566	—	—	—	—	—	—
1980	49	.692	70	.502	—	—	—	—	—	—
1981	—	—	65	.521	—	—	—	—	—	—
1982	—	—	63	.570	—	—	—	—	—	—
1983	—	—	62	.576	—	—	—	—	80	.525

Year	GDP		GNP		GNP-PPP		Real GDP		GDP	
	N	r	N	r	N	r	N	r	N	r
1984	—	—	64	.566	—	—	—	—	80	.532
1985	—	—	66	.575	—	—	—	—	80	.524
1986	—	—	65	.615	—	—	—	—	80	.602
1987	—	—	66	.632	—	—	68	.759	80	.606
1988	—	—	66	.669	—	—	66	.763	80	.627
1989	—	—	68	.629	—	—	74	.726	80	.631
1990	77	.728	70	.616	—	—	74	.735	80	.626
1991	—	—	70	.628	—	—	74	.758	80	.631
1992	48	.720	72	.622	—	—	75	.709	80	.630
1993	—	—	72	.644	—	—	76	.595	80	.649
1994	—	—	71	.652	—	—	77	.725	80	.655
1995	—	—	75	.655	68	.721	76	.731	80	.656
1996	—	—	—	—	—	—	—	—	81	.663
1997	—	—	78	.670	69	.755	77	.726	—	—
1998	—	—	81	.664	65	.775	81	.733	—	—

Table 7.2

Spearman Rank-Order Correlations between National IQs and the GDP Per Capita, GNP Per Capita, GNP Per Capita Measured at PPP, Real GDP Per Capita (PPP), and GDP Per Capita during the Period 1820 to 1998 in 81 Countries

Year	GDP		GNP		GNP-PPP		Real GDP		GDP	
	N	r	N	r	N	r	N	r	N	r
1820	24	.544	—	—	—	—	—	—	—	—
1850	19	.750	—	—	—	—	—	—	—	—
1870	30	.550	—	—	—	—	—	—	—	—
1890	28	.541	—	—	—	—	—	—	—	—
1900	37	.514	—	—	—	—	—	—	—	—

Table 7.2   continued

Year	GDP N	GDP r	GNP N	GNP r	GNP-PPP N	GNP-PPP r	Real GDP N	Real GDP r	GDP N	GDP r
1910	41	.513	—	—	—	—	—	—	—	—
1920	30	.371	—	—	—	—	—	—	—	—
1930	40	.466	—	—	—	—	—	—	—	—
1940	39	.545	—	—	—	—	—	—	—	—
1950	78	.617	—	—	—	—	—	—	—	—
1960	49	.689	—	—	—	—	—	—	—	—
1970	48	.699	—	—	—	—	—	—	—	—
1976	—	—	74	.730	—	—	—	—	—	—
1977	—	—	74	.739	—	—	—	—	—	—
1978	—	—	72	.730	—	—	—	—	—	—
1980	49	.731	70	.739	—	—	—	—	—	—
1981	—	—	65	.743	—	—	—	—	—	—
1982	—	—	63	.747	—	—	—	—	—	—
1983	—	—	62	.746	—	—	—	—	80	.725
1984	—	—	64	.738	—	—	—	—	80	.731
1985	—	—	66	.729	—	—	—	—	80	.705
1986	—	—	65	.752	—	—	—	—	80	.761
1987	—	—	66	.765	—	—	68	.859	80	.769
1988	—	—	66	.807	—	—	66	.835	80	.778
1989	—	—	68	.788	—	—	74	.830	80	.776
1990	77	.832	70	.780	—	—	74	.821	80	.770
1991	—	—	70	.772	—	—	74	.854	80	.775
1992	48	.800	72	.777	—	—	75	.805	80	760
1993	—	—	72	.798	—	—	76	.756	80	.793
1994	—	—	71	.822	—	—	77	.829	80	.804
1995	—	—	75	.828	68	.822	76	.834	80	.807
1996	—	—	—	—	—	—	—	—	81	.804

Year	GDP N	r	GNP N	r	GNP-PPP N	r	Real GDP N	r	GDP N	r
1997	—	—	78	.827	69	.859	77	.826	—	—
1998	—	—	81	.816	65	.839	81	.827	—	—

Tables 7.1 and 7.2 show that all the correlations between national IQs and the five measures of per capita income are positive over the 180-year period and are moderate or strong, with one exception. For 1950, the Pearson correlation is only .257. This low correlation for 1950 is principally due to the very high per capita GDP for Qatar (29,257) in Maddison's data, arising from its high oil revenue and small population. When Qatar is excluded, the correlation for 1950 rises from .257 to .570. Thus, the results of the correlation analysis support our hypothesis that differences in national intelligence have been an important factor contributing to the differences in the wealth and poverty of nations from 1820 up to the last decade of the twentieth century.

The explanatory power of the correlations between national IQs and the measures of per capita national income is measured by the coefficient of determination (r^2), which indicates the explained part of the variation. In the case of Maddison's data, the strength of the correlations remained more or less stable from 1820 to 1950 and have become stronger since 1960. The explained part of variation in Pearson correlations was 29 percent in 1820, 37 percent in 1960, and 52 percent in 1992. In the corresponding Spearman rank correlations, the explained part of variation was 30 percent in 1820, 47 percent in 1960, and 64 percent in 1992. The average increase of correlations over time also can be measured by correlating the 15 correlations of the period 1820-1992 (Maddison's data) with year. The Pearson correlation for the period of 1820 to 1992 is .330 and the Spearman rank correlation .543. These correlations are positive but only moderate. When the anomalous correlation for 1950 is excluded, the Pearson correlation rises to .540. The bivariate line chart shown in Figure 7.1 illustrates the relationship between the 15 Spearman correlations and the years of comparison in the 81 countries over the period of 1820 to 1992. This figure shows that the correlations have increased significantly since 1920. The exceptionally high correlation for 1850 may be due to the fact that Maddison's data for 1850 cover only 18 out of the 24 countries.

Another way to measure this relationship is to limit the comparison to the original group of 24 countries for which Maddison has per capita data for 1820. This method eliminates the variation caused by differences in the samples of countries. The Pearson correlation between the 15 Pearson correlations of the period 1820–1992 and the years of comparison in the 24 original countries is .630 and with the 15 Spearman rank correlation is .761. These results show that correlations have increased in the original group of 24 countries during the period 1820-1992 more than in the total group of 81 countries.

Figure 7.1

Bivariate Line Chart of the Spearman Correlations and the Years of Comparison during the Period of 1820 to 1992 (Maddison's data) in the Group of 81 Countries

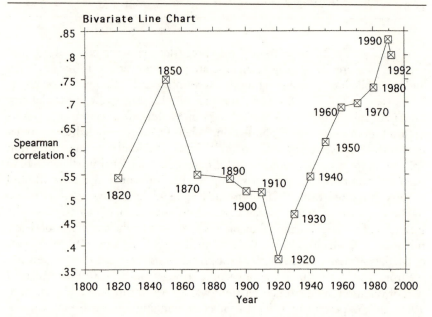

In the cases of the other four data sets, the periods of comparison are so short that it is not justifiable to make any definitive conclusions on the trends of change. In most cases, however, the correlations seem to have become stronger over time. In the case of GNP per capita, the explained part of variation increased from 29 percent in 1976 to 44 percent in 1998; in the case of GNP per capita (PPP) from 52 percent in 1995 to 60 percent in 1998; in the case of real GDP, it slightly decreased from 58 percent in 1987 to 54 percent in 1998; and in the case of GDP per capita, it increased from 28% in 1983 to 44% in 1996.

Table 7.2 indicates that the Spearman rank correlations are significantly higher than Pearson correlations from the 1950s onward. Because the Spearman rank correlation is resistant to outliers, it is .617 for 1950, whereas the corresponding Pearson correlation is only .257. In the period 1976–1998, the Spearman rank correlation coefficients vary from .725 to .859 and the explained part of variation ranges from 53 to 74 percent. It is approximately 20 percentage points more than in the Pearson correlations. Thus, the results of correlation analysis based on Spearman rank correlations support the hypothesis more strongly than those of the Pearson correlations. Less than half of the variation in per capita income remains unexplained.

CORRELATIONS OF NATIONAL IQs AND ECONOMIC GROWTH

The correlations between national IQs and economic growth rates are shown in Table 7.3. These correlations are based on the economic growth rates provided in Appendix 2.

Table 7.3

National IQs Correlated with Economic Growth Rates in 81 Countries

Economic growth rate	Period of comparison	N	Pearson correlation	Spearman rank correlation
GDP per capita (Maddison)	1820–1992	24	.643	.500
GDP per capita (Maddison)	1820–1900	24	.468	.350
GDP per capita (Maddison)	1910–1992	41	.535	.530
GDP per capita (Maddison)	1950–1990	78	.568	.643
GDP per capita (Maddison)	1890–1910	28	.209	.173
GNP per capita (World Bank data)	1976–1998	74	.566	.602
GDP per capita (United Nations data)	1983–1996	80	.599	.658
Real GDP per capita (UNDP data)	1987–1998	68	−.072	.090
GNP per capita measured at PPP	1995–1998	62	.184	.174

Table 7.3 shows that national IQs are significantly and quite highly correlated with long-term economic growth rates during the period 1820–1992 (rs = .643 and .500), 1910–1992; (rs = .535 and .530); and 1950–1990 (rs = .568 and .643); national IQs are also significantly and quite highly correlated with economic growth during the shorter time periods: 1976–1998 (rs = .566 and .602) and 1983–1996 (rs = .599 and .658). On the other hand, national IQs do not show any significant correlations with the short-term economic growth rates over the periods 1890–1910 (rs = .209 and .173), 1987–1998 (rs = -.072 and .090), and 1995–1998 (rs = .184 and .174). The correlations between national IQs and long-term economic growth rates are approximately as strong as the correlations between national IQs and measures of per capita income, whereas short-term economic growth rates are only weakly correlated with national IQs. There are no significant differences between the Pearson and Spearman correlation coefficients in the data shown in Table 7.3.

The results of the correlation analyses presented in the previous sections indicate that positive correlations between national IQs and per capita income and long-term economic growth have existed since 1820 and that the correlations between national IQs and measures of per capita income have become somewhat stronger during more recent decades. Thus, differences in national intelligence provide a powerful explanation for the persistent and increasing gap between rich and poor countries over the period from 1820 to the end of the twentieth century.

We now use regression analysis to identify the countries whose per capita incomes deviate only slightly or moderately from the values predicted from their populations' IQs and to identify the countries whose per capita incomes deviate greatly from their predicted values. The countries in the first category lie around the regression line of per capita income on national IQ, and their positive or negative residuals are small or only moderate. The countries in the second category lie above or below the regression line, and their positive residuals or their negative residuals are large.

Although it is possible to make separate regression analyses for all of the correlations shown in Table 7.1, it would take too much space and would not be reasonable because different measures of per capita income are highly inter-correlated and the relative changes over time have been small in most cases. Table 7.4 illustrates the strength of the correlations between the different measures of per capita income and Table 7.5 illustrates the consistency over time of relative differences among countries.

Table 7.4 shows that all the cross-sectional correlations are extremely high. The explained part of variation (co-variance) varies from 90 to 98 percent. Table 7.5 indicates that the correlation between GDP per capita in 1820 and 1992 is quite high (.691), and that the strength of correlations rises when the period of comparison becomes shorter. Thus, it does not make much difference which measure of per capita income is used in the regressions. However, it is interesting to compare the situations at the most extreme points of time. Hence, we limit our regression analysis to the first and the last years of comparison (1820 and 1998). Only Maddison's data on GDP per capita are available from 1820, whereas GNP per capita, GNP per capita (PPP), and real GDP per capita are available from 1998. Data on GNP per capita and real GDP per capita cover all 81 countries. Because the correlation between national IQs and real GDP per capita in 1998 is higher (.733) than the correlation between IQs and GNP per capita in 1998 (.664), we use real GDP per capita 1998 as the dependent variable in the second regression analysis. The interval between 1820 and 1998 is 178 years, but despite this distance the correlation between GDP per capita in 1820 and real GDP per capita in 1998 is .688 (N = 24).

We examine first the data for 1820. The number of countries is small (24) and the correlation between national IQs and per capita income is weaker than in 1998 (see Tables 7.1 and 7.2). However, it is still interesting to see which

Table 7.4

Some Cross-Sectional Correlations between the Different Measures of Per Capita Income in 1990 and 1998 in the Group of 81 Countries

Variable/year	GNP per capita	Real GDP per capita	GDP per capita
1990			
GDP (Maddison) 1990	.951 (N =70)	.991 (N = 73)	.948 (N = 76)
GNP per capita 1990		.953 (N = 68)	.991 (N = 69)
Real GDP per capita 1990			.952 (N = 74)
GDP per capita 1990			

	GNP per capita PPP	Real GDP per capita	GDP per capita
1998			
GNP per capita 1998	.968 (N = 65)	.952 (N = 81)	.987 (N = 81)
GNP per capita (PPP) 1998		.992 (N = 65)	.958 (N = 65)
Real GDP per capita 1998			.938 (N = 81)
GDP per capita 1996			

Table 7.5

Correlations of the Five Measures of Per Capita Income in the Group of 81 Countries

Variable/years	N	Correlation
GDP per capita (Maddison) between 1820 and 1992	24	.691
GNP per capita between 1976 and 1998	74	.832
GNP per capita (PPP) between 1995 and 1998	60	.992
Real GDP per capita between 1987 and 1998	68	.975
GDP per capita between 1983 and 1996	80	.860

countries deviated from the average relationship between national IQ and per capita income at that time and whether they were still deviant cases in 1998. The results of regression analysis are shown in Table 7.6 and in Figure 7.2.

Table 7.6

The Results of the Regression Analysis in which GDP Per Capita 1820 is Used as the Dependent Variable and National IQ is Used as the Independent Variable for 24 Countries

	Country	IQ	GDP per capita 1820	Residual GDP	Fitted GDP
8	Australia	98	1,528	466	1,062
9	Austria	102	1,295	108	1,187
16	Belgium	100	1,291	166	1,125
22	Brazil	87	670	–47	717
30	Canada	97	893	–137	1,030
35	China	100	523	–602	1,125
45	Czech. Republic	97	849	–181	1,030
46	Denmark	98	1,225	163	1,062
58	Finland	97	759	–271	1,030
59	France	98	1,218	156	1,062
63	Germany	102	1,112	–75	1,187
76	India	81	531	3	528
77	Indonesia	89	614	–165	779
80	Ireland	93	954	49	905
82	Italy	102	1,092	–95	1,187
84	Japan	105	702	–579	1,281
111	Mexico	87	760	43	717
119	Netherlands	102	1,561	374	1,187
124	Norway	98	1,004	–58	1,062
137	Russia	96	751	–248	999
151	Spain	97	1,063	33	1,030
159	Sweden	101	1,198	42	1,156
175	United Kingdom	100	1,756	631	1,125
176	United States	98	1,287	225	1,062

Figure 7.2

The Results of the Regression Analysis of GDP Per Capita 1820 on National IQ for 24 Countries in the Group of 81 Countries

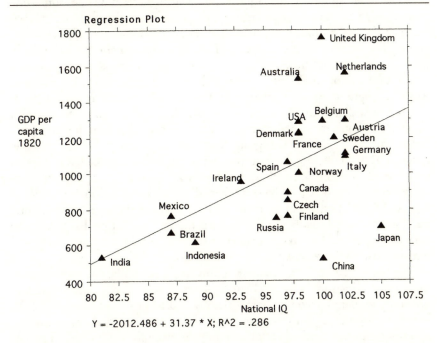

Y = -2012.486 + 31.37 * X; R^2 = .286

Table 7.6 gives the estimated national IQs and GDP per capita in 1820 for the 24 countries as well as, on the basis of the regression equation, the residuals and fitted values of GDP per capita. "Fitted GDP" is the value of GDP per capita at the regression line. "Residual GDP" indicates how much the actual value of GDP per capita deviates from the predicted (fitted) value. A positive residual indicates that the actual level of per capita income is higher than expected on the basis of the regression equation and a negative residual indicates that it is lower than expected. A small residual indicates that the level of national IQ provides a satisfactory explanation for the country's actual level of per capita income, whereas a large residual implies that, in addition to national IQ, some other factors have affected the level of economic development significantly. It is not necessary to discuss relatively small residuals because they do not seriously contradict the hypothesis and because they may be due to measurement errors.

Table 7.6 shows that there is considerable variation in the size of residuals. This means that not all countries conformed equally well to the relationship between national IQ and GDP per capita. In some countries, the actual level of the GDP per capita was much higher than expected on the basis of their national IQs, and in some other countries it was much lower than expected. A problem is how to separate the countries close to the regression line from those with large positive and negative residuals. There is no clear distinction between small and large deviations. We have to determine the borderline arbitrarily. In this case, it seems reasonable to use residuals of +200 and −200 to separate large outliers from small and moderate deviations. This criterion yields 16 countries in the category of small and moderate deviations and leaves 8 countries as outliers of large positive and large negative deviations.

The category of small and moderate deviations includes the countries of Austria, Belgium, Brazil, Canada, the Czech. Republic, Denmark, France, Germany, India, Indonesia, Ireland, Italy, Mexico, Norway, Spain, and Sweden. It should be noted that some of these countries were not independent countries in 1820. The group includes countries with high and low national IQs. However, the countries with the lowest national IQs are not represented in this group, while countries with high national IQs are over-represented. This bias may have weakened the correlation between national IQs and GDP per capita to some extent. Because the level of economic development was broadly consistent with the level of national IQs in these countries, it would have been reasonable to expect that these countries would remain close to the regression line in the future.

The countries with large positive residuals are Australia, the Netherlands, the United Kingdom, and the United States. These four countries had significantly higher per capita incomes than would be predicted from their IQs. While the wealth of Australia was based largely on its agricultural exports and not on industry, the three other countries were the leaders in industrialization and technological development. Because of their high positive residuals, it would have been reasonable to predict in 1820 that their relative position would decline in the future in accordance with the economic principle of convergence. However, their technological advantage was an additional factor that helped them to maintain a much higher-than-expected level of economic development and per capita income.

The countries with the large negative residuals are China, Finland, Japan, and Russia. Based on their high negative residuals, it would have been reasonable to predict in 1820 that per capita incomes would increase in these countries more rapidly than in other countries and that they would ultimately achieve the level of per capita income predicted from their national IQs. However, it would have been necessary to modify this prediction by taking into account the effects of additional variables. First, new industrial technologies had not yet spread to these countries to any significant extent. Second, China, Japan, and Russia were traditional autocracies at that time, and Finland belonged to Russia as an autonomous Grand Duchy. The countries with the large positive residuals were not yet full democracies, but democratic institutions were emerging in all of them. The comparison of the countries with large positive and large negative residuals implies that differences in political and economic systems may have affected the level of per capita income independently from national IQs because the countries with the large positive and large negative residuals were at approximately the same level of national IQ.

Figure 7.2 shows the results of regression analysis and the position of the most extreme outliers. It can be seen that the differences between the large positive and large negative outliers cannot be explained by national IQs, which are approximately the same for both categories. On the other hand, the figure shows that national IQs explain the relatively low level of per capita income in India, Mexico, Brazil, and Indonesia quite satisfactorily. India's extreme position has strengthened the correlation between national IQs and GDP per capita. When India is excluded from the group, the correlation falls from .535 to .456. This implies that if more countries with low national IQs were included in this comparison group, the correlation between national IQ and GDP per capita might be higher than .535.

REGRESSION OF NATIONAL INCOME IN 1998 ON IQs

Real GDP per capita in 1998 is used as the dependent variable in the second regression analysis. Because real GDP per capita in 1998 and GNP per capita in 1998 are highly inter-correlated (.952, N = 81), it makes virtually no difference which of these two variables is used as the dependent variable. Real GDP per capita is selected because it may be a better measure of per capita income differences than GNP per capita and because it is more strongly correlated with national IQs than GNP per capita. The results of the regression analysis are presented in Table 7.7 and in Figure 7.3.

Again the problem with the results set out in Table 7.7 is how to separate countries with large deviations from those with small and moderate deviations. In this case, it seems reasonable to use the criterion of +5,000 and −5,000 to separate the largest deviations from the smaller ones. In the countries for which residuals are smaller than the criterion value, the level of per capita income is approximately consistent with the national IQs. The residuals are larger than +5,000 for 16 countries and larger than −5,000 for 18 countries. We focus on these 34 countries with the largest deviations. The problem is what kinds of additional factors may have caused these deviations. They could be global or local, domestic or international, cultural, social, political, economic, historical, geographical, or some other environmental factors.

The 16 countries with large positive outliers are Australia, Austria, Barbados, Belgium, Canada, Denmark, Equatorial Guinea, Finland, France, Ireland, Norway, Qatar, Singapore, South Africa, Switzerland and the United States. Equatorial Guinea can be excluded from this group because its large positive residual is a technical consequence of the linear regression line (see Figure 7.3). Its predicted value is highly negative (−5,096) because of its

Table 7.7

The Results of the Regression Analysis in Which Real GDP Per Capita 1998 is Used as the Dependent Variable and National IQ is Used as the Independent Variable for 81 Countries

	Country	IQ	Real GDP per capita 1998	Residual real GDP	Fitted real GDP
6	Argentina	96	12,013	–2,094	14,107
8	Australia	98	22,452	7,307	15,145
9	Austria	102	23,166	5,945	17,221
14	Barbados	78	12,001	7,236	4,765
16	Belgium	100	23,223	7,040	16,183
22	Brazil	87	6,625	–2,811	9,436
24	Bulgaria	93	4,809	–7,741	12,550
30	Canada	97	23,582	8,956	14,626
35	China	100	3,105	–13,078	16,183
36	Colombia	89	6,006	–4,468	10,474
38	Congo (Brazzaville)	73	995	–1,175	2,170
39	Congo (Zaire)	65	822	2,804	–1,982
42	Croatia	90	6,749	–4,244	10,993
43	Cuba	85	3,967	–4,431	8,398
45	Czech. Republic	97	12,362	–2,264	14,626
46	Denmark	98	24,218	9,073	15,145
50	Ecuador	80	3,003	–2,800	5,803
51	Egypt	83	3,041	–4,319	7,360
53	Equatorial Guinea	59	1,817	6,913	–5,096
56	Ethiopia	63	574	3,594	–3,020
57	Fiji	84	4,231	–3,648	7,879
58	Finland	97	20,847	6,221	14,626
59	France	98	21,175	6,030	15,145
63	Germany	102	22,169	4,948	17,221

	Country	IQ	Real GDP per capita 1998	Residual real GDP	Fitted real GDP
64	Ghana	71	1,735	603	1,132
65	Greece	92	13,943	1,912	12,031
67	Guatemala	79	3,505	−1,779	5,284
68	Guinea	66	1,782	3,245	−1,463
73	Hong Kong	107	20,763	946	19,817
74	Hungary	99	10,232	−5,432	15,664
76	India	81	2,077	−4,245	6,322
77	Indonesia	89	2,651	−7,823	10,474
78	Iran	84	5,121	−2,758	7,879
79	Iraq	87	3,197	−6,239	9,436
80	Ireland	93	21,482	8,932	12,550
81	Israel	94	17,301	4,232	13,069
82	Italy	102	20,585	3,364	17,221
83	Jamaica	72	3,389	1,738	1,651
84	Japan	105	23,257	4,478	18,779
87	Kenya	72	980	−671	1,651
90	Korea, South	106	13,478	−5,820	19,298
95	Lebanon	86	4,326	−4,591	8,917
104	Malaysia	92	8,137	−3,894	12,031
108	Marshall Islands	84	3,000	−4,879	7,879
111	Mexico	87	7,704	−1,732	9,436
115	Morocco	85	3,305	−5,093	8,398
118	Nepal	78	1,157	−3,608	4,765
119	Netherlands	102	22,176	4,955	17,221
120	New Zealand	100	17,288	1,105	16,183
123	Nigeria	67	795	1,739	−944
124	Norway	98	26,342	11,197	15,145
130	Peru	90	4,282	−6,711	10,993

Table 7.7   continued

	Country	IQ	Real GDP per capita 1998	Residual real GDP	Fitted real GDP
131	Philippines	86	3,555	–5,362	8,917
132	Poland	99	7,619	–8,045	15,664
133	Portugal	95	14,701	1,113	13,589
134	Puerto Rico	84	8,000	121	7,879
135	Qatar	78	20,987	16,222	4,765
136	Romania	94	5,648	–7,421	13,069
137	Russia	96	6,460	–7,647	14,107
139	Samoa (Western)	87	3,832	–5,604	9,436
144	Sierra Leone	64	458	2,959	–2,501
145	Singapore	103	24,210	6,470	17,740
146	Slovakia	96	9,699	–4,408	14,107
147	Slovenia	95	14,293	705	13,588
150	South Africa	72	8,488	6,837	1,651
151	Spain	97	16,212	1,586	14,626
156	Sudan	72	1,394	–257	1,651
157	Suriname	89	5,161	–5,313	10,474
159	Sweden	101	20,659	3,957	16,702
160	Switzerland	101	25,512	8,810	16,702
162	Taiwan	104	13,000	–5,260	18,260
164	Tanzania	72	480	–1,171	1,651
165	Thailand	91	5,456	–6,056	11,512
167	Tonga	87	3,000	–6,436	9,436
170	Turkey	90	6,422	–4,571	10,993
172	Uganda	73	1,074	–1,096	2,170
175	United Kingdom	100	20,336	4,153	16,183
176	United States	98	29,605	14,460	15,145
177	Uruguay	96	8,623	–5,484	14,107

Country	IQ	Real GDP per capita 1998	Residual real GDP	Fitted real GDP
184 Zambia	77	719	–3,527	4,246
185 Zimbabwe	66	2,669	4,132	–1,463

Figure 7.3

The Results of the Regression Analysis of Real GDP Per Capita 1998 on National IQ for 81 Countries in the Group of 81 Countries

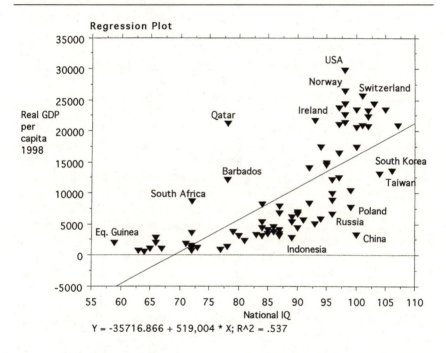

exceptionally low national IQ. The predicted negative per capita income is unrealistic because per capita income cannot be negative for any country. Out of the other 15 countries, 12 are the technologically and highly developed Western and East Asian countries. The most reasonable explanation for their much higher-than-expected level of per capita income is that this is principally because they are technologically developed market economies. Note that the residuals are positive yet are not as large as nearly all other western and East Asian countries that have technologically developed market economies.

The remaining countries with large positive residuals are Barbados, Qatar, and South Africa. Barbados' highly positive residual can be attributed to its well-established tourist industry and financial services, which are owned, controlled, and managed mainly by American and European companies. Thus, the people from countries of higher national IQs play a significant role in these industries (cf. *South America, Central America and the Caribbean 1999*, pp. 95–97). The explanation for Qatar's position lies in its lucrative oil industry, which raises its per capita income substantially above what would be predicted from its IQ. Its oil industry is based on western technologies and is controlled and managed largely by Europeans or Orientals. Thus, the unexpectedly high per capita income in Qatar, as well as in several other oil producing countries, is principally due to the contributions and technologies from countries whose national IQs are higher than the IQs of their domestic populations. For this reason, it is questionable whether Qatar and other similar countries are really deviant cases from the perspective of our hypothesis (cf. *The Middle East and North Africa 1998*, pp. 869–875). South Africa's much higher-than-expected per capita income is mainly due to the contributions of its significant white minority. Most productive industries are still owned and controlled by the white minority and by international corporations (cf. *Africa South of the Sahara 2000*, pp. 1006–1013).

Three of the positive outliers (Australia, the United Kingdom, and the United States) had large positive residuals already in 1820. Residuals were also positive for Austria, Belgium, Denmark, France, Ireland, and Sweden in 1820. Residuals in 1820 were highly negative for Finland and slightly negative for Norway. Comparison of the residuals for 1820 and 1998 shows that nearly all countries for which residuals were positive in 1820 also had positive residuals in 1998. Mexico is the only country whose slightly positive residual in 1820 had turned negative by 1998. Thus, the relative position of the countries has remained stable in most but not in all cases. Some countries have been able to improve their relative position significantly while the relative position of some others has dropped.

The group of 18 large negative outliers in 1998 consists of Bulgaria, China, Hungary, Indonesia, Iraq, South Korea, Morocco, Peru, Philippines, Poland, Romania, Russia, Samoa (Western), Suriname, Taiwan, Thailand, Tonga, and Uruguay. Six of these countries are present or former socialist countries (Bulgaria, China, Hungary, Poland, Romania, and Russia). These countries have large negative residuals because their socialist, political, and economic systems hindered their economic development and kept these countries poorer than expected on the basis of their high national IQs. The fact that the residuals are also negative for all other present or former socialist countries supports this interpretation. The economic system has evidently been a relevant negative factor for the growth of national per capita income in all of these socialist and former socialist countries. It is quite probable that the negative residuals will decline in most of the former European socialist countries as a consequence of the establishment of market economies. Per capita income has already risen significantly especially in the three Baltic states, Croatia, the Czech. Republic, Hungary, Poland, Slovakia, and Slovenia (see Appendix 2).

It is not as easy to identify the factors that have caused the negative residuals of the other 12 countries. Indonesia may be only a temporarily deviant case. As a consequence of Asia's economic crisis in the 1990s, Indonesia's GDP per capita declined sharply in 1998. The same is true for Thailand. The economic development of Iraq has been hampered by the sanctions imposed by the United Nations since 1991. In addition to those sanctions, Iraq has also experimented with a version of socialism. The per capita incomes of South Korea and Taiwan have risen rapidly since the 1960s, although they have not yet achieved the level expected on the basis of their high national IQ. It is reasonable to expect that they will cease to be negatively deviant cases within the next ten years. Samoa (Western) and Tonga are geographically isolated small island states, and this may be a factor that has hindered their economic development. Possibly unfavorable geographical conditions have hindered economic development in Morocco, too. The war in Western Sahara is an additional factor (cf. *The Middle East and North Africa 1998*, pp. 817–830). Peru experienced a high rate of inflation of 33.7 percent a year during 1990 to 1998, which probably had an adverse effect on its economic growth. It also suffered from ethnic conflict and civil strife. The Philippines and Suriname also had problems of ethnic conflict and much lower than expected per capita incomes. Direct evidence for the association between the amount of ethnic conflict and low economic growth has been provided by W. Easterly and R. Levine (1997). They estimate that a one-standard deviation increase in ethnic conflict is associated with a decrease of approximately 30 percent of a standard deviation in growth rate across countries. The poor economic performance of Uruguay is probably partly attributable to its very high rate of inflation of 40.5 percent per annum over the years 1990 to 1998, which hampered economic activities. We should also note that residuals are negative for all other Latin American countries, although they are not as large as for Uruguay. It seems probable that some unidentified regional factors have hampered economic development throughout the Latin American countries.

Figure 7.3 illustrates graphically the results of the regression analysis. Several of the most deviant countries are identified in this figure. The regression line is shown expressing the average relationship between the two variables.

It can be seen from the regression plot shown in Figure 7.3 that the relationship between national IQ and per capita income becomes weaker when the national IQ rises above 90 and disappears completely at higher IQ levels. The decline of this relationship was measured by correlating real GDP per capita 1998 with national IQ at different levels of IQ. In the countries with national IQs of 90 and above, this correlation is still high at .540 (N = 42);

in the group of countries with a national IQ of 93 and above, it is .345 (N = 36); in the group of countries with a national IQ of 95 and above, the correlation declines to .275 (N =32); and in the group of countries with a national IQ of 97 and above, the positive correlation disappears completely (–.022, N = 26). Corresponding correlations between national IQ and the four other measures of per capita income are approximately similar. Part of the explanation for the decline of correlations at higher levels of national IQs is that there is a restriction of the IQ range, but in addition there are differences in economic and political systems that explain the major part of the variation in economic development and per capita income among countries with higher levels of national IQs. There are several countries in this group that were socialist or communist autocracies for most of the second half of the twentieth century, and this is the factor that has retarded their economic development. Following the collapse of the Soviet Union in 1991, many of these countries have attempted with varying degrees of success to introduce market economies and democratic institutions, but this transition has been difficult and takes time. As these reforms progress, we can predict rapid economic development and the rise of per capita incomes in the high IQ countries that successfully reform their economic and political systems. In addition, the historically late start of modern economic development in East Asia, especially in the case of China, has weakened the correlation between national IQ and per capita income at the higher levels of national IQ.

The fact that the number of rich countries increases steeply above the level of a national IQ of 90 raises an interesting question: is a national IQ of 90 or higher needed to adopt modern technologies effectively? Of course, because IQs vary within populations, there are some people who are capable of learning the skills needed in modern technologies in all societies. However, if a certain IQ threshold is needed to learn such skills, the relative number of such people is many times higher in societies in which the mean national IQ is 90 or higher than in societies in which it is below 80 (cf. Chapters 4, "Intelligence and Further Economic and Social Phenomena," and 5, "The Sociology of Intelligence, Earnings, and Social Competence"). In this group of nations, Qatar is the only country whose national IQ is slightly below 80 but the per capita income is as high as in technologically advanced market economies. However, as noted earlier, this is due to the rich oil industry that is based on Western technologies and is managed or controlled by Europeans and Orientals.

SUMMARY

In this chapter, we have tested the hypothesis that there is a positive relationship between national intelligence and economic development assessed by various measures of per capita income in 81 countries for which we have direct evidence of their national IQs based on intelligence tests. The relationship between national IQs and the measures of per capita income was measured by correlation and regression analyses. The results of the correlation analyses provide strong support to the hypothesis. Per capita income has been positively correlated with national IQs since 1820. The correlation between national IQs and per capita income increases from .540 (the average of the Pearson and Spearman correlations) in 1820 to .720 in 1997 to 1998 (the average of six Pearson correlations). Thus, national IQs explain 29 percent of the variance in per capita income in 1820 and 52 percent of the variance in per capita income in 1997-1998. The average of six Spearman correlations in 1997 to 98 rises to .833 and the explained part of variation rises to 69 percent. We conclude that differences in national intelligence provide the most powerful and fundamental explanation for the gap between rich and poor countries.

Regression analysis was used to identify the countries in which the level of per capita income is approximately consistent with the level of national IQ and the countries that deviate greatly from the expected relationship. The examination of the most deviant countries identified some other relevant factors. We found that differences in economic and probably also in political systems have affected economic development significantly in countries with national IQs above 90. In this group of countries with a narrow range of IQs, there are considerable differences in per capita incomes between market economy democracies and present and former socialist countries. It seems justifiable to conclude that the socialist command economies have been much less favorable for economic development than market economies.

The sample of 81 countries analyzed in this chapter consists of countries from all parts of the world including Western and Eastern Europe, North and sub-Saharan Africa, the Near East and the Middle East, South Asia, North East Asia, the Pacific Islands, Australasia, North and South America, and the Caribbean. Although it is not a random sample, it can be regarded as a representative sample of the world's nations. Furthermore, practically all the large countries are included, and thus it represents the major part of the world population. For these reasons, the strong associations found in this sample may be regarded as providing persuasive evidence for a causal effect of national IQs on economic growth and development.

8

National IQs and Economic Development in 185 Countries

The 185 countries analyzed in this chapter consist of the 81 countries for which we have direct evidence of their national IQs and the 104 other countries for which we have estimated their national IQs as explained in Chapter 6, "Data on Variables and Methods of Analysis." The national IQs of all these countries are presented in Table 6.4 in Chapter 6. This group includes all contemporary and independent countries, except for Bosnia and Herzegovina, whose population in 1990 was 50,000 inhabitants or more, and, in addition to them, Hong Kong, Puerto Rico, and Taiwan. Because this group comprises virtually all contemporary countries, our hypothesis can be tested more definitively in this total world group than in the previous sample of 81 countries. However, there is one weakness in this world group. We had to estimate the national IQs for 104 countries due to the lack of direct evidence of intelligence tests.

CORRELATIONS BETWEEN NATIONAL IQs AND PER CAPITA INCOME, 1820–1998

We begin with an examination of the correlations between national IQs and the measures of per capita income used in the previous chapter for the sample of 81 countries. The results of this examination will show whether the hypothesized relationship is stronger or weaker in the total world group than in the 81 countries. If our estimated national IQs are biased to favor the hypothesis, it can be assumed that the relationships should be stronger in the 185 countries than in the 81 countries. If correlations are weaker in this group, our estimated national IQs are not biased to favor the hypothesis, although they may include other errors.

The results of correlation analysis using the Pearson product-moment correlations are shown in Table 8.1. The results of correlation analysis using the Spearman rank correlations are shown in Table 8.2.

Table 8.1

National IQs Correlated with GDP Per Capita (Maddison), GNP Per Capita, GNP Per Capita Measured at PPP, Real GDP Per Capita (PPP), and GDP Per Capita during the Period of 1820 to 1998 in the Group of 185 Countries (Pearson product-moment correlations)

Year	GDP N	GDP r	GNP N	GNP r	GNP-PPP N	GNP-PPP r	Real GDP N	Real GDP r	GDP N	GDP r
1820	26	.627	—	—	—	—	—	—	—	—
1850	19	.669	—	—	—	—	—	—	—	—
1870	30	.481	—	—	—	—	—	—	—	—
1890	28	.489	—	—	—	—	—	—	—	—
1900	42	.566	—	—	—	—	—	—	—	—
1910	47	.532	—	—	—	—	—	—	—	—
1920	34	.490	—	—	—	—	—	—	—	—
1930	46	.538	—	—	—	—	—	—	—	—
1940	45	.478	—	—	—	—	—	—	—	—
1950	166	.273	—	—	—	—	—	—	—	—
1960	56	.606	—	—	—	—	—	—	—	—
1970	55	.658	—	—	—	—	—	—	—	—
1976	—	—	148	.463	—	—	—	—	—	—
1977	—	—	150	.486	—	—	—	—	—	—
1978	—	—	148	.509	—	—	—	—	—	—
1980	58	.713	143	.493	—	—	—	—	—	—
1981	—	—	139	.507	—	—	—	—	—	—
1982	—	—	132	.528	—	—	—	—	—	—
1983	—	—	132	.539	—	—	—	—	181	.466
1984	—	—	131	.532	—	—	—	—	181	.474

Year	GDP N	GDP r	GNP N	GNP r	GNP-PPP N	GNP-PPP r	Real GDP N	Real GDP r	GDP N	GDP r
1985	—	—	140	.551	—	—	—	—	181	.470
1986	—	—	138	.606	—	—	—	—	181	.561
1987	—	—	141	.621	—	—	129	.695	181	.565
1988	—	—	141	.643	—	—	128	.730	182	.580
1989	—	—	138	.625	—	—	159	.643	183	.583
1990	163	.677	139	.628	—	—	159	.679	183	.577
1991	—	—	157	.588	—	—	174	.671	183	.574
1992	56	.730	153	.575	—	—	174	.622	184	.539
1993	—	—	159	.563	—	—	175	.544	184	.547
1994	—	—	158	.584	—	—	175	.595	184	.556
1995	—	—	165	.579	141	.641	173	.591	184	.561
1996	—	—	—	—	—	—	—	—	185	.570
1997	—	—	174	.583	146	.672	174	.608	—	—
1998	—	—	185	.567	141	.696	185	.623	—	—

Table 8.2

National IQs Correlated with GDP Per Capita (Maddison), GNP Per Capita, GNP Per Capita Measured at PPP, Real GDP Per Capita (PPP), and GDP Per Capita during the Period of 1820 to 1998 in the Group of 185 Countries (Spearman rank correlations)

Year	GDP N	GDP r	GNP N	GNP r	GNP-PPP N	GNP-PPP r	Real GDP N	Real GDP r	GDP N	GDP r
1820	26	.617	—	—	—	—	—	—	—	—
1850	19	.750	—	—	—	—	—	—	—	—
1870	30	.550	—	—	—	—	—	—	—	—
1890	28	.541	—	—	—	—	—	—	—	—
1900	42	.620	—	—	—	—	—	—	—	—
1910	47	.609	—	—	—	—	—	—	—	—

Table 8.2   continued

Year	GDP N	GDP r	GNP N	GNP r	GNP-PPP N	GNP-PPP r	Real GDP N	Real GDP r	GDP N	GDP r
1920	34	.493	—	—	—	—	—	—	—	—
1930	46	.546	—	—	—	—	—	—	—	—
1940	45	.609	—	—	—	—	—	—	—	—
1950	166	.590	—	—	—	—	—	—	—	—
1960	56	.700	—	—	—	—	—	—	—	—
1970	55	.723	—	—	—	—	—	—	—	—
1976	—	—	148	.678	—	—	—	—	—	—
1977	—	—	150	.665	—	—	—	—	—	—
1978	—	—	148	.670	—	—	—	—	—	—
1980	58	.774	143	.716	—	—	—	—	—	—
1981	—	—	139	.685	—	—	—	—	—	—
1982	—	—	132	.709	—	—	—	—	—	—
1983	—	—	132	.710	—	—	—	—	181	.649
1984	—	—	131	.707	—	—	—	—	181	.659
1985	—	—	140	.693	—	—	—	—	181	.643
1986	—	—	138	.710	—	—	—	—	181	.673
1987	—	—	141	.708	—	—	129	.794	181	.653
1988	—	—	141	.707	—	—	128	.798	182	.668
1989	—	—	138	.728	—	—	159	.720	183	.673
1990	163	.723	139	.719	—	—	159	.732	183	.658
1991	—	—	157	.686	—	—	174	.739	183	.648
1992	56	.834	153	.657	—	—	174	.698	184	.490
1993	—	—	159	.631	—	—	175	.652	184	.533
1994	—	—	158	.655	—	—	175	.660	184	.565
1995	—	—	165	.655	141	.732	173	.652	184	.590
1996	—	—	—	—	—	—	—	—	185	.600
1997	—	—	174	.654	146	.717	174	.651	—	—
1998	—	—	185	.636	141	.713	185	.678	—	—

Tables 8.1 and 8.2 show that the correlations in the total world group are, in nearly all cases, somewhat weaker than in the sample of 81 countries (cf., Tables 7.1 and 7.2). The difference in the means of the correlations is clear. The arithmetic mean of all 64 Pearson correlations is .620 and of all Spearman correlations is .745 in the 81 countries. The corresponding arithmetic means of 64 correlations are respectively .577 and .667 in the 185 countries. This implies that our estimated national IQs are not biased to favor the hypothesis. It is more probable that errors in the estimates weakened the correlations in the analyses of the 185 countries. The correlations with Maddison's historical data deviate from this pattern. Most of them are slightly stronger in 185 countries than in the 81 countries group. The arithmetic mean of the 15 Pearson correlations is .550 in the 81 countries and is .575 in 185 countries. The arithmetic means of the corresponding 15 Spearman correlations are .611 and .645. These small differences in correlations are probably caused by the fact that the total world group includes relatively more countries with low national IQs.

The results of the correlation analyses support the hypothesis consistently and strongly. The Spearman rank-order correlations are again somewhat stronger than the Pearson correlations. The Pearson correlations (except for the low correlation for 1950, which was explained in the previous chapter) are positive and relatively strong. The explained part of variation in Maddison's data, when the correlation for 1950 is omitted, varies from 23 to 53 percent; in the GNP per capita data (World Bank) from 21 to 41 percent; in the GNP per capita measured at PPP (World Bank) from 41 to 48 percent; in the real GDP per capita (UNDP data) from 30 to 53 percent; and in the GDP per capita (United Nations) from 22 to 34 percent. The explained part of variation in the Spearman rank correlations varies from 24 to 70 percent in Maddison's data, from 40 to 53 percent in the GNP per capita data; from 51 to 54 percent in the GNP per capita (PPP) data; from 42 to 64 percent in real GDP per capita data; and from 24 to 45 percent in the GDP per capita data. The variation in these correlations is partly caused by the fact that the number of countries in each sample varies from year to year and from variable to variable. In most cases, the explained part of variation is less than 50 percent, which indicates that other factors affect economic development and the gap between rich and poor countries. However, the explained part of the variation in per capita income is sufficiently high for the differences in national intelligence to be regarded as an important factor that determines economic growth and development.

The correlations seem to have become somewhat stronger over time, although they have not risen regularly. Maddison's data make it possible to examine this problem over the period of 172 years from 1820 to 1992. The correlation between the 15 Pearson correlations for the period 1820 to 1992 and the years of comparison is .221. When the anomalous year of 1950 is excluded, this correlation rises to .458. The corresponding correlation for the

15 Spearman correlations is .467. Figure 8.1 illustrates the changes of the Spearman correlations during the period of 1820 to 1992. The Spearman correlations have increased almost regularly since 1920. The periods of comparison are also much shorter in the cases of the other four data sets, and it is difficult to see any systematic changes in the strength of correlations over time.

There are differences in the explanatory power of national IQs for the five measures of per capita income. GNP per capita and GDP per capita measured at current exchange rates are not as strongly correlated with national IQs as GNP per capita measured at PPP (purchasing power parity) dollars and real GDP per capita (PPP). The arithmetic mean of 21 GNP per capita Pearson correlations is .560 and of 14 GDP per capita (United Nations) correlations .546. The corresponding arithmetic means of the three GNP per capita (PPP) correlations and of the 11 real GDP per capita correlations are .670 and .636, respectively. This indicates that the real differences in the level of economic development are more strongly related to the differences in national intelligence than the differences in per capita incomes based on partly artificial exchange rate dollars. However, despite differences between the five measures of per capita income, they are strongly inter-correlated both cross-sectionally and longitudinally. We examine some examples shown in Table 8.3 and 8.4.

Figure 8.1

Bivariate Line Chart of Spearman Correlations and the Years of Comparison during the Period of 1820 to 1992 (Maddison's data) in the Group of 185 Countries

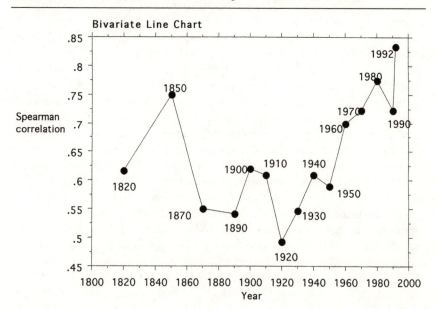

Table 8.3

Some Cross-Sectional Correlations between the Different Measures of Per Capita Income in 1990 and 1998 in the Group of 185 Countries

Variable/year	GNP per capita	Real GDP per capita	GDP per capita
1990			
GDP (Maddison) 1990	.948 (N =137)	.963 (N = 156)	.935 (N = 162)
GNP per capita 1990		.956 (N = 135)	.991 (N =138)
Real GDP per capita 1990			.946 (N = 159)
GDP per capita 1990			

	GNP per capita PPP	Real GDP per capita	GDP per capita
1998			
GNP per capita 1998	.967 (N = 141)	.953 (N = 185)	.988 (N = 185)
GNP per capita PPP 1998		.989 (N = 141)	.960 (N = 141)
Real GDP per capita 1998			.942 (N = 185)
GDP per capita 1996			

Table 8.4

Correlations over time of the Five Measures of Per Capita Income in the Group of 185 Countries

Variable/years	N	Correlation
GDP per capita (Maddison) between 1820 and 1992	26	.744
GDP per capita 1820 and GNP per capita 1998	26	.675
GDP per capita 1820 and real GDP per capita 1998	26	.743
GDP per capita 1820 and GDP per capita 1996	26	.646
GNP per capita between 1976 and 1998	148	.779
GNP per capita (PPP) between 1995 and 1998	120	.989
Real GDP per capita between 1987 and 1998	129	.971
GDP per capita between 1983 and 1996	181	.805

These correlations are nearly as high as the corresponding correlations in the group of 81 countries that were presented in Tables 7.4 and 7.5. Because the various measures of per capita income are highly inter-correlated, it does not make much difference which variable is used to measure per capita income. However, the correlations over time are somewhat weaker, which indicates that the relative position of several countries has changed over time.

Differences in national intelligence have consistently explained approximately 40 to 50 percent of the gap between rich and poor countries, sometimes somewhat more and sometimes somewhat less. Until now, researchers have not found any other factor that is as strongly and consistently correlated with the variation in per capita income.

CORRELATIONS BETWEEN NATIONAL IQs AND ECONOMIC GROWTH

We now examine the hypothesis that national IQs should be positively correlated with long-term economic growth rates. In the previous chapter, this hypothesis was tested and confirmed in the sample of 81 countries. The corresponding correlations for the 185 nations are shown in Table 8.5.

The correlations presented in Table 8.5 differ only slightly from the corresponding correlations for 81 countries shown in Table 7.3 (81 countries). The correlations for the long time periods are positive, and it can be seen

Table 8.5

National IQs Correlated with Economic Growth Rates in 185 Countries

Economic growth rate	Period of comparison	N	Pearson correlation	Spearman rank correlation
GDP per capita (Maddison)	1820–1992	26	.728	.607
GDP per capita (Maddison)	1820–1900	26	.573	.470
GDP per capita (Maddison)	1910–1992	47	.531	.567
GDP per capita (Maddison)	1950–1990	166	.449	.506
GDP per capita (Maddison)	1890-1910	28	.209	.167
GNP per capita (World Bank data)	1976–1998	148	.451	.478
GDP per capita (United Nations data)	1983–1996	181	.280	.330
Real GDP per capita (UNDP data)	1987–1998	127	–.012	.105
GNP per capita measured at PPP	1995–1998	121	–.006	–.107

that the strength of the correlations declines when the period of comparison shortens. In fact, the correlations decrease to zero in the two shortest periods of comparison. The fact that the longest period of comparison (1820–1992) has produced the highest correlation indicates the continuity of the gap between rich and poor countries.

REGRESSION OF PER CAPITA INCOME IN 1900 ON IQs

We now use regression analysis to identify the countries that deviate the most from the average relationship between national IQs and the measures of per capita income and to identify the countries for which it was possible to predict the level of per capita income relatively well from their population IQs. Because the correlations in the total world group are somewhat lower than in the group of 81 countries, the predictions produced by the regression equations will also be less accurate than in the group of 81 countries. Because it is not reasonable to carry out all possible regression analyses, the problem is again to determine which years of comparison and dependent variables to select. The data sets of per capita income (see Appendix 2, "Data on Per Capita Income and Economic Growth in 185 Countries") enable us to examine the relationship between national IQs and per capita income at several different historical points in time. We have selected four years for the regression analyses. Because the number of countries in the world group for 1820 is only two higher (26) than in the 81 nation sample (24), the results would be nearly the same. Therefore, we omit 1820 and examine first the situation for the year 1900. This year provides a good historical comparison point from the period before the establishment of socialist economic and political systems. In later sections of this chapter, we report the regressions of national income and IQs for 1930, 1960, and 1998.

The results of the regression analysis for 1900 are presented in Table 8.6 and in Figure 8.3. The number of countries for which there are national income data has increased from 26 in 1820 to 42 in 1900. For 37 of these countries, our data on national IQs are based on the direct evidence of intelligence tests. Ghana is the only sub-Saharan African country represented in this sample. Other major regions of the world are better represented.

The great variation of the residuals reflects the fact that the correlation between national IQs and GDP per capita is only moderately strong (.566). Only 32 percent of the variation in national income is due to variation in national IQs. The variation in the residuals is greatest at higher levels of national IQ. The problem is again to define the distinction between large and small residuals. In this case, it seems reasonable to use the criterion of +700 and −700 to distinguish large residuals from moderate and small ones. When this criterion is adopted, there are nine large positive outliers and seven large negative outliers. We can use the results of the regression analysis

Table 8.6

The Results of the Regression Analysis in which GDP Per Capita 1900 (Maddison) Is Used as the Dependent Variable and National IQ as the Independent Variable for 42 Countries

Country	IQ	GDP per capita 1900	Residual GDP	Fitted GDP
6 Argentina	96	2,756	721	2,035
8 Australia	98	4,299	2,084	2,215
9 Austria	102	2,901	326	2,575
13 Bangladesh	81	581	−102	683
16 Belgium	100	3,652	1,257	2,395
22 Brazil	87	704	−520	1,224
26 Burma	86	647	−487	1,134
30 Canada	97	2,758	633	2,125
34 Chile	93	1,949	185	1,764
35 China	100	652	−1,743	2,395
36 Colombia	89	973	−431	1,404
45 Czech Republic	97	1,729	−396	2,125
46 Denmark	98	2,902	687	2,215
51 Egypt	83	509	−354	863
58 Finland	97	1,620	−505	2,125
59 France	98	2,849	634	2,215
63 Germany	102	2,134	559	2,575
64 Ghana	71	452	680	−218
74 Hungary	99	1,682	−623	2,305
76 India	81	625	−58	683
77 Indonesia	89	745	−659	1,404
80 Ireland	93	2,495	731	1,764
82 Italy	102	1,746	−829	2,575
84 Japan	105	1,135	−1,710	2,845

Country	IQ	GDP per capita 1900	Residual GDP	Fitted GDP
90 Korea, South	106	850	–2,085	2,935
111 Mexico	87	1,157	–67	1,224
119 Netherlands	102	3,533	958	2,575
120 New Zealand	100	4,320	1,925	2,395
124 Norway	98	1,762	–453	2,215
126 Pakistan	81	687	4	683
130 Peru	90	817	–677	1,494
131 Philippines	86	1,033	–101	1,134
133 Portugal	95	1,408	–536	1,944
137 Russia	96	1,218	–817	2,035
151 Spain	97	2,040	–85	2,125
159 Sweden	101	2,561	76	2,485
160 Switzerland	101	3,531	1,046	2,485
162 Taiwan	104	759	–1,996	2,755
165 Thailand	91	812	–772	1,584
175 United Kingdom	100	4,593	2,198	2,395
176 United States	98	4,096	1,881	2,215
180 Venezuela	89	821	–583	1,404

given in Table 8.6 to test the previous predictions made based on the situation in 1820 (refer to Table 7.6) and to make predictions on the prospects of economic development in these 42 countries. It should be noted that Maddison's data set covers not only independent states but also several countries that were not independent in 1900.

There are 26 countries with moderate and small residuals. Within this category, residuals are positive for nine countries (Austria, Canada, Chile, Denmark, France, Germany, Ghana, Pakistan, and Sweden), and negative for 17 countries (Bangladesh, Brazil, Burma, Colombia, the Czech Republic, Egypt, Finland, Hungary, India, Indonesia, Mexico, Norway, Peru, the Philippines, Portugal, Spain, and Venezuela). On the basis of these residuals, it would have been reasonable to predict in 1900 that these countries would remain near the regression line in the near future. However, if we had been aware of the effects of some additional variables, especially of the significance of technological and industrial development, it would have been possible to modify this general prediction.

In addition, it would have been reasonable to predict in 1900 that the countries which were able to adopt modern industrial technologies would have the best chances of increasing their per capita incomes and that the countries which were not able to adopt modern technologies would fall behind. In accordance with this expectation, it is interesting to note that several countries near the core area of original industrialization had already achieved positive residuals in 1900. Six of the nine countries with positive residuals (Austria, Canada, Denmark, France, Germany, and Sweden) belong to this group. These countries were industrializing and their per capita income was rising. Chile is a neighbor of Argentina, for which the residual was highly positive in 1900. Ghana was an anomalous case among the countries with positive residuals. It is the only sub-Saharan African country in this group. Its per capita income was low (452 dollars) in 1900, but not as low as expected on the basis of the linear regression equation (–218 dollars). This negative predicted per capita income is an impossible consequence of the linear regression line. Therefore, Ghana's real deviation was smaller than its residual indicates. Its small positive deviation was due principally to its agricultural exports. Pakistan was also on the regression line.

Eleven of the 17 countries with small or moderate negative residuals are Latin American and Asian countries that had not yet begun the process of industrialization. There are also six European countries in this group. These are the Czech Republic, Finland, Hungary, Norway, Portugal, and Spain. Their common feature is that they were geographically separated from the core area of industrialization in Northwest Europe, and they were industrializing more slowly. However, because the national IQs in these countries were at the same or nearly at the same level as in the more industrialized countries, it could have been predicted that per capita incomes would increase in these countries faster than average. It would not have been possible to make the same prediction for the 11 Latin American and Asian countries in this category, because the national IQs for these countries are lower than those of the European countries. The level of per capita income in the European countries was somewhat lower than expected on the basis of IQs in 1900, and there would not have been any special grounds to predict significant changes up or down.

The countries with the largest positive residuals consisted of Argentina, Australia, Belgium, Ireland, the Netherlands, New Zealand, Switzerland, the United Kingdom, and the United States. Of these countries, Argentina, Australia, and New Zealand are European offshoot countries in which agriculture and livestock production were efficient. The other seven countries constituted the geographically compact European core area of industrialization. At that time, Australia, New Zealand, the United Kingdom, and the United States were the richest countries in the world, and positive residuals were highest for them. Because the per capita income in all these nine countries was much higher than expected on the basis of the average relationship between national IQs and per capita income, it would have been reasonable to predict a decline in their relative position. However, it would have been necessary to make such a prediction technologically conditional. Because they had achieved their high position in 1900 with the help of modern technologies, these countries would not lose their pre-eminence if they were able to maintain their technological advantage compared to other countries and regions of the world. If they were not able to retain this lead, their relative status would decline, and their residuals would become smaller in the future.

The countries with the largest negative residuals consisted of China, Italy, Japan, South Korea, Russia, Taiwan, and Thailand. This is an interesting group from the perspective of our hypothesis that national IQ is a determinant of economic growth and development. The national IQs for these countries, except for Russia and Thailand, are above 100. Their high negative residuals are inconsistent with our hypothesis. The highest negative residuals are for the four East Asian countries of China, Japan, South Korea, and Taiwan. These countries were relatively poor despite the high level of intelligence of their populations. The explanation for these anomalies is that for various historical reasons, technological advances and industrialization began first in Northwest Europe and were only adopted slowly in the rest of the world. In 1900, Japan had started to adopt modern technologies, but this had barely begun in the three other East Asian countries. In several of these countries, the adoption of European technologies and industrialization was retarded by autocratic political systems. This was notably the case in China whose despotic rulers and the mandarinate and imperial court stifled dissent and were hostile to technological innovation (Landes, 1998, pp. 35–38).

Russia is another example of a country with autocratic political rulers who were slow to adopt the political and economic institutions needed to promote economic development. Italy's high negative residual is also attributable to its inadequately developed political and economic institutions. Thailand's negative residual reflects the situation throughout the whole of East Asia, where all the residuals were negative in 1900.

Next, we examine the extent to which the predictions made on the basis of the relation between national IQs and economic development in 1820 had become realized by 1900. In the 1820 group of countries there are 24 in the 1900 group. Nearly all of the 15 countries that were moderate and small outliers in 1820 were in the same category in 1900. This reflects the stability of the relationship between national IQ and per capita income over time and the slowness of the process of industrialization. However, the position of some of these countries changed significantly. Belgium and Ireland had risen to the category of large positive outliers in 1900, whereas Italy had dropped to the category of large negative outliers. Belgium and Ireland had joined the core of the industrialized world.

The most interesting predictions concern the countries with large positive or negative residuals in 1820. What had happened to them? All the five countries with large positive residuals—Australia, France, the Netherlands, the United Kingdom, and the United States—were still among the largest positive outliers in 1900. This implies that they had succeeded in maintaining their technological lead. Of the four countries with large negative residuals in 1820, China, Japan and Russia were still among the largest negative outliers. Finland had moved to the category of moderate negative residuals. In 1900, Finland still belonged to Russia as an autonomous Grand Duchy, but the results of the regression analysis imply that industrialization had progressed faster in Finland than in Russia.

Figure 8.2 illustrates graphically the results of the regression analysis. The regression line in the figure indicates the average relationship between national IQs and the GDP per capita in 1900. According to the regression equation, per capita income rose 90 dollars on the average for each index point increase in national IQ.

Figure 8.2 shows that in 1900 there was virtually no correlation between national IQs and per capita income among countries with national IQs above 90 (r = .142, N = 30). However, when the four East Asian countries

Figure 8.2

The Results of the Regression Analysis of GDP Per Capita 1900 on National IQ for 42 Countries in the Group of 185 Countries

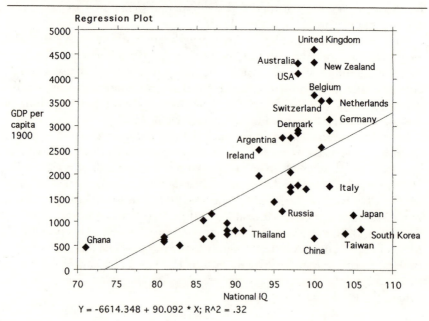

$Y = -6614.348 + 90.092 * X; R^2 = .32$

are excluded, the correlation rises to .589 (N = 26). The extreme deviation of the four East Asian countries reduces the strength of the correlation drastically. In fact, without the four East Asian countries, the correlation between national IQs and GDP per capita would have been .765 in 1900 as compared to .566 in this group of 42 countries. The difference in the explained part of the variation in per capita income is 26 percentage points.

The countries with national IQs below 90 deviate from the regression line only moderately. Nearly all of them are below the regression line. The moderate positive correlation between national IQs and per capita income in the 42 countries is entirely due to the fact that the position of the countries with IQs below 90 is in accordance with our hypothesis. The level of per capita income was relatively low in all of them, as expected on the basis of their low IQs.

REGRESSION OF PER CAPITA INCOME IN 1930 ON IQs

We use the year 1930 as the second historical point of comparison. The situation in 1930 indicates how the relation between national IQs and per capita income changed during the period of thirty years since 1900. The number of countries for which Maddison gives data on GDP per capita has increased from 42 to 46. Egypt and Ghana disappeared from the 1930 group. Bulgaria, Greece, Poland, Romania, Turkey, and Yugoslavia were new countries. The correlation between national IQs and per capita income is .534 in this group of 46 countries, virtually the same as the correlation of .566 in 1900. The results of this regression analysis are presented in Table 8.7 and in Figure 8.4.

Table 8.7

The Results of the Regression Analysis in which GDP Per Capita 1930 (Maddison) Is Used as the Dependent Variable and National IQ as the Independent Variable for 46 Countries

Country	IQ	GDP per capita 1930	Residual GDP	Fitted GDP
6 Argentina	96	4,080	1,279	2,801
8 Australia	98	4,792	1,711	3,081
9 Austria	102	3,610	−32	3,642
13 Bangladesh	81	619	−78	697
16 Belgium	100	4,873	1,511	3,362

Table 8.7   continued

Country	IQ	GDP per capita 1930	Residual GDP	Fitted GDP
22 Brazil	87	1,061	–477	1,538
24 Bulgaria	93	1,284	–1,096	2,380
26 Burma	86	836	–562	1,398
30 Canada	97	4,558	1,617	2,941
34 Chile	93	3,143	763	2,380
35 China	100	786	–2,576	3,362
36 Colombia	89	1,474	–345	1,819
45 Czech Republic	97	2,926	–15	2,941
46 Denmark	98	5,138	2,057	3,081
58 Finland	97	2,589	–352	2,941
59 France	98	4,489	1,408	3,081
63 Germany	102	4,049	407	3,642
65 Greece	92	2,300	60	2,240
74 Hungary	99	2,404	–817	3,221
76 India	81	654	–43	697
77 Indonesia	89	1,198	–621	1,819
80 Ireland	93	3,034	654	2,380
82 Italy	102	2,854	–788	3,642
84 Japan	105	1,780	–2,283	4,063
90 Korea, South	106	1,173	–3,030	4,203
111 Mexico	87	1,371	–167	1,538
119 Netherlands	102	5,467	1,825	3,642
120 New Zealand	100	4,985	1,623	3,362
124 Norway	98	3,377	296	3,081
126 Pakistan	81	735	38	697
130 Peru	90	1,417	–542	1,959
131 Philippines	86	1,564	166	1,398

Country	IQ	GDP per capita 1930	Residual GDP	Fitted GDP
132 Poland	99	1,994	−1,227	3,221
133 Portugal	95	1,536	−1,124	2,660
136 Romania	94	1,219	−1,301	2,520
137 Russia	96	1,448	−1,353	2,801
151 Spain	97	2,802	−139	2,941
159 Sweden	101	3,937	435	3,502
160 Switzerland	101	6,160	2,658	3,502
162 Taiwan	104	1,112	−2,811	3,923
165 Thailand	91	799	−1,300	2,099
170 Turkey	90	985	−974	1,959
175 United Kingdom	100	5,195	1,833	3,362
176 United States	98	6,220	3,139	3,081
180 Venezuela	89	3,444	1,625	1,819
183 Yugoslavia	93	1,325	−1,055	2,380

The results of the regression analysis shown in Table 8.7 can be used to examine the predictions proposed on the basis of the situation in 1900 and to consider what had happened to the countries with extremely large positive or negative residuals in 1900. In this case, we use the criterion of ±1,200 to distinguish the countries with the largest positive and negative residuals from the countries whose GDP per capita departed less from the regression line. According to these criteria, 12 countries had large positive residuals and eight countries large negative residuals in 1930.

There were 26 countries with small or moderate residuals in 1930. Nearly all of these 26 countries that belonged to this category in 1900 have remained near the regression line. Only three countries—Canada, Denmark, and Venezuela—have left this group and moved to the category of large positive residuals. Thus, the predictions made for the countries of this category on the basis of the situation in 1900 were quite accurate. Their level of national IQ approximately explained their level of per capita income in 1930.

The same cannot be said of the countries with extremely large positive or negative residuals. Of the nine countries with large positive residuals in 1900, eight had remained in this category. Only Ireland had dropped to the category of moderate positive residuals, and Canada, Denmark, and

Venezuela were new entrants. Of the seven countries with large negative residuals in 1900, six had remained in this category. Italy had improved its relative position and risen to the category of moderate negative residuals. Poland and Romania, which were not included in the comparison group 1900, were new countries with large negative residuals. The stability of both extreme groups implies the existence of powerful additional variables that affected the relationship between national IQs and per capita income. The most probable explanation is that modern technologies invented and introduced in the West produced and maintained the much higher-than-expected level of economic development in the core region of industrialization, whereas the slowness to adopt outside knowledge and technologies obstructed economic development in East Asia.

Next we examine what kinds of predictions it would have been possible to make in 1930 for these countries on the basis of the results of this regression analysis. Let us start with the group of 26 countries with small or moderate residuals. Residuals were positive for eight of these countries (Chile, Germany, Greece, Ireland, Norway, Pakistan, the Philippines, and Sweden) and negative for 18 countries (Austria, Bangladesh, Brazil, Bulgaria, Burma, Colombia, the Czech Republic, Finland, Hungary, India, Indonesia, Italy, Mexico, Peru, Portugal, Spain, Turkey, and Yugoslavia). The geographical position of these countries illustrates the spreading of technological innovations from the core region of Northwest Europe to neighboring countries and other parts of the world. Of the eight countries with positive residuals, Germany, Ireland, Norway, and Sweden are immediate neighbors of the original core region of the technological revolution. The positive residuals of Greece, Pakistan, and Philippines are insignificant. Chile is a neighbor of Argentina. It would have been reasonable to predict in 1930 that the prospects of economic development were best in the four neighboring countries (Germany, Ireland, Norway, and Sweden) of the industrial core region and that, consequently, the residuals for these countries might increase rather than decrease. Chile would probably have remained near the regression line.

Eight of the 18 countries with small or moderate negative residuals were European countries on the periphery of the original industrial core region of Northwest Europe (Austria, Bulgaria, the Czech Republic, Finland, Hungary, Italy, Portugal, and Spain). The diffusion of new technologies had reached them only partially. It would have been reasonable to predict that their negative residuals would decrease as a consequence of the diffusion of technology from their neighboring countries. The other ten countries were Latin American and Asian countries that until then had only partially adopted modern technologies. Thus, there were no special reasons to expect any radical changes in their relative positions in the near future.

The group of 12 countries with large positive residuals in 1930 included three European offshoot countries that had been highly successful in agricultural exports (Argentina, Australia, and New Zealand) and eight countries of the European and North American industrial core region (Belgium, Canada, Denmark, France, the Netherlands, Switzerland, the United Kingdom and the United States). Compared to the situation in 1900, Canada and Denmark were new entrants to this group. Because these countries had been able to maintain their technological lead, it could have been reasonably predicted in 1930 that they would remain as highly deviant cases in the future. Venezuela was a surprising new entrant to this group in 1930. Venezuela's GDP per capita had increased from 821 dollars in 1900 to 3,444 dollars in 1930, and the negative residual −583 in 1900 had changed into the highly positive residual of 1,625. Venezuela had achieved an unexpectedly high level of per capita income in 1930 due to the start of petroleum production in 1921. Most of Venezuela's petroleum was produced by giant North American and European petroleum companies (Blank, 1973, pp. 31–32).

Six of the eight countries with the largest negative residuals in 1930 (China, Japan, South Korea, Russia, Taiwan, and Thailand) were the same as in 1900. On the basis of their high negative residuals, we should have predicted a rapid decrease of negative residuals for all of them, but economic development in these countries was also influenced by other factors. China suffered from serious political instability, and Korea and Taiwan were colonies of Japan. The Communist party had established a socialist system in Russia, and it was difficult to predict in 1930 how it would affect the country's economic development. Because Poland and Romania are geographically close to the wealthy western and central European industrial countries, it would have been reasonable to expect the diffusion of technology from the West and, consequently, the decrease of negative residuals.

Figure 8.3 shows the results of the regression analysis. The basic structure of the figure is the same as in 1900, although some of the most extremely deviant countries have changed. The four East Asian countries and the richest Western countries now show large deviations from the regression line. Some factors other than national IQs must explain the great difference of per capita income between these two extreme groups of countries, for which the level of per capita income should be approximately the same according to national IQs. Figure 8.3 also shows that the East European countries tended to have much lower-than-expected levels of per capita income before the imposition of socialist systems implemented after the World War II. Although the diffusion of new technologies from Western Europe progressed slowly, this was not the only reason for their slow economic development. Political instability and unfavorable domestic political and social institutions probably hampered economic development. The establishment of a socialist political and economic system in Russia retarded its relative position, although the process of industrialization accelerated. Its negative residual was higher in 1930 than in 1900. It is remarkable that for nearly all countries with national IQs below 90, the residuals were negative.

Figure 8.3

The Results of the Regression Analysis of GDP Per Capita 1930 on National IQ for 46 Countries in the Group of 185 Countries

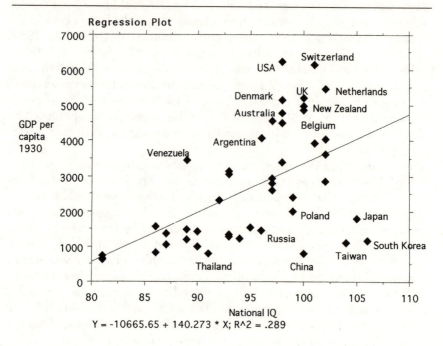

Y = -10665.65 + 140.273 * X; R^2 = .289

Venezuela was an exception, but as noted its higher-than-expected level of per capita income was principally due to the impact of petroleum production started by American and European oil companies.

REGRESSION OF PER CAPITA INCOME IN 1960 ON IQs

It will be interesting to see whether World War II changed the relationship between national IQs and GDP per capita to any significant extent and whether the diffusion of Western knowledge and technology reduced the gap between rich and poor countries and helped some of the poor countries below the regression line to achieve the level of per capita income expected on the basis of their national IQ. Maddison's data on GDP per capita cover 56 countries in 1960. Our data on national IQs are based on direct evidence for 50 of these countries. The correlation between national IQs and GDP per capita (.606) in 1960 is closely similar to that in 1930 (.538) and 1900 (.566). The results of regression analysis are shown in Table 8.8 and in Figure 8.4.

Figure 8.4

The Results of the Regression Analysis of GDP Per Capita 1960 on National IQ for 56 Countries in the Group of 185 Countries

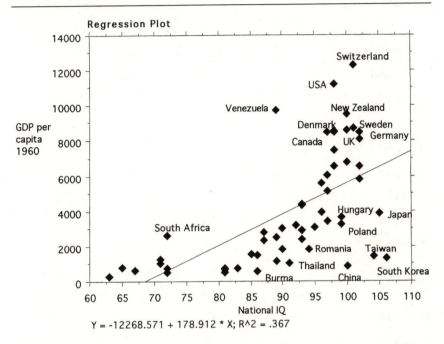

$Y = -12268.571 + 178.912 * X; R^2 = .367$

The accuracy of predictions is slightly better in this regression analysis than in the previous ones, but many residuals are extremely high, which reflects the fact that national IQs do not explain more than 37 percent of the variation in GDP per capita. In this case, it seems reasonable to use the criterion of ±2,000 to separate the countries with the largest positive or negative residuals from the countries which deviate less from the regression line. According to this criterion, 13 countries had large positive residuals and 10 countries had large negative residuals in 1960. The residuals were moderate or small for the other 33 countries.

We examine first what happened to the predictions that were made based on the situation in 1930. It was assumed that the 12 countries with large positive residuals in 1930 would remain as highly deviating cases if they succeeded in maintaining their technological advantage. In fact, ten of them still belonged to this group in 1960. Argentina and Belgium had dropped out of the group, but their residuals remained moderately positive. Germany, South Africa, and Sweden were new entrants. Germany is the most interesting case. Despite the devastation caused by the defeat in World War II, Germany was

Table 8.8

The Results of the Regression Analysis in which GDP Per Capita 1960 (Maddison) Is Used as the Dependent Variable and National IQ as the Independent Variable for 56 Countries

Country	IQ	GDP per capita 1960	Residual GDP	Fitted GDP
6 Argentina	96	5,559	652	4,907
8 Australia	98	8,539	3,274	5,265
9 Austria	102	6,561	581	5,980
13 Bangladesh	81	536	−1,687	2,223
16 Belgium	100	6,779	1,156	5,623
22 Brazil	87	2,335	−962	3,297
24 Bulgaria	93	2,912	−1,458	4,370
26 Burma	86	549	−2,569	3,118
30 Canada	97	8,459	3,373	5,086
34 Chile	93	4,304	−66	4,370
35 China	100	874	−4,745	5,623
36 Colombia	89	2,499	−1,156	3,655
39 Congo (Zaire)	65	808	1,447	−639
41 Cotê d'Ivoire	71	1,051	617	434
45 Czech Republic	97	5,108	22	5,086
46 Denmark	98	8,477	3,212	5,265
51 Egypt	83	712	−1,869	2,581
56 Ethiopia	63	302	1,299	−997
58 Finland	97	6,051	965	5,086
59 France	98	7,472	2,207	5,265
63 Germany	102	8,463	2,483	5,980
64 Ghana	71	1,232	798	434
65 Greece	92	3,204	−987	4,191
74 Hungary	99	3,649	−1,795	5,444

Country	IQ	GDP per capita 1960	Residual GDP	Fitted GDP
76 India	81	735	−1,488	2,223
77 Indonesia	89	1,131	−2,524	3,655
80 Ireland	93	4,368	−2	4,370
82 Italy	102	5,789	−191	5,980
84 Japan	105	3,879	−2,638	6,517
87 Kenya	72	717	104	613
90 Korea, South	106	1,302	−5,394	6,696
111 Mexico	87	2,781	−516	3,297
115 Morocco	85	1,511	−1,428	2,939
119 Netherlands	102	8,085	2,105	5,980
120 New Zealand	100	9,491	3,868	5,623
123 Nigeria	67	645	926	−281
124 Norway	98	6,549	1,284	5,265
126 Pakistan	81	661	−1,562	2,223
130 Peru	90	3,023	−811	3,834
131 Philippines	86	1,488	−1,630	3,118
132 Poland	99	3,218	−2,226	5,444
133 Portugal	95	3,095	−1,633	4,728
136 Romania	94	1,844	−2,705	4,549
137 Russia	96	3,935	−972	4,907
150 South Africa	72	2,624	2,011	613
151 Spain	97	3,437	−1,649	5,086
159 Sweden	101	8,688	2,886	5,802
160 Switzerland	101	12,286	6,484	5,802
162 Taiwan	104	1,399	−4,939	6,338
164 Tanzania	72	498	−115	613
165 Thailand	91	1,029	−2,983	4,012
170 Turkey	90	1,801	−2,033	3,834

Table 8.8   continued

Country	IQ	GDP per capita 1960	Residual GDP	Fitted GDP
175 United Kingdom	100	8,571	2,948	5,623
176 United States	98	11,193	5,928	5,265
180 Venezuela	89	9,726	6,071	3,655
183 Yugoslavia	93	2,401	–1,969	4,370

able to recover in 15 years and enter the group of the most wealthy countries. This indicates the significance of the general intelligence of the population. The group of countries with large negative residuals also remained stable. Seven of the eight countries with large negative residuals in 1930 remained in the same category in 1960. Russia had risen to the group of countries with moderate negative residuals. Burma, Indonesia, and Turkey were new entrants to this category. In 1930, their negative residuals had been moderate. The stability of these two categories of the most deviating countries indicates that some additional factors were responsible for the much higher-than-expected level of per capita income in the countries showing positive residuals, and they also hindered economic development in the countries showing negative residuals.

Because the levels of economic development and per capita income were approximately consistent with the level of national IQ in the 33 countries with small and moderate residuals, it would have been reasonable to predict in 1960 that most of these countries would remain in the same category in the near future. The residuals were slightly or moderately positive for 12 countries (Argentina, Austria, Belgium, Congo (Zaire), Coté d'Ivoire, the Czech Republic, Ethiopia, Finland, Ghana, Kenya, Nigeria, and Norway). The prospects of economic development were best for the five European market economy countries (Austria, Belgium, Finland, Ireland, and Norway), because they were close neighbors of the European core of technological development. Positive residuals for the five sub-Saharan African countries with national IQs below 72 were partly misleading due to the fact that they were caused, because of the linear regression line, by negative or unrealistically low predicted per capita income values. The relative decline of Argentina's per capita income was probably caused by political instability that characterized Argentina's political development following the military coup in 1930 (Kantor, 1969, pp. 573–616).

The residuals were slightly or moderately negative for 21 other countries: Bangladesh, Brazil, Bulgaria, Chile, Colombia, Egypt, Greece, Hungary, India, Ireland, Italy, Mexico, Morocco, Pakistan, Peru, Philippines, Portugal,

Russia, Spain, Tanzania, and Yugoslavia. One could have argued in 1960 that the prospects of economic development were best for Italy and Portugal, and perhaps also for Greece and Spain, because these countries are situated closely to the developed European industrial countries. It is probable that Spain's authoritarian political system established after the civil war in the 1930s was responsible for its relative underdevelopment. Portugal with its slightly smaller negative residual was handicapped by the same problems. It would have been more difficult to predict the prospects of economic development in the four countries of the European socialist block (Bulgaria, Hungary, Russia, and Yugoslavia), because it was not yet self-evident that the socialist economies would lose the contest for economic development with the democracies and market economies. There were also not any special reasons to expect significant changes in the relative position of the four Asian countries (Bangladesh, India, Pakistan, and the Philippines), in the three African countries (Egypt, Morocco, and Tanzania), and in the five Latin American countries (Brazil, Chile, Colombia, Mexico, and Peru). It would have been reasonable to assume that they would remain relatively close to the regression line.

The group of the 13 countries with the largest positive residuals had remained nearly the same as in 1930. Nine of these countries (Canada, Denmark, France, Germany, the Netherlands, Sweden, Switzerland, the United Kingdom, and the United States) constituted the central core of technological development and democratic market economies. Because they had retained their scientific and technological lead, it could have been predicted that they would remain as highly deviating countries above the regression line. Australia and New Zealand are European offshoots that had maintained close contact with technological development in Europe and North America and, therefore, had been able to achieve a much higher-than-expected level of per capita income. Venezuela had risen to this category of highly deviant countries in 1930 as a result of its lucrative petroleum industry; however, its position was insecure due to its dependence on foreign technology and oil companies and because of the international supply and demand for oil. South Africa had a significant positive residual (2,011), which reflects the economic contribution of its large European minority.

The 10 countries with large negative residuals were also relatively stable. Because of their high negative residuals, we would have predicted in 1960 that their negative residuals would decrease, and they would achieve higher per capita incomes consistent with their national IQs. However, the operation of various additional variables would have made it necessary to modify this general prediction. The four East Asian countries with the highest national IQs (China, Japan, South Korea, and Taiwan) were the most deviant cases. Japan's negative residual was decreasing as a consequence of the effective adoption of western technologies, whereas the three other countries were still far behind. It might have been possible to predict in 1960 that their residuals would begin to decrease in the future if they followed the example of Japan in the adoption and application of western technological knowledge. Burma, Indonesia, Thailand, and Turkey were other Asian countries for which negative residuals had become high. Thailand was already in this category in 1930, whereas the residuals for Burma, Indonesia, and Turkey had been only moderately negative in 1930. Contrary to expectation, they had dropped further from the expected level of per capita income. It is probable that political instability in Burma, Indonesia, and Thailand hindered economic development. Poland and Romania continued in this category as highly deviant cases. The imposition of the socialist system after World War II hindered the improvement of their relative position.

Figure 8.4 shows that the position of the most highly deviant countries in the regression plot had not changed much from the situation in 1930. World War II did not affect the relationship between national IQs and per capita income or reduce the gap between rich and poor countries. The most significant change is that of Japan, which became the first East Asian country to approach the regression line. China, Taiwan, and South Korea were still well below the regression line. Venezuela, the United States, and Switzerland were the most extreme deviant countries above the regression line. Without these six countries, the correlation between national IQs and GDP per capita increases from .606 to .750. The explained part of the variation increases by 20 percentage points. This indicates the significance of extreme deviating countries. It is remarkable that nearly all the countries whose national IQs are between 80 and 93 are below the regression line. Does this imply that it is difficult for countries at that level of national IQ to adopt new technologies? As previously discussed, there is only a weak positive correlation between national IQ and per capita income in the group of countries whose national IQ is 90 or higher ($r = .338$, $N = 36$). This correlation drops to zero in the group of countries with national IQs 95 or higher ($r = -.129$, $N = 27$).

REGRESSION OF PER CAPITA INCOME IN 1998 ON IQs

The results of the three previous regression analyses indicate how individual countries conformed to the average relationship between national IQs and per capita income in 1900, 1930, and 1960. The stability of that relationship has been surprisingly strong at least since 1900, for which we have data on the GDP per capita for 42 countries. During the last 100 years, only a few countries were able to change their position in the regression plot substantially. In other words, a country's position in the regression plot in 1900 predicted relatively well its position in 1930 and in 1960. We turn now to the contemporary situation on the basis of data on real GDP per capita in 1998. The data are for all 185 countries in the world. The results of the regression analysis are presented in Table 8.9 and in Figure 8.5.

Table 8.9

The Results of the Regression Analysis in which Real GDP Per Capita 1998 Is Used as the Dependent Variable and National IQ as the Independent Variable for 185 Countries

	Country	IQ	Real GDP per capita 1998	Residual GDP	Fitted GDP
1	Afghanistan	83	1,200	−5,314	6,514
2	Albania	90	2,804	−6,589	9,383
3	Algeria	84	4,792	−2,133	6,925
4	Angola	69	1,821	1,065	756
5	Antigua and Barbuda	75	9,277	6,053	3,224
6	Argentina	96	12,003	152	11,861
7	Armenia	93	2,072	−8,555	10,627
8	Australia	98	22,452	9,769	12,683
9	Austria	102	23,166	8,837	14,329
10	Azerbaijan	87	2,175	−5,984	8,159
11	Bahamas	78	14,614	10,156	4,458
12	Bahrain	83	13,111	6,597	6,514
13	Bangladesh	81	1,361	−4,331	5,692
14	Barbados	78	12,001	7,543	4,458
15	Belarus	96	6,319	−5,542	11,861
16	Belgium	100	23,223	9,717	13,506
17	Belize	83	4,566	−1,948	6,514
18	Benin	69	867	111	756
19	Bhutan	78	1,536	−2,922	4,458
20	Bolivia	85	2,269	−5,068	7,337
21	Botswana	72	6,103	4,113	1,990
22	Brazil	87	6,625	−1,534	8,159
23	Brunei	92	16,765	6,549	10,216
24	Bulgaria	93	4,809	−5,818	10,627

Table 8.9   continued

	Country	IQ	Real GDP per capita 1998	Residual GDP	Fitted GDP
25	Burkina Faso	67	870	936	–66
26	Burma	86	1,199	–6,549	7,748
27	Burundi	70	570	–597	1,167
28	Cambodia	89	1,257	–7,725	8,982
29	Cameroon	70	1,474	307	1,167
30	Canada	97	23,582	11,310	12,272
31	Cape Verde	78	3,233	–1,225	4,458
32	Central African Republic	68	1,118	773	345
33	Chad	72	856	–1,134	1,990
34	Chile	93	8,787	–1,840	10,627
35	China	100	3,105	–10,401	13,506
36	Colombia	89	6,006	–2,976	8,982
37	Comoros	79	1,398	–3,471	4,869
38	Congo (Brazzaville)	73	995	–1,406	2,401
39	Congo (Zaire)	65	822	1,711	–889
40	Costa Rica	91	5,987	–3,817	9,804
41	Cotê d'Ivoire	71	1,598	19	1,579
42	Croatia	90	6,749	–2,644	9,393
43	Cuba	85	3,967	–3,370	7,337
44	Cyprus	92	17,482	7,266	10,216
45	Czech Republic	97	12,362	90	12,272
46	Denmark	98	24,218	11,535	12,683
47	Djibouti	68	1,266	921	345
48	Dominica	75	5,102	1,878	3,224
49	Dominican Republic	84	4,598	–2,327	6,925
50	Ecuador	80	3,003	–2,277	5,280
51	Egypt	83	3,041	–3,473	6,514

	Country	IQ	Real GDP per capita 1998	Residual GDP	Fitted GDP
52	El Salvador	84	4,036	–2,889	6,925
53	Equatorial Guinea	59	1,817	5,174	–3,357
54	Eritrea	68	833	488	345
55	Estonia	97	7,682	–4,590	12,272
56	Ethiopia	63	574	2,286	–1,712
57	Fiji	84	4,231	–2,694	6,925
58	Finland	97	20,847	8,575	12,272
59	France	98	21,175	8,492	12,683
60	Gabon	66	6,353	6,831	–478
61	Gambia	65	1,453	2,342	–889
62	Georgia	93	3,353	–7,274	10,627
63	Germany	102	22,169	7,840	14,329
64	Ghana	71	1,735	156	1,579
65	Greece	92	13,943	3,727	10,216
66	Grenada	75	5,838	2,614	3,224
67	Guatemala	79	3,505	–1,364	4,869
68	Guinea	66	1,782	2,260	–478
69	Guinea-Bissau	66	616	1,094	–478
70	Guyana	84	3,403	–3,522	6,925
71	Haiti	72	1,383	–607	1,990
72	Honduras	84	2,433	–4,492	6,925
73	Hong Kong	107	20,763	4,378	16,385
74	Hungary	99	10,232	–2,863	13,095
75	Iceland	98	25,111	12,427	12,683
76	India	81	2,077	–3,615	5,692
77	Indonesia	89	2,651	–6,331	8,982
78	Iran	84	5,121	–1,804	6,925
79	Iraq	87	3,197	–4,962	8,159

Table 8.9   continued

	Country	IQ	Real GDP per capita 1998	Residual GDP	Fitted GDP
80	Ireland	93	21,482	10,855	10,627
81	Israel	94	17,301	6,263	11,038
82	Italy	102	20,585	6,256	14,329
83	Jamaica	72	3,389	1,399	1,990
84	Japan	105	23,257	7,695	15,562
85	Jordan	87	3,347	−4,812	8,159
86	Kazakhstan	93	4,378	−6,249	10,627
87	Kenya	72	980	−1,010	1,990
88	Kiribati	84	3,000	−3,925	6,925
89	Korea, North	104	3,000	−12,151	15,151
90	Korea, South	106	13,478	−2,476	15,974
91	Kuwait	83	25,314	18,800	6,514
92	Kyrgyzstan	87	2,317	−5,842	8,159
93	Laos	89	1,734	−7,248	8,982
94	Latvia	97	5,728	−6,544	12,272
95	Lebanon	86	4,326	−3,422	7,748
96	Lesotho	72	1,626	−364	1,990
97	Liberia	65	1,200	2,089	−889
98	Libya	84	6,697	−228	6,925
99	Lithuania	97	6,436	−5,836	12,272
100	Luxembourg	101	33,500	19,583	13,917
101	Macedonia	93	4,254	−6,375	10,627
102	Madagascar	79	756	−4,113	4,869
103	Malawi	71	523	−1,056	1,579
104	Malaysia	92	8,137	−2,079	10,216
105	Maldives	81	4,083	−1,609	5,692

	Country	IQ	Real GDP per capita 1998	Residual GDP	Fitted GDP
106	Mali	69	681	–75	756
107	Malta	95	16,448	4,997	11,450
108	Marshall Islands	84	3,000	–3,925	6,925
109	Mauritania	74	1,563	–1,250	2,813
110	Mauritius	81	8,312	2,620	5,692
111	Mexico	87	7,704	–455	8,159
112	Micronesia	84	3,000	–4,525	6,925
113	Moldova	95	1,947	–9,503	11,450
114	Mongolia	98	1,541	–11,142	12,683
115	Morocco	85	3,305	–4,032	7,337
116	Mozambique	72	782	–1,208	1,990
117	Namibia	72	5,176	3,186	1,990
118	Nepal	78	1,157	–3,301	4,458
119	Netherlands	102	22,176	7,847	14,329
120	New Zealand	100	17,288	3,782	13,506
121	Nicaragua	84	2,142	–4,783	6,925
122	Niger	67	739	805	–66
123	Nigeria	67	795	861	–66
124	Norway	98	26,342	13,659	12,683
125	Oman	83	9,960	3,446	6,514
126	Pakistan	81	1,715	–3,977	5,692
127	Panama	85	5,249	–2,088	7,337
128	Papua New Guinea	84	2,359	–4,566	6,927
129	Paraguay	85	4,288	–3,049	7,337
130	Peru	90	4,282	–5,111	9,393
131	Philippines	86	3,555	–4,193	7,748
132	Poland	99	7,619	–5,476	13,095

Table 8.9   continued

Country	IQ	Real GDP per capita 1998	Residual GDP	Fitted GDP
133 Portugal	95	14,701	3,251	11,450
134 Puerto Rico	84	8,000	1,075	6,925
135 Qatar	78	20,987	16,529	4,458
136 Romania	94	5,648	–5,390	11,038
137 Russia	96	6,460	–5,401	11,861
138 Rwanda	70	660	–507	1,167
139 Samoa (Western)	87	3,832	–4,327	8,159
140 Sao Tome and Principe	59	1,469	4,826	–3,357
141 Saudi Arabia	83	10,158	3,644	6,514
142 Senegal	65	1,307	2,196	–889
143 Seychelles	81	10,600	4,908	5,692
144 Sierra Leone	64	458	1,758	–1,300
145 Singapore	103	24,210	9,470	14,740
146 Slovakia	96	9,699	–2,162	11,861
147 Slovenia	95	14,293	2,843	11,450
148 Solomon Islands	94	1,940	–4,985	6,925
149 Somalia	68	1,000	655	345
150 South Africa	72	8,488	6,498	1,990
151 Spain	97	16,212	3,940	12,272
152 Sri Lanka	81	2,979	–2,713	5,692
153 St. Kitts and Nevis	75	10,672	7,448	3,224
154 St. Lucia	75	5,183	1,959	3,224
155 St. Vincent and the Grenadines	75	4,692	1,468	3,224
156 Sudan	72	1,394	–596	1,990
157 Suriname	89	5,161	–3,821	8,982
158 Swaziland	72	3,816	1,825	1,990

	Country	IQ	Real GDP per capita 1998	Residual GDP	Fitted GDP
159	Sweden	101	20,659	6,742	13,917
160	Switzerland	101	25,512	11,595	13,917
161	Syria	87	2,892	−5,267	8,159
162	Taiwan	104	13,000	−2,151	15,151
163	Tajikistan	87	1,041	−7,118	8,159
164	Tanzania	72	480	−1,510	1,990
165	Thailand	91	5,456	−4,348	9,804
166	Togo	69	1,372	616	756
167	Tonga	87	3,000	−5,159	8,159
168	Trinidad and Tobago	80	7,485	2,205	5,280
169	Tunisia	84	5,404	−1,521	6,925
170	Turkey	90	6,422	−2,971	9,393
171	Turkmenistan	87	2,550	−5,609	8,159
172	Uganda	73	1,074	−1,327	2,401
173	Ukraine	96	3,194	−8,667	11,861
174	United Arab Emirates	83	17,719	11,205	6,514
175	United Kingdom	100	20,336	6,830	13,506
176	United States	98	29,605	16,922	12,683
177	Uruguay	96	8,623	−3,238	11,861
178	Uzbekistan	87	2,053	−6,106	8,159
179	Vanuatu	84	3,120	−3,805	6,925
180	Venezuela	89	5,808	−3,174	8,982
181	Vietnam	96	1,689	−10,172	11,861
182	Yemen	83	719	−5,795	6,514
183	Yugoslavia	93	4,000	−6,627	10,627
184	Zambia	77	719	−3,327	4,046
185	Zimbabwe	66	2,669	3,147	−478

Figure 8.5

The Results of the Regression Analysis of Real GDP Per Capita 1998 on National IQ for 185 Countries in the Group of 185 Countries

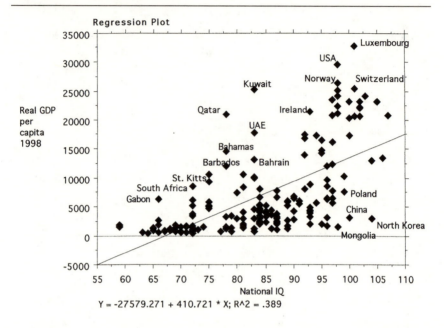

$Y = -27579.271 + 410.721 * X; R^2 = .389$

There are three measures of per capita income for 1998: GNP per capita, GNP per capita measured at PPP dollars, and real GDP per capita (PPP). GNP-PPP is more highly correlated with national IQs (.696) than the two other measures of per capita income, but because data on the GNP-PPP cover only 141 countries, we leave it out. Data for the other two variables are available for all 185 countries. Because GNP per capita and real GDP per capita are highly inter-correlated (.953), the results would be closely similar in both regression analyses. Therefore, it is sufficient to present the results of only one regression analysis. We have adopted real GDP per capita as the dependent variable in this regression analysis because its correlation with national IQs (.623) is higher than the correlation between national IQs and the GNP per capita (.567).

The regression analysis shown in Table 8.9 can be usefully compared with those obtained from the group of 81 countries (presented in Chapter 7, "National IQs and Economic Development in 81 Countries"). We can compare the two populations for the highly deviant and less deviant countries, analyze the relationship between national IQs and per capita income at the level of individual countries, consider what other factors may have affected the variation in per capita income in addition to national IQs, and consider the prospects of economic development in individual countries.

We start by comparing the results of this regression analysis to the corresponding results in the group of 81 countries presented and discussed in the previous chapter. The two regression equations differ from each other to some extent. Real GDP per capita is used as the dependent variable in both regression equations, but the intercept is lower and the regression line is steeper in the regression equation for 81 countries (Y = –35716 + 519*X) than in the regression equation for 185 countries (Y = –27579 + 411*X). Consequently, in the first regression the predicted values of real GDP per capita are lower for countries with low national IQs and are higher for countries with high national IQs than in this regression. The principal reason for this difference seems to be that countries with low national IQs (especially African countries) are under-represented in the group of 81 countries as well as countries in which the real GDP per capita is relatively low while the national IQ is high (especially the new states separated from the former Soviet Union). Because of this difference, the positive residuals are considerably higher for the countries with low national IQs in the group of 81 countries than in the 185 countries and are much lower for the countries with high national IQs. For example, the positive residual of Ethiopia is 3,594 in the group of 81 countries and 2,286 in the 185 countries, and the positive residual of the Netherlands is 4,955 in the group of 81 countries and 7,847 in the 185 countries. Correspondingly, negative residuals for countries with high national IQs are smaller in the 185 countries than in the group of 81 countries. For example, the negative residual of China is –13,078 in the group of 81 countries and –10,401 in the group of 185 countries. The residuals are approximately the same for the countries in the middle of the range of IQs. Despite these differences, the most deviant countries are approximately the same in both regression equations. The major exception is South Korea, which is not a significantly deviant country in this analysis (–.2,496), although it was a highly deviant case in the group of 81 countries (–. 5,820).

ANALYSIS OF INDIVIDUAL COUNTRIES

Because the number of countries in this regression analysis is much greater than in the previous regression analyses, we divide the significantly deviant countries into three subgroups according to the size of residuals. The criterion adopted for extremely deviant countries as a residual in 1998 was greater than ±8,000. Twenty-five countries fall into this category. The second category of significant deviations comprises the countries for which the residual in 1998 was between ±5,000 and 7,999. This category consists of 43 countries. The third category of minor deviations comprises the countries for which the residual in 1998 was between ±3,500 and 4,999. This category consists of 31 countries. For the other 86 countries the residuals were smaller than ±3,500. These countries deviate from the regression line only slightly, and the direction of deviations may be partly due to errors in measurements. Therefore, it is not reasonable to pay any special attention to the slight deviations of this group.

Extreme Deviations

Of the 25 extremely deviant countries, residuals are positive for 18 countries and are negative for 7 countries. The group of countries with high positive residuals consists of Australia, Austria, the Bahamas, Belgium, Canada, Denmark, Finland, France, Iceland, Ireland, Kuwait, Luxembourg, Norway, Qatar, Singapore, Switzerland, the United Arab Emirates, and the United States. With four exceptions, these countries are European and East Asian high technology market economies. The national IQ for these 14 countries is 93 or higher, and all of them are democracies. However, it is questionable whether these characteristics are enough to explain the much higher-than-expected level of per capita income. Some other European and East Asian countries with similar IQs are less developed and poor. There are many democracies that are less developed and belong to the category of poor countries. There are also market economy countries that are not rich. The fact that these countries are technologically highly developed seems to separate them from other countries more effectively. It may be that a combination of a relatively high national IQ, a market economy system, and a democracy has been needed to create the circumstances in which it has been possible to invent and effectively adopt the modern technologies necessary to produce high per capita income. Perhaps if any of these characteristics is missing, the chances of exceptionally high per capita income decrease sharply. A high national IQ seems to be a necessary, but not a sufficient, condition of an exceptionally high per capita income. The same may concern the nature of economic and political systems. A market economy is better suited to promote economic development than a command economy, and a democratic political system may provide a more suitable framework for economic development than an authoritarian system, in which individual property rights are not as well protected and contracts enforceable as in democracies as argued by Olson (2000). Certainly, the combination of a high national IQ, a market economy, and a democracy characterizes the group of these 14 countries with extremely high positive residuals. So our preliminary conclusion is that the combination of market economy systems and democracy has helped these 14 countries to produce a much higher per capita income than expected on the basis of national IQ.

The four other countries of this category (the Bahamas, Kuwait, Qatar, and the United Arab Emirates) differ from the pattern of the 14 high technology market economies. The national IQs of these countries are much lower (ranging from 78 to 83) than in the group of 14 countries. The

Bahamas is a democracy, but the three other countries are autocracies. The economic systems in all these countries are some kind of market economies. In other words, one or two of the three characteristics of high technology market economies are missing from these countries, but these missing characteristics have not prevented them from producing much higher-than-expected levels of per capita income. To explain these anomalies, we have to examine the structure of their economies. It seems to us that significant contributions from technologically highly developed countries have helped these countries to deviate from the regression line and to produce much higher-than-expected per capita incomes.

In the Bahamas, tourism is the basis of prosperity. It employed some 30 percent of the population in 1994. In 1996, the tourism sector directly contributed 55 percent of GDP and net travel receipts covered 92 percent of the cost of goods imported. Many of the hotel properties in the Bahamas belong to international chains, and their technology is imported from the United States and Europe. Banking is another important sector of the economy. Agriculture and manufacturing are poorly developed (*South America, Central America and the Caribbean 1999*, pp. 83–85). Because the tourism and off-shore finance industries are primarily owned and controlled by foreign corporations, it is reasonable to conclude that the much higher-than-expected level of per capita income is principally due to the contributions of people from countries with high national IQs.

Kuwait's prosperity is completely based on petroleum industries that have been established and operated by European and American oil corporations since the 1930s. Petroleum's share of the GDP is approximately 50 percent and crude petroleum and petroleum products account for over 90 percent of the value of export earnings each year. Although the government now controls petroleum production, foreign companies, persons, and technologies have a crucial role in the operation of oil industries (*The Middle East and North Africa 1998*, pp. 684–692). It is reasonable to assume that Kuwait's higher-than-expected level of real GDP per capita is principally due to the contribution of foreign companies and technologies.

Qatar is a similar Middle Eastern country whose prosperity since the 1930s has been based on petroleum and natural gas production carried out by foreign companies (*The Middle East and North Africa 1998*, pp. 869–875). As in the case of Kuwait, Qatar's much higher-than-expected level of real GDP per capita is due to the contribution of technologies and expertise of people from countries whose national IQs are significantly higher than the national IQ of Qatar. The prosperity of the United Arab Emirates is also completely based on the petroleum and gas industries managed by European and American companies (*The Middle East and North Africa 1998*, pp. 1067–1079). It seems justified to conclude that for all of these countries with large positive residuals, the much higher-than-expected level of GDP per capita is principally due to the contribution of foreign people and technologies.

These 18 countries with large positive residuals indicate that, in addition to national IQ, several other factors affect the prosperity of countries. We believe that a combination of high national IQ, a competitive market economy system, and a democracy made it possible for European and European offshoot nations (and later also for East Asian nations) to invent and adopt more advanced technologies than countries in other parts of the world. In addition, these same skills and technologies helped the Caribbean tourist countries and the Middle East oil countries to achieve much higher-than-expected levels of per capita income.

It is interesting to compare the seven countries with extremely large negative residuals (Armenia, China, North Korea, Moldova, Mongolia, Ukraine, and Vietnam) to the countries with extremely large positive residuals. Although the national IQs of the countries with large negative residuals are approximately at the same level as the IQs of the group of 14 high technology market economies discussed above, there is a striking difference in economic systems. It seems that when some components of the combination of a high national IQ, a market economy system, and a democracy are missing, the country is not able to achieve an unexpectedly high level of per capita income, or even the expected level. All of these seven countries with large negative residuals are contemporary or former socialist countries. At the present time, Armenia, Moldova, Mongolia, and Ukraine are democracies or are moving toward democracy, but until quite recently all of them were autocracies. It is evident that these differences in economic and political systems have affected economic development. In the 1990s, all of them introduced economic reforms intended to replace the structures of the socialist command economy with those of market economy, but it takes time to implement these reforms and to stabilize the institutions of the market economy and democracy. For these reasons, their economic performance is still far below the level expected on the basis of their high national IQs. The highest negative residuals are for China, North Korea, Mongolia, and Vietnam, which until the 1990s have been and, with the partial exception of Mongolia, are still to varying degrees largely socialist countries and autocracies.

China has transformed its economic system since 1978 and has partially replaced the structures of a command economy by market mechanisms, but China's reforms have not yet substantially affected the key economic sector of the large and medium-sized state industrial enterprises. Its transition to a market economy is still only partial. China's authoritarian political system is dominated by the Communist Party (Chai, 1998; *The Far East and Australasia 1999*, pp. 241–250). North Korea has still one of the world's most highly centralized and planned economies, and it has the highest negative residual in the world. Its political system remains strictly authoritarian. Thus, it represents the complete opposite of the high technology market democracies (*The Far East and Australasia 1999*, pp. 538–544). Vietnam started a cautious transition from central planning to market reforms in 1979, but the structural reforms have remained more limited than the reforms in China. The political system is strictly authoritarian (*The Far East and Australasia 1999*, pp. 1180–1188). The national IQs of these three East Asian socialist countries are high, but because their economic systems are partially or wholly socialistic and their political systems are not democratic, it is highly questionable whether they will be able to follow the example of South Korea and Taiwan and achieve the expected level of per capita income.

Mongolia is a more complicated case because of its geographical isolation. It rejected the communist political system in the early 1990s and established democratic institutions. At the same time, the government initiated a series of far-reaching economic reforms aimed at achieving a market economy and the privatization of its state-controlled industries and corporations. The transition to a democracy has succeeded better than the transition to a market economy (*The Far East and Australasia 1999*, pp. 695–698). Because of its far-reaching political and economic reforms, Mongolia should have better chances of future economic growth than China, North Korea, and Vietnam; however, its geographical isolation may constitute a serious obstacle and affect its economic development.

Armenia, Moldova, and Ukraine are successor states of the former Soviet Union. Their democratic institutions established at the dawn of independence have functioned more or less successfully, but the transition from a centralized, command economy to a market-oriented system has been difficult and is still incomplete. It takes time to privatize state enterprises and to adopt and learn market mechanisms (see Dudwick, 1997; Crowther, 1997; Motyl and Krawchenko, 1997; *Eastern Europe and the Commonwealth of Independent States 1999*, 1999). However, despite serious problems of transition, we predict that economic growth will accelerate in these countries and their per capita incomes will rise toward the expected level on the regression line.

Significantly Deviant Countries

Of the 43 significantly deviant countries with residuals between ±5,000 and 7,999, the residuals are positive for 16 countries and negative for 27 countries. The countries with significant positive residuals are Antigua and Barbuda, Bahrain, Barbados, Brunei, Cyprus, Equatorial Guinea, Gabon, Germany, Israel, Italy, Japan, Malta, the Netherlands, South Africa, St. Kitts and Nevis, Sweden, and the United Kingdom. These countries are of the same general kind as those in the first category of the most extreme positive outliers discussed in the preceding section. Seven of these countries (Germany, Israel, Italy, Japan, the Netherlands, Sweden, and the United Kingdom) are high technology market economies. Their positive residuals are only slightly smaller than those found in the first category of outliers. Again we consider that the combination of a market economy and democracy enabled these countries to achieve a higher level of real GDP per capita than expected on the basis of their national IQs.

Seven of the other nine countries (Antigua and Barbuda, Bahrain, Barbados, Brunei, Cyprus, Gabon, Malta, and St. Kitts and Nevis) derive their national wealth principally from tourism or oil exports. Antigua and Barbuda is a small Caribbean island state inhabited almost entirely by black Africans. Tourism dominates its economy and accounts, directly and indirectly, for some 70 percent of the GDP and for about 35 percent of employment (*South America, Central America and the Caribbean 1999*, pp. 47–48). Their tourism industry was established by Europeans and is still mostly owned by European and American companies.

Barbados is also heavily dependent on tourism. The tourist industry employs 15 percent of the working population and produces about 50 percent of the foreign-exchange earnings (*South America, Central America and the Caribbean 1999*, pp. 95–97). St. Kitts and Nevis is another Caribbean country with a significant positive residual. Tourism is an important sector in the economy, although it is not as dominant as in the Bahamas. The islands' principal economic activity is the sugar industry, which accounted for 51.6 percent of the total export earnings in 1996 (*South America, Central America and the Caribbean 1999*, pp. 610–611). Sugar companies were established by foreigners and are still partly owned and controlled by foreigners.

The contribution of the foreign-controlled tourist and other industries explains a major part of the higher-than-expected level of per capita income in these three Caribbean states. They are democracies and their economic systems are market economies, but because national IQs are low, they could not be expected to achieve and maintain their present level of real GDP per capita without the significant contribution of foreign-owned and controlled tourist and other industries. From this perspective, it is interesting to compare these three countries and the Bahamas with the other Caribbean countries where the real GDP per capita is more consistent with the level of national IQs. The role of tourism is less prominent in countries like Dominica, Grenada, Jamaica, St. Lucia, and St. Vincent and the Grenadines, although the residuals are slightly positive for all of them (cf., *South America, Central America and the Caribbean 1999*, 1999).

Cyprus is a Mediterranean island state, which is also heavily dependent on tourism, but it is not as dependent on foreign technologies, investments, and managers as the Carribbean tourist states. Its own people are able to manage the tourist and other industries. Cyprus is a democracy, and it is closely comparable to high technology market economies.

Bahrain, Brunei, and Gabon are principally petroleum-producing countries. Bahrain is an oil country like Kuwait and Qatar, and its production of petroleum and natural gas is dependent on foreign technologies and people (*The Middle East and North Africa 1998*, pp. 332–336). Brunei's economy is based largely on wealth from natural gas and petroleum run by international companies (*The Far East and Australasia 1999*, pp. 178–186). Gabon also derives much of its wealth from petroleum. *Africa South of the Sahara 2000* (p. 485) notes that the "plentiful petroleum resources have given Gabon one of the highest incomes per head in sub-Saharan Africa." As in Bahrain and Brunei, the petroleum production is run by international oil companies. The same is true of other mining industries.

South Africa's much higher-than-expected real GDP per capita is principally due to the industries established and managed by the country's large white minority (*Africa South of the Sahara 2000*, pp. 1006–1013). Equatorial Guinea is not a really deviant country because its high positive residual (5,174) is principally due to the fact that the predicted value of real GDP is negative (–.3,357) because of the country's extremely low national IQ (59).

The 27 countries with significant negative residuals constitute a more heterogeneous group. Most of these countries are former socialist countries in Europe and Asia (Albania, Azerbaijan, Belarus, Bulgaria, Cambodia, Georgia, Kazakhstan, Kyrgyzstan, Laos, Latvia, Lithuania, Macedonia, Poland, Romania, Russia, Tajikistan, Turkmenistan and Uzbekistan). The national IQs of these 18 countries range from 87 to 99. Their national IQs do not differ greatly from those of the nine high technology market economy countries with significant positive residuals. The major difference between these two groups of countries lies in their economic systems. All of these 18 countries with significant negative residuals are former socialist countries, which started their transition from command economies to market economies only in the early 1990s. The transition process is still unfinished in most of them. Political systems have already become democratized in Albania, Bulgaria, Georgia, Latvia, Lithuania, Macedonia, Poland, Romania and Russia. The other nine countries are still in the process of transition or, in the case of Laos, have retained an authoritarian system. We predict that real GDP per capita will probably increase and negative residuals will decrease in the countries that have the most successfully established market economies and democratic institutions, whereas the prospects for economic development are not as good for countries that fail to carry out these reforms. However, unfavorable geographical conditions may hinder economic development in some cases independently from national IQ, the economic system, and the nature of the political system.

Of the other nine countries with significant negative residuals, Tonga is a small island state in the Pacific. Its geographical isolation may constitute a factor that restricts economic development because of high transportation costs. This explanation is supported by the fact that residuals are also negative for the other small Pacific island states (Fiji, Kiribati, the Marshall Islands, Micronesia, Papua New Guinea, Samoa, the Solomon Islands, and Vanuatu). Because geography is a permanent factor, it is probable that these countries will remain below the regression line at least for the short-term future. However, new developments in communications, transportation, and the tourist industries may improve their economic growth rates in the longer-term future.

The remaining eight countries constitute a heterogeneous group. However, it is possible to discern some common factors. Serious ethnic conflicts or wars may have obstructed economic development in Afghanistan, Bolivia, Burma, Indonesia, Iraq, and Peru (see Vanhanen, 1999a, 1999b). Geographical isolation may be a relevant factor at least in the cases of Afghanistan and Yemen. It is interesting to note that the residuals are negative for Jordan and Lebanon in addition to Syria and Yemen, which are the only Middle East countries without significant petroleum resources. The contrast between these four countries and the other Middle East countries shows the significance of petroleum and gas resources and Western technologies that are needed in oil industries. It is probable that in the future the level of per capita income will remain lower than expected in these countries for as long as unfavorable economic structures and undemocratic institutions obstruct their economic development.

COUNTRIES WITH MINOR DEVIATIONS

Of the 31 countries with relatively small residuals (±3,500 to 4,999), the residuals are positive for eight countries and are negative for 22 countries. These minor outliers imply the existence of some extra factors that have had relatively small effects on per capita income independently of the level of national IQ. What might those factors be? Are they similar to those of the highly and moderately deviant countries?

The group of minor positive outliers consists of Botswana, Greece, Hong Kong, Malta, New Zealand, Sao Tome and Principe, Saudi Arabia, Seychelles, and Spain. In most cases, the responsible factors seem to be the same as in the two previous categories of positive outliers. Greece, Hong Kong, Malta, New Zealand, and Spain are related to the group of high technology market economies, although Greece, Malta, and Spain are also important tourist countries and New Zealand is an efficient agricultural economy. In four of these countries, a combination of high national IQs, a market economy, and democracy has promoted economic development and produced a higher-than-expected level of real GDP per capita. Because these factors seem to be securely established in these four countries, we must predict that they will remain as positive outliers. Hong Kong seems to be the only high technology market economy that has achieved a high level of per capita income without democracy. However, it should be noted that it is not an independent country. Until 1998, the British colonial administration maintained the law and order needed for economic development while the area was under the British control as a Crown Colony.

Seychelles belongs to the group of tropical countries whose national incomes are significantly derived from tourism, which is largely managed by international companies and corporations run by Europeans and North Americans. Saudi Arabia is another country of the Middle East oil producing countries whose petroleum and natural gas industries are run by international oil companies. Saudi Arabia is by far the largest producer of petroleum within the Organization of Petroleum Exporting Countries (OPEC). The sales of petroleum and petroleum products account for more than 80 percent of the total export revenue (*The Middle East and North Africa 1998*, pp. 891–895). We predict that the residuals will remain positive for these countries, because the additional factors that have enabled them to increase their per capita incomes are relatively stable.

In Botswana, the per capita income is much higher than in other parts of sub-Saharan Africa. During the time when it gained independence in 1966, Botswana was one of the poorest countries in the world, with a predominantly subsistence economy. During the 1980s, however, Botswana's economic performance exceeded that of all the other non-petroleum producing countries in Africa. The principal factor behind its high economic growth is the discovery and development of valuable mineral resources, especially diamonds. Large-scale mineral exploitation began in 1971. The diamond mines are owned and operated by the Debswana Diamond Co., a joint venture owned equally by the Botswana government and De Beers Consolidated Mines of South Africa. By 1997, diamonds accounted for approximately 70 percent of Botswana's exports and for some 30 percent of the GDP (*Africa South of the Sahara 2000*, pp. 207–211). The contribution of European people and technologies has been crucial. Because the prospects of the mining industries remain good and because Botswana's government has used new resources to improve education and infrastructures of the country, we predict that Botswana will remain a positive outlier.

Sao Tome and Principe has also a positive residual that is higher than 3,500, but it cannot be regarded as a really deviant case because the predicted value of real GDP per capita is negative for it, as is the case for all countries with national IQs lower than 68. This anomaly is a consequence of the regression equation and the linear regression line.

From the group of 22 countries with minor negative residuals, we can identify some that have similar characteristics to the countries with larger negative residuals, which we considered in the two previous sections. Estonia's economic system was socialist during the period of Soviet occupation from 1940 to 1991. The country's transition to a market economy has progressed fairly successfully. It is quite possible that Estonia will reach the expected level of per capita income within a few years. Kiribati, the Marshall Islands, Micronesia, Papua New Guinea, Samoa (Western), and Vanuatu are Pacific island states. It was suggested in the previous section that the geographical isolation and geographical conditions of these countries may constitute unfavorable environmental factors that hinder economic development (cf., *The Far East and Australasia 1999*, pp. 816–946). Therefore, we predict that real GDP per capita in these countries will probably remain lower than expected in relation to their national IQs, but new developments in communications, transportation and tourism may change the situation. The Philippines is geographically close to the small Pacific island states and Indonesia. Despite a market economy and democracy, it has not been able to achieve a similar rate of economic growth like Taiwan or Malaysia (*The Far East and Australasia 1999*, pp. 1023–1029). However, its negative residual is only slightly higher than that for Taiwan and Malaysia and is considerably smaller than the negative residual for Indonesia.

Costa Rica, Guyana, Honduras, Nicaragua, and Suriname are Central American and Caribbean countries with negative residuals. It is interesting to note that residuals are negative for all Latin American countries, except for Argentina and Puerto Rico. This observation raises the question about possible regional factors that hamper economic development. We have to leave this question open. Unfavorable factors may be related to some cultural characteristics or to the racial heterogeneity of their populations, but we also want to draw attention to the fact that residuals are negative for most countries in the tropics. This implies that it has been difficult to adapt modern technologies to tropical conditions. It seems reasonable to assume that the five countries will remain below the regression line at least in the near future.

Jordan and Morocco, together with Lebanon, Syria, and Yemen, belong to the group of Middle Eastern countries without significant petroleum resources. None of these countries have been able to achieve the level of per capita income expected on the basis of their national IQs. It seems reasonable to expect that the residuals will remain negative for these countries. Iraq is a petroleum country, but its per capita income is lower than expected because the trade embargo imposed by the United Nations in 1990 reduced petroleum export.

Bangladesh, India and Pakistan are members of the South Asian region of poor countries in which the level of per capita income is lower than expected on the basis of national IQs. For Bhutan, Nepal and Sri Lanka the residuals are also negative, although they are slightly smaller. In the case of India, it is reasonable to argue that the semi-socialist economic system established by Jawaharlal Nehru in the 1950s has seriously hampered the economic development of the country. Indian governments have attempted to dismantle these socialist regulations, controls, and structures since the 1980s, but the transition process is still unfinished. The other South Asian countries have also implemented socialist economic policies that have impaired their economic growth

(Hossain, Islam, and Kibria, 1999; Vanhanen, 2000). It can be predicted that the dismantling of socialist controls and the adoption of market economies would create favorable conditions for faster economic growth in South Asia.

Thailand is a Southeast Asian country that has not yet achieved the expected level of per capita income, but it is adopting new technologies and industries and may improve its relative position in the future. Thailand is following the example of Malaysia. Both countries have an economically successful Chinese minority. Tourism plays a more important role in Thailand than in Malaysia (*The Far East and Australasia 1999*, pp. 1137–1146).

The two island states, Comoros and Madagascar, do not differ greatly from the other sub-Saharan states economically, but because their national IQs are somewhat higher than in the other sub-Saharan African countries, their residuals have become negative. We predict that they will remain as slightly deviant cases.

NON-DEVIANT COUNTRIES

Residuals are smaller than ±3,500 for the remaining 86 countries. They are countries in which the actual level of real GDP per capita does not differ significantly from the level expected on the basis of national IQs. It is interesting to examine how these countries are geographically distributed and whether they are dispersed randomly around the world, or are more frequently in some locations. In fact, there are large regional differences in the distribution of these countries. Most of them are in Africa and Latin America.

Residuals are smaller than ±3,500 for 45 out of the 53 African countries (at 85 percent), for 22 out of the 34 Latin American and the Caribbean countries (at 65 percent), for 12 out of the 53 Asian and the Pacific countries (at 23 percent), and for 7 out of the 45 European, North American, and European offshoot countries (at 16 percent). These large regional differences imply that it is possible to predict the actual level of real GDP per capita much more accurately for African and Latin American countries than for Asian and European countries. This result can be interpreted to mean that relatively low national IQs, independently from other variables, are enough to explain the major part of the low level of real GDP per capita in nearly all African countries and in most Latin American and the Caribbean countries, whereas in European, North American, European offshoots, Asian, and Pacific countries other factors affecting economic development are much more important.

Figure 8.5 summarizes graphically the results of the regression analysis. The pattern is similar to that in the previous regression plots except for one difference. In the earlier years, very few countries with national IQs below 90 were highly deviant cases, but in 1998 several such countries had large positive or negative residuals. The categories of extreme and significant positive deviations (residuals of 5,000 or higher) include Antigua and Barbuda, the

Bahamas, Bahrain, Barbados, Gabon, Kuwait, Qatar, St. Kitts and Nevis, South Africa, and the United Arab Emirates. The category of minor deviations includes Botswana, Equatorial Guinea, Sao Tome and Principe, Saudi Arabia, and Seychelles. In nearly all these countries international tourism, petroleum production or, in the case of Botswana, diamonds, have raised per capita income substantially above the regression line. Only South Africa deviates from this pattern. Equatorial Guinea and Sao Tome and Principe cannot be regarded as really deviant cases because their large positive residuals are technical effects of the linear regression line.

The countries with national IQs below 90 for which the negative residuals are higher than 3,500 represent opposite cases. These countries are not named in Figure 8.5, but the crowded group includes the following 34 countries: Afghanistan, Azerbaijan, Bangladesh, Bolivia, Burma, Cambodia, Comoros, Egypt, Guyana, Honduras, India, Indonesia, Iraq, Jordan, Kiribati, Kyrgyzstan, Laos, Madagascar, the Marshall Islands, Micronesia, Morocco, Nicaragua, Pakistan, Papua New Guinea, the Philippines, Samoa, Suriname, Syria, Tajikistan, Tonga, Turkmenistan, Uzbekistan, Vanuatu, and Yemen. Nearly all of them lack significant petroleum resources or extensive industrial investments from the countries of high technology, or are without international tourist industries. This group includes Middle Eastern countries without petroleum exports, geographically isolated and remote countries (such as Central Asian countries and the Pacific islands), and many countries of the Tropics in which climatic or other environmental conditions are unfavorable for modern agricultural and other technologies.

Figure 8.5 also illustrates the sharp contrast between high technology market economies with large positive residuals and contemporary and former socialist countries that have large negative residuals. There is only a moderate correlation between national IQ and real GDP per capita in the group of countries with national IQs 90 or higher (r = .505, N = 65). Within this group of countries, differences in the economic and in political systems seem to explain a major part of the differences in per capita incomes.

THE IMPACT OF ECONOMIC FREEDOM AND DEMOCRACY

In considering why a number of countries have positive or negative residuals above or below the regression lines of economic development on IQ, we have frequently invoked the effects of economic and political systems and argued that a market economy and a democracy provide more favorable conditions for economic development than socialist and command economies and authoritarian political systems. We now test these explanations more systematically. *The Economic Freedom of the World: 2000 Annual Report* (2000) provides data for national differences in "economic freedom," which are essentially differences in the extent to which countries have market economies.

Ratings are given for 122 countries for 1997. Measures of the degree of democracy in 183 countries in 1998 are provided by Vanhanen's Index of Democratization (ID), which was published in the *Polyarchy Dataset* (2000; see also Vanhanen, 1997).

Our assumptions on the effects of economic systems and democracy can be tested by correlating the measures of economic freedom (EF) and democracy (ID) with measures of per capita income and then by calculating multiple correlations in which combinations of national IQ, EF, and ID are used to explain variation in measures of per capita income. These correlational analyses are carried out for the group of 122 countries for which we have both economic freedom ratings in 1997 and democracy data for 1998. The results of simple and multiple correlation analyses are presented in Table 8.10.

Table 8.10

Four Measures of Per Capita Income Correlated with National IQs, the Economic Freedom (EF) Ratings, the Index of Democratization (ID), and Their Combinations in a Group of 122 Countries

Explanatory variable	GDP per capita (Maddison) 1990	GNP per capita 1998	GNP-PPP per capita 1998	Real GDP per capita 1998
N	114	122	102	122
National IQ	.742	.634	.749	.711
Economic Freedom (EF) 1997	.691	.644	.732	.709
Index of Democratization (ID) 1998	.622	.527	.630	.600
EF-1997 and ID-1998	.752	.684	.776	.763
IQ and EF-1997	.787	.708	.799	.787
IQ and ID-1998	.753	.639	.758	.720
IQ, EF-1997, and ID-1998	.792	.708	.803	.790

The first row of correlations in Table 8.10 shows that national IQs and measures of per capita income have somewhat higher correlations in this subgroup of 122 countries than in the total world group of 185 countries (cf., Table 8.1). National IQs and economic freedom (EF) ratings are approximately as strongly correlated with the measures of per capita income, whereas the correlations with the Index of Democratization (ID) are a little weaker. An interesting question is how much EF and ID taken together could explain the variation in the measures of per capita incomes. The results of multiple correlation analysis in which EF-1997 and ID-1998 taken together are used to explain the variation in the measures of per capita income indicate that multiple correlations are higher than the simple correlations between the measures of per capita income and EF and ID. The difference in the explained part of variation varies from six to nine percentage points compared to simple correlations with EF and from 18 to 22 percentage points compared to simple correlations with ID. The results show that EF and ID taken together can explain a little more of the variation in per capita income than national IQ. The results of the correlation analysis support the assumption that a market economy and democracy provide a more favorable environment for economic growth and development than command economies and authoritarian political systems. The problem is how much these factors could explain of the variation in measures of per capita income independently from the level of national IQ. The correlation between national IQ and EF is .629 and between national IQ and ID is .691 in this group of 122 countries. The correlation between EF and ID is weaker (.478). Because national IQ, EF and ID are strongly inter-correlated, it is clear that independent contributions of EF and ID must be much smaller than the simple correlations indicate. The multiple correlations given in the last three rows of Table 8.10 indicate how much EF and ID are able to explain of the variation in the measures of per capita income independently from national IQs.

In the first multiple correlation model national IQs and economic freedom ratings (1997) are used together to explain the variation in the four measures of per capita income. By comparing these multiple correlations to the simple correlations between national IQs and the measures of per capita income we can see how much EF increases the explained part of variation independently of the level of national IQ. In the case of GDP per capita (Maddison) 1990, the explained part of variation rises from 55 to 62 percent; in the case of GNP per capita 1998 it rises from 40 to 50 percent; in the case of GNP per capita (PPP) 1998 it rises from 56 to 64 percent; and in the case of real GDP per capita 1998 it rises from 51 to 62 percent. These are significant increases in the explained part of variation. The independent contribution of EF is approximately ten percentage points. Thus, the nature of the economic system matters, although its significance is not the same in all parts of the world. Figure 8.5 indicates that the significance of the economic system is greatest in the category of countries with national IQs above 90.

In the second multiple correlation model national IQ and the Index of Democratization (1998) are used together as the independent variables. The multiple correlations indicate the independent contribution of ID. In the case of GDP per capita (Maddison) 1990, the explained part of variation increased from 55 to 57 percent; in the case of GNP per capita 1998 it increased less than one percentage point; in the case of GNP per capita (PPP) 1998 it increased from 56 to 57 percent; and in the case of real GDP per capita it increased from 51 to 52 percent. The results of the multiple correlation analysis indicate that the independent contribution of ID is not more than one or two percentage points. In other words, the explanation provided by ID is almost completely overlapping with the explanation provided by national IQs. However, the nature of the political system is not irrelevant. Because the level of democratization is relatively highly correlated both with the measures of per capita income and national IQs, we can conclude that a high level of democratization is more favorable for economic development than a low level.

Finally, in the multiple correlations given in the last row of Table 8.10, national IQ, EF, and ID are taken together to explain the variation in the four measures of per capita income. These multiple correlations are only slightly higher than the multiple correlations in which national IQ and EF are used as explanatory variables. By comparing these multiple correlations to the simple correlations between national IQ and the measures of per capita income, we can see how much EF and ID taken together increase the explained part of variation. In the case of GDP per capita (Maddison) 1990, the explained part of variation rises from 55 to 63 percent; in the case of GNP per capita 1998 it rises from 40 to 50 percent; in the case of GNP per capita (PPP) 1998 it rises from 56 to 65 percent; and in the case of real GDP per capita 1998 it rises from 51 to 63 percent. The combined contribution of EF and ID is 8 to 12 percentage points, but only one percentage point more than the combination of national IQ and EF already explains. Thus, economic freedom (EF) ratings explain clearly more of the variation in the measures of per capita income independently of the level of national IQ than the Index of Democratization.

SUMMARY

In this chapter, we have tested our hypothesis in the total world group of 185 countries. The results are broadly similar to those found in the previous chapter, in which the hypothesis was tested in 81 countries for which we have direct evidence on their national IQs based on intelligence tests. The relationships between national IQs and the measures of per capita income are somewhat weaker in this total world group. Nevertheless, the results of the correlation analysis provide strong support for the hypothesis in the total world group. Per capita income has been positively correlated with national IQs since 1820, and this relationship seems to have become a little stronger during the last several decades. The correlation between national IQs and per capita income increases from .625 (the average of the Pearson and Spearman correlations) in 1820, to .629 (the average of six Pearson correlations), and to .675 (the average of six Spearman correlation) in 1997 to 1998. The explained part of variation is 39 percent in the Pearson correlations and 46 percent in the Spearman correlations in 1997 to 1998.

Regression analysis was again used to disclose the countries where the levels of per capita income are approximately consistent with the level of national IQs and the countries that deviate greatly from the expected relationship. Regression analysis was carried out separately for per capita data in 1900, 1930, 1960, and 1998. The results indicate that the relationship between national IQs and per capita income has remained surprisingly stable over the period of comparison. The position of most of the countries has remained approximately the same since 1900 and for a number of countries, even since 1820. However, the relative position of some countries has changed significantly. The examination of most deviant countries helped to identify some other relevant factors. Geographical and climatic conditions seem to matter to some extent. All geographical and climatic conditions are not equally favorable for economic development. It also was found that differences in economic systems and most likely in political systems affect economic development especially in the category of countries with national IQs above 90. In this group of countries, the difference in per capita income is greatest between market economies and present and former socialist countries. The evidence indicates that socialist command economies have been much less favorable for economic development than market economies.

We also measured the significance of economic and political systems using data on economic freedom ratings (1997) and an index of democratization (1998). The results of multiple correlation analyses show that these two additional variables explain 10–12 percentage points of the variation in the measures of per capita income independently from national IQs. Thus, when the three explanatory variables are taken together, the explained part of variation in the measures of per capita income increases to 52–65 percent and less than half of the variation remains unexplained. Our conclusion is that differences in national intelligence provide the most powerful and fundamental explanation for the gap between rich and poor countries.

9

Intelligence and Markets as the Determinants of Economic Development

In the last chapter it was shown that national IQs have been correlated at around .50 to .70 with economic growth and per capita income over the period 1820 to 1998. It was also shown that the degree to which nations have market economies is associated with economic growth and development at about the same magnitude. In this chapter, we consider the explanations for these associations. We begin with a further discussion of the role of national intelligence in rates of economic growth and development. We turn next to a consideration of climate theories, of economic development, and of modernization and convergence theories, and we argue that anomalies in these theories can be understood once the intelligence of populations is taken into account. The chapter concludes with discussions of the contributions of national intelligence and markets in the economic development of India, China, Japan, and the nations of sub-Saharan Africa.

INTELLIGENCE AND EARNING CAPACITY

The first explanation for the association between national intelligence and economic development lies in an extension of the principle that there is a positive association between intelligence and earnings among individuals within countries. The evidence for this has been reviewed in Chapter 3, "Intelligence and Earnings." The reason for this association is that individuals with high IQs can produce goods and services for which there is a demand and which those with low IQs are unable to provide. The result of this is that individuals with high IQs can command higher incomes. In Chapter 5, "The Sociology of Intelligence, Earnings, and Social Competence," we showed that this principle holds for regions within nations, and that in the United States, the British Isles, France, and Spain there is an association between the average intelligence levels in regions and average incomes. The positive association between national IQs and per capita incomes is a further expression of this principle. Nations are aggregates of individuals, so nations whose populations have high IQs are able to produce goods and services for which there is a demand more efficiently, and that in a number of instances cannot be produced by the populations of nations with low IQs. Goods and services for which there is a strong demand command a high value and those who are able to produce them or who can produce them most efficiently secure the highest incomes.

Considered in more detail, the economic advantages gained by nations whose populations have high IQs are secured in six principal ways. First, because intelligence is a major determinant of educational attainment (as shown for individuals in Chapter 4, "Intelligence and Further Economic and Social Phenomena"), the children of populations with high IQs perform well in schools and achieve high educational standards. Evidence for this is provided in Chapter 6, "Data on Variables and Methods of Analysis," where it is shown that there are correlations of around .5 to .8 between national IQs and educational attainment. The high educational attainments of the populations with high IQs provide the skilled labor force and human capital that are required for strong economic growth and developed economies.

Second, nations whose populations possess high IQs have a large scientific elite who are able to produce economically valuable new products. In the nineteenth century, Britain became the richest country in the world in terms of per capita income largely because the country developed new engineering products like the steam engine, railways, and steam-driven ships which the country was able to sell worldwide. In the twentieth century, the economically developed nations have achieved high rates of economic growth and increased their per capita incomes to a considerable extent through their scientific, engineering, and technological advances in the development of such products as automobiles (United States, Europe, and Japan), television, radio, and video recorders (Japan), industrial robots (Japan), airplanes (United States—Boeing; and Europe—Airbus), computers (United States—Microsoft), mobile telephones (Finland— Nokia; Britain—Vodophone) and pharmaceuticals (Britain—Glaxo-Welcome and Astra-Zeneca; and the United States—Merck and Pfizer).

Third, nations whose populations have high IQs can provide other non-scientific but complex and cognitively demanding goods and services that command high prices in international markets. These goods and services include such things as the financial services of banking, stock exchange dealing, and insurance provided by the leading financial centers of London, New York, Frankfurt, Tokyo, and Hong Kong; the fashion industry led by Paris and Milan; the film industry led by Hollywood; the perfume industry led by Paris; and the high quality wine industry led by France.

Fourth, we have reviewed in Chapter 4 the extensive research evidence showing that intelligence is positively associated with efficient work performance. Hence, nations whose populations have high IQs have large numbers of individuals of moderate to high intelligence who are able to carry out efficiently the management functions and perform the skilled work on which a successful economy depends.

Fifth, nations whose populations have high IQs have relatively few individuals with low levels of intelligence who are only able to do unskilled work, for which there is little demand. We should expect many of these individuals to be unemployed and an economic burden. As we note in Chapter 4, there is an association between low intelligence and unemployment among individuals, and as we note in Chapter 5, "The Sociology of Intelligence, Earnings, and Social Competence," this relationship also holds among regions in the United States, the British Isles, and France. We should expect the same relationship among nations. To ascertain whether this is the case, we have examined national rates of unemployment in relation to national IQs. Data on unemployment rates are taken from the United Nations' *Statistical Yearbook 1996* and from the International Labour Office's *Yearbook of Labour Statistics 1999* (pp. 441–470). These data are for the years of 1992 to 1998. The correlations between national rates of unemployment given in these two sources and national IQs are −.221 (N = 86) and −.274 (N = 92) respectively in the group of 185 countries and −.285 (N = 53) and −.397 (N = 54) in the group of 81 countries. The relationship is significantly negative as expected, although weak. It should be noted, however, that data on unemployment are missing from most poor countries and that the comparability of existing data is poor (see the *Yearbook of Labour Statistics 1999*, pp. 441–443).

Sixth, nations whose populations have low IQs have large agricultural and mining industries that do not require a high level of intelligence and for which there is in general a world surplus and weak demand. These products command only low prices in international markets, and therefore generate low incomes for the producers. The principal exceptions to this are the high price of oil and of a few relatively rare and valuable raw materials, such as diamonds and gold in the case of Botswana and manganese in the case of Gabon. Possession of these natural resources raises the per capita income of the nations concerned above what would be predicted from their national IQs, as we show in Chapter 8, "National IQs and Economic Development in 185 Countries."

INTELLIGENCE OF POLITICAL LEADERS

A second major reason why nations whose populations have high IQs achieve high rates of economic growth is that these countries normally have intelligent political leaders who manage their economies effectively.

Intelligent economic management is required to produce the right conditions for economic growth. The most important of these are the introduction and maintenance of a market economy, the promotion of competition and free trade, the prevention of the growth of monopolies, and the curtailment of restrictive practices by trade unions. It is also important for political leaders to ensure that interest rates are kept at the optimum level in order to attain full employment with minimum inflation and to promote education and vocational training in order to produce a skilled workforce.

The theory of the competitive market economy as the most efficient form of economic organization for the production of economic growth was formulated in the last quarter of the eighteenth century by Adam Smith (1776). It was well understood and implemented throughout the western world in the nineteenth century and by the more intelligent political leaders of the twentieth century. This understanding and the implementation and maintenance of competitive market economies was the foundation of the economic progress secured in the western nations in the nineteenth and twentieth centuries, and in the second half of the twentieth century by the market economies of Japan, South Korea, Taiwan, and Singapore in East Asia.

In the twentieth century, there have been numerous instances where political leaders have wrecked their countries' economies because they have been insufficiently intelligent to understand the basic principles of market economics. The most spectacular examples have been the introduction of socialism and communism by Lenin in the former Soviet Union and its maintenance by Stalin and subsequent political leaders, and by Mao in China, by Castro in Cuba, by Tito in the former Yugoslavia, and by the communist leadership in North Korea and Vietnam. In the case of Russia, Adam Smith's writings on the theory of the market economy were reasonably well known in the middle decades of the nineteenth century. The Russian writer, Nikolai Gogol, records in his autobiography that Adam Smith's work was known, read, and discussed in Russia and that he had read and discussed it with others, although he says that he was unable to understand it. Apparently the same was true of Lenin and the rest of the communist leadership. It was because of this intellectual shortcoming that Lenin and his successors prohibited private property and enterprise, replaced them with state monopolies, and collectivized agriculture. The resulting economy was hugely inefficient and led ultimately to the collapse and disintegration of the Soviet Union.

The same intellectual failure was present among a number of the political leaders of western Europe in the decades after the end of World War II. There was a particularly striking contrast between the intellectual caliber of the political leaders in Britain and in Germany. In Britain, the poorly led Attlee government of 1945 to 1951 nationalized the coal mines, civil aviation, cable and wireless services, railways, road transport, and the steel industry. They thereby created a number of inefficient, over-manned, and loss-making monopolies. They retained a large number of the wartime restrictions and controls on the operation of the free market including the rationing of food and clothing and even introduced the rationing of bread, which had not been present during the war. They instituted a system of licenses for building materials so that only registered and licensed builders were permitted to buy timber and a number of other products. They did nothing to curtail trade union restrictive practices. They also retained the conscription of 18- to 20-year-olds into the armed services. This removed from the labor force large numbers of young men who would otherwise have been productively employed. Conscription served no conceivable military purpose because in the event of the Soviet Union invading western Europe, the Americans would have undertaken the major role in the defense of the West and Britain would have provided a more effective contribution to this defense with a smaller but better trained professional army. The effect of this series of blunders was to impair British economic growth for some forty years until it was rectified in the 1980s by the Thatcher government.

The decline of the British economy from the closing decades of the nineteenth century as a result of poor industrial leadership has been described by Ord (1948) in his book, *Politics and Poverty*. His argument is that Great Britain was very wealthy in 1880, but from then on it started to decline as an economic power because of two major mistakes made by political leaders. In the 1880s, the heads of British businesses began to form trade associations, price rings, and cartels, that were intended to restrict competition. The British government allowed this to happen because it did not understand that sharp and effective competition was necessary for industrial efficiency. The second major mistake was made by trade union leaders who started to urge the workers to adopt restrictive practices and work slowly. They assured their members that there was ample wealth for all, if only it was fairly distributed. They argued for the nationalization of industry and for a "planned economy." Ord argues that from that time onward, intentionally or otherwise, British trade unions began to retard the efficiency of the economy. As a consequence, by 1914 the American people were receiving fully fifty percent more out of the same system than were the British. Together the industrial cartels, which reduced competition, and trade union policies, which reduced working efficiency, were responsible for the relative decline of British industries. Conservative governments supported the cartels for several decades. During World War II, the British government took charge of industry and set up central planning authorities in an attempt to make it more efficient, but in reality its efficiency declined. After the war, Ord argues the wisest thing for the British Government to have done would have been to reestablish free markets, as was done in the United States and West Germany, but the British Labor Government did the opposite. It nationalized industries and increased controls. The consequence was a continuation of the economic decline of Britain.

The political leadership of Germany in the post World War II years was far more intelligent. When Konrad Adenauer became chancellor in 1949, he appointed Ludwig Erhard as his finance minister. Erhard had been a professor of economics at the University of Munich and had a sound understanding of market economics. One of his first acts on becoming finance minister was "the bonfire of controls" which the occupying Allied Forces had imposed on Germany. His freeing up of the economy laid the foundation for Germany's rapid economic growth for the next five decades. As two historians have written, "He was the pioneer of the German 'economic miracle' of recovery from wartime devastation" (Thorne and Collocott, 1985, p. 463). The difference in the intellectual quality of political leadership in Britain and Germany in the post World War II decades can be seen in the economic growth and per capita income figures given in Appendix 2, "Data on Per Capita Income and Economic Growth in 185 Countries." During the years 1950 to 1990, economic growth of GDP per capita (Maddison) in Britain was 138.1 percent. In Germany, it was more than double at 336.5 percent. The GDP per capita (Maddison) in Germany in 1950 was 4,281 and in Britain it was 6,847 (in Geary-Khamis dollars). By 1998, real GDP per capita in Britain was 20,336, while in Germany it had grown to 22,169. The poor economic performance of Britain and the strong economic performance of Germany in the second half of the twentieth century provide striking testimony to the impact on economic growth and development of the intellectual quality of political leadership.

There are many other examples of the impact of the quality of political leadership on economic growth. North and South Korea had approximately the same per capita income in 1950, when North Korea's GDP per capita was $643 (Maddison) and South Korea's was $876. By 1990, GDP per capita was $2,259 in North Korea and $8,977 in South Korea (see Appendix 2). The reason for this difference in economic success is that the political leaders of North Korea adopted a communist command economy, whereas the leaders in South Korea adopted a market economy.

CLIMATE, GEOGRAPHY AND ECONOMIC DEVELOPMENT RECONSIDERED

It has long been realized that there is an association between climate and economic development in so far as countries with temperate climates are almost invariably more economically developed than those with tropical and subtropical climates (see Chapter 1, section 1). This has generally been attributed to the enervating effects of hot climates and the greater virulence of diseases such as malaria and bilharzia. The results of our study confirm that there is a substantial gap in the average per capita incomes between the countries of the tropics and sub-tropics and the countries of the temperate zones. In Table 9.1, the 185 countries of our study are divided into three geographical groups:

1.) North (north of the Tropic of Cancer), 2.) the Tropics (between the Tropic of Cancer and the Tropic of Capricorn), and 3.) South (south of the Tropic of Capricorn). This table shows that the average GNP per capita and the average real GDP per capita in 1998 were two to four times higher in the countries of temperate zones than in the countries of the tropics, and it also shows that there is a corresponding difference in the average national IQs.

Table 9.1

The Means of National IQs, GNP Per Capita 1998, and Real GDP Per Capita 1998 for the Countries of Three Geographical Zones and the Minimum and Maximum Values of These Variables in Each Zone

Zone	N	Mean IQ	GNP per capita 1998	Real GDP per capita 1998
1. North	78	92.4	9,676	10,974
Minimum		78	210	1,041
Maximum		106	43,570	33,500
2. The Tropics	97	77.9	2,322	3,737
Minimum		59	100	458
Maximum		107	30,060	24,210
3. South	10	85.6	6,517	9,348
Minimum		72	570	1,626
Maximum		100	20,300	22,452

Diamond tries to explain these extensive differences in economic development between geographical zones by various geographical characteristics and Kamarck by direct effects of hot climates and tropical diseases (see Chapter 1, "Why Are Some Countries So Rich and Others So Poor?"). Our theoretical explanation is different. We assume that differences in climatic and geographical conditions affected the evolution of human mental abilities in such a way that the average IQs are higher for the populations of temperate zones than for the populations of the tropics. This was responsible for the differences in the mean IQs between the countries of the tropics and the countries of the two temperate zones. According to our theory, this difference provides the main explanation for the gap in economic development between tropical countries and the countries of temperate zones. Climatic conditions are related to mean IQs and they affect economic development through the evolved differences in human mental abilities.

However, the fact that IQs and the measures of per capita income vary greatly within each geographical zone indicates that there are several exceptions to the average pattern. In temperate zones, the mean IQs and per capita incomes are lowest for the countries that lie on the Tropic of Cancer, on the Tropic of Capricorn, or near them. The countries with low mean IQs and low per capita incomes in the North lie on the Tropic of Cancer or near it (India, Bangladesh, Pakistan, Bhutan, and Nepal in particular, and also Egypt and Morocco). The same is true for the countries with the lowest IQs and per capita incomes in the southern temperate zone (Lesotho, Swaziland, and Paraguay). The most significant exceptions are in the zone of the tropics. Singapore and Hong Kong lie in the zone of the tropics, but they are among the richest countries in the world. On the other hand, Lesotho and Swaziland lie slightly south of the Tropic of Capricorn, but they are among the world's poorest countries. The explanation for these differences can be understood in terms of intelligence theory. The people of Singapore and Hong Kong have high IQs and the people of Lesotho and Swaziland have low IQs. These differences do not disconfirm the theory that climatic conditions have affected the evolution of human mental abilities. Hong Kong lies near the Tropic of Cancer and the Chinese people in Singapore are recent immigrants, not the original tropical people. The Bantus of Lesotho and Swaziland as well as in South Africa are relatively recent immigrants from the tropical parts of Africa. The example of Singapore shows that in some cases it has been possible for immigrants from the north to establish economically highly developed societies in the tropical latitudes. Chinese immigrants have also helped to further economic development in Brunei, Malaysia, Indonesia, and Thailand. Correspondingly, immigrants from India have helped economic development in Mauritius. On the other hand, northern immigrants have not succeeded in establishing successful colonies in any parts of tropical Africa, and their success in the tropical countries of Latin America also has been limited when compared to the temperate zones of America. The most successful colonies of Europeans are in the temperate zones of the world—in North and South America, in the southern tip of Africa, and in Australia and New Zealand, but not in the tropics.

Some other geographical conditions may also affect economic development independently from the level of IQs. Geographical isolation is one of these. It is possible that geographical isolation hinders economic development in the small island states of the Pacific and in central Asia (Mongolia, Kyrgyzstan, and Tajikistan for example), and perhaps also in some parts of Africa and Latin America. Isolated mountainous regions may also be exceptionally unfavorable environments for economic development (Afghanistan, Nepal, and Bhutan, for example). Residuals are negative for these countries, showing that per capita income is much lower than expected on the basis of national IQs.

MODERNIZATION AND CONVERGENCE THEORIES

In Chapter 1 an account was given of Rostow's "modernization theory" of economic development, according to which all nations would evolve from subsistence agriculture through various stages of urbanization and industrialization and eventually reach the final stage of economically developed mass consumption.

Later history in most of the world has not supported Rostow's theory. Most of the poor countries are still poor, and the gap between the poor countries and the rich has not decreased. The intelligence theory of economic development helps us to understand why this is so. The countries of the Pacific Rim with market economies have gone through the modernization stages because their populations have high IQs. But most of the poor countries of the world in southern Asia, the Pacific islands, Central and South America, and sub-Saharan Africa have made little progress in modernization because their populations have low IQs. It is impossible for the countries with low national IQs to rise to the same level of economic development as the countries with high national IQs. The modernization theory is based on the assumption that the peoples of all nations are equally capable of learning and adopting modern technologies, but intelligence theory tells us that this is not so.

Closely related to modernization theory is the economic theory of "convergence." This theory states that national differences in per capita income should tend to diminish over time as the poorer countries catch up on richer countries. This is known as convergence theory because of the expectation that national per capita incomes will converge. This theory was formulated by R. M. Solow (1956) and has been restated by J. B. DeLong (1988, p. 1138): "Economists have always expected the 'convergence' of national productivity levels. The theoretical logic behind this belief is powerful. The per capita income advantage of the West is based on its application of the storehouse of industrial and administrative technology of the industrial revolution. The benefits of tapping this technology are great, so nations will strain every nerve to assimilate modern technology and their incomes will converge to those of industrial nations." The major reason for expecting convergence is that the richer nations develop the new technologies. Poorer nations are able to copy these technologies and because they have lower labor costs these nations can produce these goods more cheaply. This enables them to capture the markets formerly held by the richer countries and to make higher profits, so incomes in poorer countries should increase more rapidly than those in richer countries, thus leading to convergence.

When all the nations of the world are considered, there is a general consensus that convergence has not taken place (Quah, 1996; Jones, 1997; Firebaugh, 1999). On the contrary, over the time period of approximately 180 years from 1820 to the end of the twentieth century, the inequality of incomes between nations has increased rather than diminished. According to Maddison's data (see Appendix 2), GDP per capita was lowest in China ($523) and India in 1820, but they were not the poorest countries of the world at that time. Maddison does not provide data for any sub-Saharan African country in 1820, although he estimates that GDP per capita was $450 in 1820 in Africa as a whole, which includes North and South Africa. However, because GDP per capita was less than 300 Geary-Khamis dollars in Ethiopia, Guinea, and Guinea-Bissau in 1950 (when sub-Saharan African countries were included for the first time in Maddison's dataset, with the exception of Ghana in 1900 and 1913), it is quite probable that GDP per capita was not more than approximately 150 Geary-Khamis dollars in the poorest sub-African countries in 1820. This means that GDP per capita in the richest countries of Europe was about 10 times higher than in the poorest countries of sub-Saharan Africa already in 1820. *World Development Report 2000-2001* (p. 45) interprets the same data differently: "As late as 1820 per capita incomes were quite similar around the world—and very low, ranging from around $500 in China and South Asia to $1,000–1,500 in the richest countries of Europe." Jeffrey Sachs (2000, p. 29) claims on the basis of the same Maddison data that in 1820 "the gap between Western Europe and the world's poorest region (sub-Saharan Africa) was only three to one, according to Maddison's estimates." We think that these are misleading statements. The gap between the richest and the poorest countries of the world was already extensive in 1820. By the closing decades of the twentieth century, average incomes in the richest countries were around thirty times greater than those in the poorest countries (see Appendix 2). Although economic theory predicts convergence in national per capita incomes, what has actually occurred is divergence.

Nevertheless, if the nations of the world are divided into homogeneous geographical groups, it becomes clear that during the second half of the twentieth century the convergence theory has worked well for some groups of countries but not for others. In the 1950s and 1960s, the United States was the richest nation in the world. In relation to this yardstick, the convergence theory has worked well for western Europe and for the market economies of the Pacific Rim, consisting of Japan, South Korea, Hong Kong, Taiwan, and Singapore. This is shown in Appendix 2, which provides data on per capita income for individual countries and economic growth rates for different periods of comparison, and also in Table 9.2, which summarizes the regional differences in GDP per capita during 1950–1990 and in GNP per capita during 1976–1998 and the corresponding economic growth rates over these periods.

Table 9.2 shows that economic growth in the second half of the twentieth century was greater in western Europe and substantially greater in the Pacific Rim than in the United States, leading to a convergence of per capita incomes. For example, in 1950 GDP per capita in western Europe was 53.6

Table 9.2

Regional Means for IQs, GDP Per Capita in 1950–1990, GNP Per Capita in 1976–1998, and the Corresponding Economic Growth Rates

Variable	United States	Western Europe	Pacific Rim	Latin America	Pacific Islands	South Asia	Sub-Saharan Africa
Number of countries	1	17	5	20	9	8	42
National IQ	98.0	99.1	104.4	86.3	84.7	80.9	69.2
GDP per capita 1950	9,573	5,126	1,534	2,232	1,683	614	711
GDP per capita 1990	21,866	16,540	13,926	3,483	2,279	1,424	1,105
Growth 1950–1990 %	128.7	222.7	807.8	56.0	35.4	131.9	55.4
Number of countries	1	17	5	20	3	8	41
National IQ	98.0	99.1	104.4	86.3	84.7	80.9	69.2
GNP per capita 1976	7,890	5,710	2,292	917	663	133	331
GNP per capita 1998	29,340	25,972	21,463	2,800	1,340	548	574
Growth 1976–1998 %	271.8	354.8	836.4	205.3	102.1	312.0	73.4

percent of that in the United States, but by 1990 this had grown to 75.6 percent. Similarly, in 1950 GDP per capita in the nations of the Pacific Rim was 16.0 percent of that in the United States, but by 1990 this had increased to 63.7 percent. Similar convergence occurred for GNP per capita from 1976 to 1998. It should be noted, however, that despite convergence, the absolute differences in dollars between the United States and the other two regional groups have not yet decreased. They have remained approximately the same, or have only slightly increased.

While the convergence theory has worked well for western Europe and the Pacific Rim, it has not worked for other groups of countries including those of South Asia, the Pacific Islands, Latin America, and sub-Saharan Africa. Table 9.2 shows that economic growth was consistently lower in these four regions than in the United States, except during the period of 1976–1998, when the growth rate was slightly higher in South Asia. In Latin America, GDP per capita was 23.3 percent of that in the United States in 1950, but it was only 15.9 percent in 1990, and GNP per capita was 11.5 percent in 1976 and 9.5 percent in 1998 of that in the United States. For the small group of Pacific island states, the trend was similar. The group of southern Asian countries retained its low percentage throughout these periods of comparison, whereas sub-Saharan Africa's share declined. In sub-Saharan Africa, GDP per capita was 7.4 percent of that in the United States in 1950, but it was only 5.0 percent in 1990, and the GNP per capita was 4.2 percent of that in the United States in 1976, but only 2.0 percent in 1998. There has not been any convergence between the United States and these four regions. These differences in per capita income have continued to increase. The gap is the greatest for sub-Saharan Africa. The difference in GDP per capita between the United States and sub-Saharan Africa was $8,862 in 1950, but was $20,761 in 1990. Instead of convergence, an increasing divergence has occurred. The same is true also in the cases of Latin America, the Pacific Islands, and South Asia.

Table 9.3 shows the strength of the relationship between the regional mean IQs and the regional means of different measures of per capita income and economic growth rates in the seven regions. In this analysis, the seven regional groups are used as units of analysis.

Table 9.3 shows that most correlations based on regional means are much higher than the correlations based on the values of individual countries (cf., Chapter 7, "National IQs and Economic Development in 81 Nations," and Chapter 8). This is because the use of regional averages reduces the effects of outliers. The explained part of the variation varies from 30 percent (GDP per capita 1950) to 73 percent (GNP per capita 1998).

Figure 9.1 illustrates the strong relationship between the regional mean IQs and the regional means of GNP in 1998. Most regions are relatively close to the regression line. However, the United States deviates greatly from the regression line. Its GNP per capita in 1998 was much higher than expected.

How can the success of the convergence theory for western Europe and the Pacific Rim and its failure for the remaining four groups of nations be explained? We believe that the answer to this question lies in the intelligence levels of the populations. The convergence theory works for western Europe and the Pacific Rim because the peoples of these nations have approximately the same average IQs—in the case of Europe—or somewhat higher IQs—in the case of the Pacific Rim—as that in the United States. The convergence theory does not work for the other four groups of nations because their populations have lower IQs than those in the United States. Although these countries have an economic advantage in terms of lower labor costs, this is offset by the disadvantage of their lower IQs. The net result of these advantages and disadvantages is that virtually no convergence has taken place for

Table 9.3

Correlations between Regional Mean IQs and Regional Means of Per Capita Income and Economic Growth Rates

Regional means of variables	N	Regional mean IQs
GDP per capita 1950	7	.546
GDP per capita 1990	7	.840
Growth of GDP per capita in 1950–1990	7	.669
GNP per capita 1976	7	.679
GNP per capita 1998	7	.857
Growth of GNP per capita in 1976–1998	7	.748

Figure 9.1

The Results of the Regression Analysis of Regional Means of GNP Per Capita 1998 on Regional Mean IQ in Seven Regions of the World

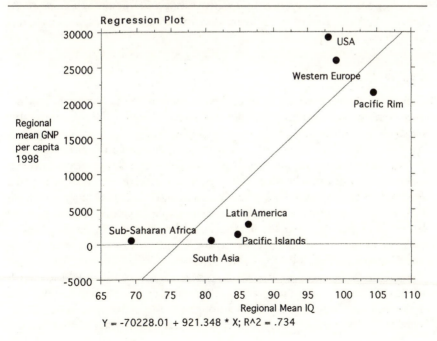

$$Y = -70228.01 + 921.348 * X; R^2 = .734$$

the nations of South Asia, the Pacific Islands, Latin America, and sub-Saharan Africa. In fact, divergence has taken place in the sense that the absolute gap in per capita dollars has increased between the United States and these four regional groups. This divergence has been most conspicuous in the case of sub-Saharan Africa and is only slightly smaller in the cases of the other three regional groups.

Because of the large gap in per capita incomes between nations, the achievement of equal economic growth rates would not mean that the gap would remain the same. It would mean that the gap continued to grow. For example, in the period 1950 to 1990, the growth rate of GDP per capita in sub-Saharan Africa was approximately the same as in Latin America, but the gap in per capita dollars increased from $1,521 to $2,059. In the case of the Pacific Islands, the gap increased from $972 to $1,174, although the growth rate in the Pacific Islands was much lower (35.4 percent) than in sub-Saharan Africa. Compared to other regional groups, the growth rate in sub-Saharan Africa was lower in 1950 to 1990, and the gaps between sub-Saharan Africa and the other regions increased steeply.

The strongly positive correlations between the regional mean IQs and regional means of per capita income and economic growth rates shown in Table 9.3 indicate that divergence, not convergence, has taken place in both periods of comparison. Positive correlations indicate that the higher the IQs of the populations, the faster the rate of economic growth has tended to be and the greater the degree of divergence. Correlations should be highly negative to produce convergence. In other words, economic growth rates would have to be much higher in the regions of low mean IQs than in the regions of high mean IQs.

INDIA

India had quite a poor rate of economic growth in the second half of the twentieth century averaging 2.5 percent a year of GNP. This is attributable partly to the low intelligence level of the population (India's average IQ is 81), but even when this is taken into account, our regression analysis of real GDP per capita 1998 on the national IQs shown in Table 8.9 indicates that per capita income in India has been lower than predicted on the basis of national intelligence (India has a negative residual of –3,615). The principal explanation for this lies in the over-regulated socialist-style economic policies pursued by Jawaharlal Nehru and his successors. Nehru became Prime Minister of India in 1947. He was inspired by British Fabian socialism, the socialist program being introduced by the Labor government of the time in Britain, and communist economic planning in the Soviet Union. He adopted these types of government as a model for his economic policy in India. The state attempted to control the economy through a series of five-year plans, which were modeled on those of the Soviet Union and an extensive license permit system that restricted and restrained private economic activities, distorted free competition, and created a favorable environment for corruption (Gardner, 1998, pp. 579–582). Thus, Nafziger (1997, pp. 544–545) notes that once "the licensing system was created, politicians, bureaucrats, and sheltered businesses and their workers used centralized planning logic to define their own interest and to oppose reform, and Indian economists also rationalized the system." These policies were continued by Nehru's successors and hampered private industrial efficiency in many ways (for poor Indian economic policies, see also Bhuleshkar, 1972; Datt and Sundharam, 1979; Ghosh, 1979; Singh 1998a, 1998b). Yergin and Stanislaw (1999, p. 218) write that inspired "by idealism and ideologies, India initially embraced a program that held back development that could have alleviated its massive poverty"; the leaders of the Congress Party "believed that central planning, strong state control, and government knowledge would do a better job of allocating investment and determining output than would many millions of individual decision makers." They describe the consequences of this set of policies as follows: "India developed a thoroughly complex and enormously cumbersome system. It operated through a Byzantine maze of quantitative regulations, quotas and tariffs, endless permits, industrial licenses, and a host of other controls—a maze in which incentives and initiative and entrepreneurship either were lost or became hopelessly distorted. All of this made the economy increasingly inefficient; bureaucratic dispensation took over the functions of the marketplace . . . . The restrictions brought economic stagnation" (Yergin and Stanislaw, 1999, p. 74).

Thus, Nehru's admiration of the socialist system and Soviet planning led him to establish a semi-socialistic planning and control system that stifled private economic activities and retarded India's economic development. There is widespread agreement among economists that India would now be a considerably richer country if India's political leaders had adopted a market economy (Nafziger, 1997, p. 58; Yergin and Stanislaw 1999, pp. 67–75, 217–222). Tavleen Singh writes of Nehru's economic policies: "While Jawaharlal Nehru undoubtedly made good speeches about trysts with destiny and other such romantic things, he appears to have been singularly wrong in choosing the bus India needed to take", and she continues that India "missed the most important bus" when Rajiv Gandhi became prime minister: "As the prime minister with the largest mandate in independent India's history he could have done anything he wanted—liberalised the economy, invested heavily in infrastructure, insisted on compulsory primary education, changed healthcare methods, brought about massive judicial reforms—and today we could have been a rich country instead of languishing among the 50 poorest in the world" (Singh, 1999). India has been slow to correct its socialist economic policies. It was not until 1991 that Narasimha Rao's government started to dismantle what became known as India's "Permit Raj" system, although these reforms are still incomplete (see Vanhanen, 2000).

CHINA

One of the most perplexing problems for our theory is why the peoples of East Asia with their high IQs lagged behind the European peoples in economic growth and development until the second half of the twentieth century. The two major problems are in regard to China and Japan. As far as China is concerned, the country's science and technology generally were more advanced than the science and technology of Europe for around two thousand years from about 500 B.C. up to around the fifteenth century A.D. During this period, "the Chinese were well ahead of anyone else—and certainly of Europe" (Landes, 1998, p. 342). In about 500 B.C., the Chinese achieved a major engineering feat by constructing a canal linking the Huang Ho and Yangtze rivers (Landes, 1998). A more extensive canal system was built in the eighth century A.D., including a northwards extension to Jojin (Beijing) (Blunden and Elvin, 1983). The first canal lock was designed and built in 984 by Ch'iao Wei-yo. In Europe, it was not until the fourteenth century that canals were dug in the Netherlands and the first locks were not built until the 1370s. It was not until 1681 that the first major canal was built in France—the Canal du Midi—linking the Atlantic and the Mediterranean. It was not until a century later that canals were built in Britain.

Chinese science and technology were generally more advanced than those in Europe up to around the year 1500 A.D. In astronomy, the first recorded observations of stars, planets, constellations, and comets were made in China around 2300 B.C. It was not until around 2,000 years later that comparable observations were made in Greece. Haley's comet was recorded by Chinese astronomers in 240 B.C. and again in 1066 A.D., but it was not known in Europe until 1450 when it was discovered by the German astronomer, Johan Muller, and again in 1607, when it was recorded by the English astronomer, Thomas Herriot. In 185 A.D., Chinese astronomers were the first to record a supernova explosion. In 365 A.D., they discovered the moons of Jupiter, which were not known in Europe until they were discovered independently by the German astronomer, Simon Marius, in 1609 and by Galileo in 1610.

In agricultural technology, the Chinese were the first to invent the collar and harness for horses around 250 B.C. In 80 A.D., they invented the chain pump for lifting water for irrigation, winnowing machines, and multi-tube seed drills. In 240 A.D., they invented the wheel barrow, which did not appear in Europe until 1250. In 530 A.D., the Chinese invented a water-powered mill for shaking and sifting flour.

In printing and paper technology, the production of paper from bark and rags was developed in China about the year 105 A.D. by Tsai Lun; paper was not produced in the West until 790, when it began to be made in Iraq. Printing from engraved wooded blocks was invented in China about 650 A.D. This technology spread to Japan where the first printed text was produced in 767. In China, the first printed book (a Buddhist scripture) was produced in 868. Around 1040, the Chinese developed movable type, made of ceramic, for printing, and in 1100, color printing was invented in China for printing paper money. In Europe, printing was first developed in Germany about 1440 by Johannes Gutenberg and printed paper money was not introduced until the nineteenth century.

In mathematics, the abacus was invented independently by the Chinese and the Babylonians around 3000 B.C. It was introduced into Europe about 950 A.D. The Chinese invented the decimal point around 1350 B.C. and negative numbers in 100 B.C.

In military technology, the Chinese invented the stirrup in 475 A.D. The stirrup enabled soldiers on horseback to sit securely in the saddle and to attack enemies more effectively with swords and lances. The most important Chinese discovery in military technology was the invention of the formula for making gunpowder, which was published in a Chinese military text in 1044. The Chinese used gunpowder to build rockets in 1200, to make bombs producing shrapnel in 1230, to make small firearms shooting bullets from bamboo and metal tubes in 1260 to 1275, and to fire a cannon in 1280. In Europe, gunpowder was first used for firing cannon in France in 1324 and was first used in warfare by the French and the English in the 1340s. In 1380, rockets powered by gunpowder were first used in warfare in Europe.

In marine technology, the Chinese were building ships with several masts by 200 B.C., about the same time as similar ships were being built in Greece. The Chinese ships were equipped with rudders, which the Chinese were the first to invent, and which were not used in Europe until 1190. The most important Chinese invention in marine technology was the magnetic compass for navigation at sea, which was invented around the year 1000. The magnetic compass was first described in Europe in 1180 by Alexander Neckam.

A number of other important inventions were first made in China. Around 300 B.C., the Chinese invented cast iron. In 350 A.D., they developed the technology for using methane gas for lighting. In 580, they built the first suspension bridge supported with iron chains. In 1035, they invented the spinning wheel, which was adopted in Europe in the 1280s. In 1088, the Chinese astronomer, Su Song, invented the water-powered mechanical clock. It was three centuries later, in the 1380s, that mechanical clocks were invented in Europe. Around 840, the Chinese developed porcelain and for many centuries produced high quality china, which Europeans were not able to match until porcelain was reinvented in 1708 by the German chemist, Johann Bottger, and its use for making fine quality ceramics was perfected in the second half of the eighteenth century.

In the fifteenth century, Chinese inventiveness in science and technology came to an end and from this time to the second half of the twentieth century virtually all important advances were made by Europeans, first in

Europe and later in the United States. The reasons why Chinese science and technology petered out and the lead passed to Europe have baffled many historians. As one leading historian has written: "The failure by the Chinese to exploit their great advantages will remain one of the great problems of history" (Thomas, 1981, p. 271). And, in the words of another, "The mystery lies in China's failure to realize its potential" (Landes, 1998, p. 55).

We believe that the major factor responsible for the stagnation of China from around the year 1500 is that the Chinese failed to develop a market economy of the kind that evolved in Europe. This is the principal reason why Europe, and later the United States, assumed the lead in economic, scientific, and technological development. This is the conclusion reached by the European historian, Etienne Balazs, who states, "Chinese society was highly authoritarian . . . . There was a whole array of state monopolies, which comprise the great consumption staples: salt, iron, tea, alcohol and foreign trade . . . there were clothing regulations, a regulation of public and private construction of the dimensions of houses . . . it was the state that killed technological progress in China" (Balazs, 1968, pp. 22–23). The same conclusion has been reached by the American historian Landes who states, "I would stress the market. Enterprise was free in Europe. Innovation worked and paid, and rulers and vested interests were limited in their ability to prevent or discourage innovation" (Landes, 1998, p. 59). The reason that Europe developed a market economy is probably because it consisted of a large number of independent and competing states, in some of which market institutions were able to evolve, were seen to be effective, and were adopted by others, whereas China was a single state whose rulers were able to impose state controls over the whole national economy. This analysis extends historically our conclusion for the twentieth century that the presence of a market economy is a major determinant of economic growth and development. It shows that a population with a high level of intelligence is not sufficient to secure economic growth and development in the absence of a free market. However, an effective market economy is frequently associated with democracy, because, as Olson (2000) notes, individual rights to property and private contracts can be enforced much more effectively in democracies than in autocracies. Democratic reforms with freedom to invent and experiment evolved in Europe, but not in China.

JAPAN

The failure of Japan to develop economically until the late nineteenth century is largely attributable to a regulated economy and to isolation from the rest of the world. This isolation was deliberately imposed by the rulers because of their fear of the potentially subversive effects of foreign influences. Portuguese traders established contact with Japan in the sixteenth century. Missionaries followed and began to convert the Japanese to Christianity. The

Japanese rulers perceived this as a threat, and in 1637 they prohibited all foreigners from Japan and all Japanese from traveling abroad. The only exceptions to this prohibition were that Dutch merchants were allowed to call once a year to trade on the island of Deshima in the Bay of Nagasaki, and Chinese merchants were allowed to trade in Nagasaki city. The importation of European books was banned and those from China were checked by censors before being allowed in. These prohibitions lasted until 1854, when an American naval officer, Commander Perry, forced the Japanese to open the country up to American and other traders.

In 1867-68, a revolution occurred and the Meiji Restoration re-established the control of the emperor. The new rulers embarked on a program to modernize the country by adopting Western education and technology and by freeing up the economy. Compulsory education for four years was introduced and was increased to six years in 1907. There were no universities in Japan until 1877, when the University of Tokyo was established, shortly followed by six more universities in major cities. These were modeled after the German universities with their strong departments of science, engineering, and technology. The economy was liberalized by the abolition of a number of state monopolies that were transferred to private corporations. As a result of these reforms, industries grew rapidly and by the end of the nineteenth century Japan had become a formidable industrial and military power. In 1895, Japan fought and defeated China and annexed Taiwan. In 1904, Japan fought and won a war with Russia. In World War I, Japan fought on the side of Britain and France and at its conclusion annexed Korea. "Henceforth Japan was a world power, with a first-class economy" (Thomas, 1981, p. 661). In World War II, Japan was an ally with Germany. Japan was initially successful in the war in eastern Asia, where she defeated the British and occupied the British colonies of Hong Kong, Singapore, and Malaysia. She also occupied the Philippines. Despite ultimate defeat as a result of the atom bomb, Japan rapidly rebuilt its industrial and economic strength and by the 1980s had achieved approximately the same per capita GDP as Britain, Germany, France, and the rest of northwest Europe.

Much of the Japanese economic success in the twentieth century was built on adopting the inventions made in the West, improving them, and then selling them more competitively in world markets. In the second half of the century, Japan developed its motorcycle, automobile, shipbuilding, and electronic industries to the point where they competed successfully with those in Europe and the United States. It has sometimes been asserted that the Japanese have not made any significant scientific and technological innovations but have been merely copiers of the technologies made in the West. This assertion underestimates the Japanese technological achievements. *Philip's Science and Technology Encyclopedia* (1998) lists a number of important discoveries and technological innovations made by the Japanese in the second half of the twentieth century. In 1960, the Japanese produced the fiber-tipped pen; in 1963, they produced the Wankel-engined car; in 1964, they produced the high speed "bullet" trains traveling at 210 kilometers per hour—much faster than any Western trains; in 1966, they invented laser radar; and in 1967, they produced the first quartz watch. From the 1970s onwards, the Japanese have made several important discoveries in television and radio products. In 1976, the Japanese JVC company produced the video home system (VHS) for videotape; in 1979, the Matsushita company produced the flat screen television using a liquid crystal display; in 1979, the Japanese produced the Walkman personal stereo; in 1980, Sony produced video discs; in 1985, Sony produced CD-ROM (read only memory) disks; in 1987, the Japanese produced the digital audio tape (DAT); in 1988, they produced the International Services Digital Network (ISDN) for sending signals along coaxial cables and optical fibers; and in 1993, Sony produced the digital audio Mini Disc.

The rapid economic development of Japan in the nineteenth and twentieth centuries was replicated by that of Taiwan, Hong Kong, and Singapore in the second half of the twentieth century. All of these countries achieved high rates of economic growth and are textbook examples of the convergence theory working well for countries whose populations have high levels of intelligence.

SUB-SAHARAN AFRICA

The nations of sub-Saharan Africa are the greatest anomaly for the convergence theory. The low rate of economic growth of these countries following their independence from colonial rule in the 1960s is one of the major problems in development economics. During the years 1976 to 1998, the average economic growth rate of per capita GNP of the 41 nations of sub-Saharan Africa for which the data are available was much lower than in the rest of the world (see Table 9.2). While all other countries in the world have been growing richer in absolute terms, many African countries are now poorer than they were in the early 1970s (Alemayehu, 2000, p. 1).

Several economists have attempted to explain the poor economic performance of sub-Saharan Africa including J. R. Barro (1991), W. Easterly and R. Levine (1997), and P. Collier and J. W. Gunning (1999). Their common approach to this problem has been to quantify all possible factors such as climate, geography, mismanagement of the economies, large proportions of economically inactive young people and the like and to examine how far these factors are capable of explaining the low economic growth in the countries of sub-Saharan Africa as compared with other economically underdeveloped countries, which are principally located in Asia. All three studies conclude that these factors cannot provide a complete explanation and conclude that there is some "missing element" contributing to the low economic growth rate in sub-Saharan Africa.

In the most recent of these analyses, Collier and Gunning (1999) consider that five factors have contributed to the problem. These are the low level of what they call "social capital," which is the widespread corruption and lack of trust in commercial relationships; the "lack of openness of trade," which places restrictions on the free market such as the widespread imposition of price controls, minimum wage regulations, and monopolies; the "deficient public services," such as poor roads and railways, unreliable telephones, and electricity supplies; "geography," such as the relative lack of access to sea ports and consequent high transportation costs, and the prevalence of tropical diseases like malaria; and the "lack of financial depth," such as the poorly developed and monopolistic banking services. They conclude that although these five factors can explain some fraction of the low economic growth in sub-Saharan Africa, they do not provide a complete explanation. The data presented in the last chapter and the first sections of the present chapter suggest that the "missing element" in these analyses is the low level of intelligence of the populations.

In addition to low intelligence as a "missing element," some of the factors that Collier and Gunning propose as contributing to the low economic growth of sub-Saharan Africa are themselves attributable to a low level of intelligence in the populations. One of the major factors identified by economists as responsible for the low economic growth in sub-Saharan Africa is the poor quality of the political leadership that has generally instituted socialistic, protectionist, regulatory, and monopolistic programs. Collier and Gunning conclude that this has been the single most important factor retarding economic growth in sub-Saharan Africa and write that "the degree of hostility of many African governments to private product markets is surely astonishing" (p. 99). A similar conclusion has been reached by Sachs and Warner (1999, p. 335) who conclude that "We find that poor economic policies have played an especially important part in the slow growth, most importantly in Africa's lack of openness to international markets." However, these economists have not asked why the political leaders in sub-Saharan Africa have so consistently mismanaged their countries' economies. In the last resort, much of this mismanagement must be attributed to the political leaders' inadequate intelligence and their failure to understand that free markets are the most efficient form of economic organization.

In addition to the mismanagement of the economies in sub-Saharan Africa by political leaders, Collier and Gunning note the widespread inefficiency of the public services, "Africa experienced the paradox of poor public services despite relatively high public expenditure" (p. 10). One of the most serious of the inefficient public services is the unreliable telephones, "the telephone system has triple the level of faults of Asia's" (p. 71) and "inadequate telephone services were identified by 47 percent of Zimbabwean firms as their most serious problem; one export firm in the survey had to make a 30 mile journey in order to make a telephone call" (p. 88). Another public service that is inefficient in many African countries is the electricity supply that is plagued by frequent breakdowns and insufficient power. "Electricity supply is unreliable, so firms must rely on their own generators" (p. 88). A survey of Ugandan firms found that the shortage of electricity was identified as the single most important constraint upon the firms' growth. These inefficient public services can be attributed to the low level of intelligence among those responsible for their delivery.

There is also widespread inefficiency in much of the private sector of the economies in sub-Saharan Africa. Collier and Gunning note that agricultural yields in sub-Saharan Africa "compare very unfavourably with those achieved elsewhere, even allowing for poorer soils; for example, cocoa and palm oil yields are typically only half those recorded in Asia, and yields are also relatively low for livestock and for food crops" (p. 81). They describe the poor quality of the advice frequently provided by government advisory services. These "have often given inappropriate advice;" for instance in East Africa they "have long been hostile towards the traditional practice of intercropping, yet research shows that there are many advantages: maize-bean mixtures offer better protection against poor rains than pure strands" (p. 82). Government agencies also are frequently inefficient. For instance, "inefficiency on the part of the Kenyan Maize Marketing Board led to localized shortages, inducing farmers to retain subsistence production" (p. 98).

These factors that Collier and Gunning identify are some of the proximate determinants of the poor economic performance of sub-Saharan Africa, but they do not go to the heart of the problem. Collier and Gunning do not ask why the telephone services and electricity supplies are so inefficient in sub-Saharan Africa; why the agricultural yields are so low; and why the government agricultural advisory officials give inappropriate advice and government agencies are incompetent. Inefficiency throughout the economy is precisely what would be expected in populations where the average IQ is 70. With this level of cognitive capacity, the populations of sub-Saharan Africa cannot be expected to match the rates of economic growth achieved elsewhere in the world.

SUMMARY

In this chapter, we have considered further the role of a population's intelligence and markets for economic growth and development. We began with a discussion of the contribution of national intelligence and proposed that there are two principal reasons why rates of economic growth and development are significantly determined by population IQs. The first reason is that nations whose populations have high IQs have high aggregate earning capacities in international markets. This generates a high rate of economic growth over a period of decades or even centuries, resulting in high per capita incomes. The second reason is that nations whose populations have high IQs are normally run by intelligent political leaders who provide an economic environment that is favorable to economic growth and who avoid making the mistakes in economic policy that retard economic development. Next, we discussed the theory of economic convergence, which states that national incomes should converge over time because of the economic advantages of nations with low per capita incomes. We showed that the convergence theory has not worked for many countries during the nineteenth and twentieth centuries and that the differences in national wealth between nations have generally increased rather than converged during this period. We argued that the convergence theory only works for countries whose populations have high IQs, most notably those of East Asia and Europe, and it does not work for most of the economically developing countries of Latin America, South Asia, the Pacific islands, and sub-Saharan Africa because their populations' low IQs offset their economic advantages of low labor costs. The chapter concludes with several discussions on the contributions of national intelligence and markets in the economic development of India, China, Japan, and the nations of sub-Saharan Africa. In the case of India, the population's moderately low intelligence has been compounded during the second half of the twentieth century by poor economic management and an over-regulated economy. China has a highly intelligent population but has been economically retarded for many centuries by a command economy and autocratic political systems. Japan also has a highly intelligent population but was economically retarded until the closing decades of the nineteenth century because of its over-regulated economy and isolation from the rest of the world. The nations of sub-Saharan Africa have had exceptionally low and, in many cases, negative economic growth in the last three decades of the twentieth century that is attributable to both the over-regulated economies and the low intelligence of the populations.

10

The Future of the Wealth of Nations

The results of our study indicate that the gap between rich and poor countries, which is still increasing, is strongly related to national differences in intelligence. We believe that our theory of the causal relationship between national intelligence and differences in the wealth and poverty of nations measured by per capita income and economic growth rates provides a more fundamental and theoretically more satisfactory explanation for the gap between rich and poor countries than any previous theory. In general, although not without exceptions, nations with more intelligent populations have been able to achieve a higher level of per capita incomes than less intelligent nations. This is a major reason why economic inequalities among nations are so great. In the contemporary economically, culturally, and politically integrated world, the existence of large economic disparities among nations and world regions has become a serious political, economic, and moral problem. There is a virtually universal consensus that it would be better if the poor nations could catch up with the rich nations and there were no gap between rich and poor nations. Unfortunately, the results of our study imply that it will be impossible to eradicate the gap between rich and poor nations and that there is very little hope for most poor nations ever to catch up with the rich nations.

Persistent poverty and economic inequality are serious political and economic problems in the world in which all nations are formally equal and are equally entitled to utilize the scarce resources necessary to maintain human life. It is difficult for the poorer nations to accept the unequal sharing of the wealth in the world, and it is difficult for rich and poor nations to agree on environmental regulations and restrictions necessary to keep this world inhabitable. As a consequence, many types of interest conflicts tend to arise and become violent, causing people from poor countries to try to migrate to rich countries which find it necessary to tighten their border controls. These interest conflicts also bring about environmental degeneration, which is caused by increasing economic growth and consumption in rich countries and industrialization in numerous poor countries. Persistent poverty and economic inequality are also a moral problem for rich nations, whose populations feel morally disturbed by the presence of so much poverty in the world and feel obligated to provide help. For both economic and moral reasons, the rich nations have given the poor nations economic assistance in the form of financial aid and loans in an endeavor to help them to overcome their poverty. However, this aid has not solved the problems of poverty and inequality. In fact, the gap between rich and poor nations is now much greater than it was some decades ago. Our theory explains why so many attempts to eradicate this gap have failed and why it is still growing.

In this chapter, we start by considering various possibilities on how to increase the populations' intelligence of poor nations. We also consider what the rich nations could do to help the poor nations in this matter as well as what the poor nations themselves could and should do from the perspective of our theory. We then come to the other factors affecting economic inequalities and to the question of how to live with this problem if it is impossible to solve it.

Our theory that intelligence is a major determinant of economic growth implies that one way to increase the economic growth rates of the poor nations is to raise the intelligence levels of their populations. Because intelligence is determined by both environmental and genetic factors, it would be possible in theory to work on either of these in order to increase the intelligence of the populations in the poor nations. In this chapter, we consider the possibility of interventions in order to achieve this objective, beginning with environmental measures and turning later to genetic measures.

NUTRITION

No general consensus exists on what the environmental factors are that determine intelligence. The factors that have been proposed can be divided into biological and psychological. We believe there is strong evidence that one of the major biological factors affecting intelligence is the nutritional quality of the diets of pregnant women, and the nutrition obtained by the fetus, and by babies, young children, and adolescents; this affects the growth of the brain, which in turn, affects intelligence. This conclusion rests on a number of different kinds of study. Some of the most persuasive evidence for an effect of the prenatal nutritional quality comes from studies of twins with different birth weights, among whom it has been found that the heavier twin at birth has a higher IQ in adolescence. Twins sometimes differ in their birth weights because one twin received better nutrition than the other, which results not only in a greater birth weight but also in a larger head and brain. This apparently gives the infant an intelligence advantage that persists into adolescence. The evidence on these twin studies is reviewed in Lynn (1990 and 1998). This evidence is confirmed by other studies, which show that infants with low birth weights have lower-than-average intelligence by around 6 IQ points (Martorell, 1998).

In further support of the theory that the quality of nutrition obtained by young children affects their intelligence is the finding that infants who were fed breast milk had higher average IQs at the age of 8 years by 8.3 IQ points than those who were fed on formula milk (Lucas et al., 1992). This study controlled for differences in socio-economic status, mother's age and education, and the infant's birth weight, gestational age, birth order, sex, and number of days in a respirator. The explanation for this difference is apparently that breast milk contains nutrients missing from formula milk.

The effect of nutrition on intelligence has also been shown in several nutritional supplement studies. In the first of these, which was carried out in New York in the 1950s, vitamin and mineral supplements were given to a sample of low income pregnant women; it was found that their children at the age of four years had gained 8 IQ points, when compared to a control group of children whose mothers had been given placebos (Harrel, Woodyard, and Gates, 1955). A number of studies have given nutritional supplements to samples of children for a number of weeks and have been found that they register gains in intelligence, when compared to control groups of children who were given placebo supplements. The general methodology employed in these studies has been to give multi-vitamin and mineral supplements containing some twenty-five nutrients. Eysenck and Schoenthaler (1997) have reviewed ten of these studies and shown that in all of them, the children who were given the supplements showed some increase in their IQs; the average was 3.5 IQ points. In a subsequent study, it was found that a sample of children who were deficient in iron registered a gain of 5.8 IQ points after receiving iron supplements for a sixteen-week period (Lynn and Harland, 1998).

Finally, the secular rises in intelligence that occurred in Western populations during the twentieth century are largely attributable to improvements in nutrition. Many people who have discussed these rises have advanced a number of responsible factors including increases in education, greater availability of children's games and toys, greater familiarity with intelligence tests, smaller family sizes, greater educational attainment of parents, increased urbanization, and changes in parental styles of child rearing (Williams, 1998). All of these factors can be ruled out on two grounds. First, the increases in intelligence have taken place in four-year-olds, and increases of similar magnitude have occurred in the early cognitive development of two-year-olds (Hanson, Smith, and Hume, 1985; Lynn, 1990). This shows that the causal factors in the secular rise of intelligence must have operated before the age of two, and it rules out virtually all the effects suggested above such as improvements in education, greater availability of children's games and toys, and so forth. Second, there have been two studies of pairs of biologically unrelated children who were adopted and reared in the same family and these have found that there are effectively zero correlations for intelligence between these pairs of children when they are adolescents and adults. The actual correlations are −0.03 (Scarr and Weinberg, 1978) and −0.09 (Loehlin *et al.*, 1989). These small negative correlations do not differ significantly from zero. The implication of these results is that common family influences, such as the extent to which some parents have fewer children, sent their children to better schools, give them cognitively stimulating toys and computers and so forth, have no long term effects on intelligence, because if they did the correlations between pairs of biologically unrelated children reared in the same family would be positive. The environmental factors determining intelligence must be operating before children are adopted, which points to the quality of prenatal and early post-natal nutrition. There were substantial improvements in the quality of nutrition of the populations of the western nations during the twentieth century that were responsible for increases in average heights of about one standard deviation. The increases in intelligence have been of about the same order. Improvements in nutrition brought about increases in average brain size and probably also in the brain's neurological development.

We are by no means alone in concluding that the quality of nutrition is a major environmental determinant of intelligence. This conclusion has been reached by a number of researchers. For instance, "Inadequate levels of vitamins and minerals in the blood stream reduce a child's IQ below the optimum level" (Eysenck and Schoenthaler, 1997, p. 387); "The evidence suggests that nutrition and intelligence are linked in that children with better diets, in terms of both quantity and quality of food, show superior performance on developmental and cognitive tests than children who are less well fed" (Sigman and Whaley, 1998, p. 172). The implication of this conclusion is that measures to improve the quality of nutrition in poor countries would be one way to increase the intelligence levels of their populations.

MALNUTRITION IN UNDERDEVELOPED NATIONS

There is extensive malnutrition in the poorest and least developed countries and substantial evidence that this reduces the intelligence of significant proportions of the population. The two most visible signs of the presence of malnutrition are the large numbers of babies with low birth weight and of growth stunted children. Babies with low birth weight in underdeveloped countries are largely caused by chronic malnutrition in utero, which is itself caused by the mother's poor nutrition (Kramer, 1987). In Bangladesh, one of the poorest nations in the world, approximately half of the babies born in the early 1990s had low birth weights (defined as less that 2500 grams) and in the least developed countries as a whole, approximately 24 percent of babies are born with low birth weights, as compared with approximately 6 percent in Western Europe (UNICEF, 1996). Low birth weight in economically underdeveloped countries is largely caused by poor nutrition, but in developed countries it is largely caused by prematurity (Villar and Belizan, 1982).

The extensive presence of malnutrition in poor countries is also responsible for the high prevalence of stunted growth (defined as height more than two standard deviations below the median) and for "wasting" (defined as low weight for height). In the least economically developed nations in the early 1990s, around 50 percent of children under 5 years of age were stunted and about 10 percent were wasted (UNICEF, 1996). From the age of 5 years onward, there is some catch up in physical growth, but many adults remain to some degree stunted, largely due to their poor nutrition in utero and infancy.

There is little doubt that the extensive poor quality of nutrition in economically underdeveloped countries has an adverse effect on the intelligence of the populations. In addition to the evidence on the effect of nutrition on intelligence in developed countries, there have been several studies showing similar effects in developing countries. For instance, studies in Jamaica and Mexico have examined the IQs of children who were admitted to the hospital for malnutrition and found that the average IQs of these children were 4 points lower (Jamaica) and 11 points lower (Mexico) than the IQs of their less severely malnourished siblings (Hertzig, Birch, Richardson, and Tizard, 1972; Birch, Pineiro, Alcalde, Toca, and Cravioto, 1971). Further evidence for the adverse effects of poor nutrition on intelligence in developing countries has been reported for Kenya by Sigman (1995).

There is growing consensus among experts in this field that poor nutrition is a significant factor responsible for low intelligence in poor countries. For instance, Mackintosh (1998) writes that "It seems virtually certain that severe, chronic malnutrition, of the sort common to many developing countries, has deleterious effects on the IQ of the children" (p. 123). Similarly, Martorell (1998) writes that "There is considerable evidence from today's poor countries that links poor nutrition to impaired cognitive development" (p. 201).

There are four major nutritional deficiencies in poor countries. The first of these is protein-energy malnutrition (Waterlow, 1992). Protein consumption in the economically developed countries in the late 1990s averaged about 100 grams a day per person, while in the least economically developed countries it averaged 51 grams per day per person (*Human Development Report,* 2000). The other three major nutritional deficiencies are iron deficiency anemia (Yip and Dallman, 1996), Vitamin A deficiency (Sommer and West, 1996) and iodine deficiency (Hetzell, Dunn, and Stanbury, 1987). There is reasonably strong evidence that all of these deficiencies have some adverse impact on intelligence. Thus, programs to improve the nutrition of pregnant women, infants, and children in developing countries should do something to raise the population's intelligence levels.

HEALTH

It is probable that a number of diseases impair intelligence. Some diseases, such as diphtheria, whooping cough, and measles, can have this effect by damaging the nervous system. Others, such as malaria, cause damage by impairing the absorption of nutrients and hence causing malnutrition (Jensen, 1998; Mackintosh, 1998). Many of these diseases are prevalent in the developing countries. For instance, the percentages of the population contracting malaria in 1997 was 37 percent in Zambia, 27 percent in Gambia, 26 percent in Namibia, 20 percent in Rwanda, and between 5 and 20 percent in Benin, Ghana, Guinea, the Ivory Coast, Niger, the Solomon Islands, Sudan, and Yemen. In 27 of the least economically developed countries, the prevalence of anemia among pregnant women during the period of 1975 to 1991 ranged between 24 percent in Mauritania to 80 percent in Gambia.

According to 1997 figures, more than 10 percent of adults have HIV or AIDS in a number of the economically developing countries including Botswana (25 percent), Central African Republic (10.8 percent), Djibouti (10.3 percent), El Salvador (13 percent), the Ivory Coast (10.1 percent), Kenya (12 percent), Malawi (15 percent), Mozambique (14 percent), Namibia (20 percent), Rwanda (13 percent), Swaziland (18 percent), Zambia (19 percent), and Zimbabwe (26 percent) (*Human Development Report*, 2000).

Health care is seriously deficient in many poor nations. For example, it is estimated that in the least developed countries, an average of only 55 percent of one-year-olds were immunized against measles during 1995 to 1998 (*Human Development Report*, 2000). The prevalence of disease in economically developing countries could be substantially reduced by better health care. It can be anticipated that better health care would have some beneficial impact on the intelligence of the populations.

EDUCATION

It has frequently been asserted that education increases intelligence. For instance, Jensen (1998, p. 324) writes of "the strong evidence that schooling affects IQ" and Mackintosh (1998, p. 132) states that "additional schooling is beneficial for children's IQ scores." This assertion rests on two lines of evidence. First, there are a number of studies showing that the amount of schooling children receive is positively related to their IQs. For example, a study by A. D. De Groot (1951) of a number of children who were prevented from attending school in Holland during World War II found that the children's IQs were depressed by about 5 IQ points. A study in Sweden by Harnqvist (1968) obtained the IQs for a sample of 13-year-olds, some of whom left school at the age of 13 while others remained in school until the age of 18. When IQs were obtained for the two groups at the age of 18, it was found that those who had remained in school gained approximately 10 IQ points when compared with those who had left. Further evidence in support of the effect of education on intelligence comes from studies of children who started school early. These children have been found to have higher IQs than those who started school late. A study of this kind carried out in Israel estimated that the effect of one additional year of schooling is an increase in verbal reasoning by about 5 IQ points and in non-verbal reasoning by about 2 IQ points (Cahan and Cohen, 1989). These and other studies suggesting a positive effect of schooling on intelligence have been reviewed by S.J. Ceci (1991).

There are two problems with these studies. The first is that the advantageous effect of education on intelligence may be only temporary and may fade out after a few years. The second is that education provides training and practice for the kinds of problems contained in intelligence tests, and that the increases may be confined to this type of intelligence rather than to intelligence that is more broadly considered as a general learning and problem solving ability. Several writers distinguish between increases in IQs, which are defined as the test scores that improve with education, and increases in intelligence, which may not improve. For instance, Ceci writes that "Although schooling helps prop up IQ scores, this is not equivalent to claiming that it props up intelligence" (Ceci, 1992, p. 8). Jensen (1998) and Mackintosh (1998) express similar reservations.

Although there may be some doubt about the extent to which education improves intelligence in the sense of general learning and problem-solving ability, the cognitive skills of literacy and numeracy imparted by education are likely to contribute to economic growth and development. In the least economically developed countries in the late 1990s, 50 percent of the adult population were illiterate, only 60 percent attended primary school, and only 31 percent attended secondary school (*Human Development Report*, 2000).

DYSGENIC FERTILITY

Many countries in sub-Saharan Africa experienced negative economic growth during the last three decades of the twentieth century. If this continues, nutrition, health, and education are likely to deteriorate and the intelligence of the populations is likely to decline. Apart from sub-Saharan Africa, most of the remainder of the economically developing world experienced positive economic growth during the second half of the twentieth century. This growth is likely to continue and to produce rising living standards. The impact of these should be that nutrition, health, and education should improve, and should raise the intelligence levels of the populations.

However, the advantageous effects of rising living standards for intelligence will be offset by dysgenic fertility. This consists of the tendency of the less intelligent to have greater numbers of children than the more intelligent. The intelligence of parents and children is highly correlated. The correlation between the average of the intelligence of the two parents and that of their children is .72 (Bouchard, 1993). Hence when the less intelligent have more children, the number of children with low intelligence increases and the average intelligence level of the population declines. Intelligence is determined both environmentally and genetically. Thus, the decline of the intelligence of a population that is experiencing dysgenic fertility is both environmental and genetic.

It has been shown that in the economically developed nations pronounced dysgenic fertility appeared in the last quarter of the nineteenth century and persisted throughout the twentieth century (Lynn, 1996a). During this time, fertility among the least educated and least intelligent women was two to three times greater than among the most educated. Over the course of the twentieth century, dysgenic fertility slackened, and by the second half of the twentieth century, fertility among the least educated was only around 10 to 20 percent higher than fertility among the most educated. Dysgenic fertility has been a feature of the demographic transition from high to low fertility, which began in France in the early nineteenth century and in the remainder of the economically developed nations in the second half of the nineteenth century. The demographic transition from large to small families invariably occurred first among the most highly educated and most intelligent. The reason for this is that the better educated and more intelligent were the first to use contraception, which began to be understood in the nineteenth century, particularly from the early 1870s when the latex condom was developed. In the later stages of the demographic transition, contraception became increasingly used by the less educated and the less intelligent, with the result that their fertility declined almost, although not quite, to the same level as that of the more educated and intelligent. The effect of this was that dysgenic fertility was greatly reduced, although it did not disappear entirely.

The economically developing countries are in the early stages of the demographic transition with high fertility among the least educated and lower fertility among the most educated. Some statistics illustrating these phenomena are given in Table 10.1. The table shows that in Brazil, the Dominican Republic, and Nicaragua fertility among women with secondary education in the late 1990s lay between 1.8 and 2.2, while among those with least education it lay between 5.0 and 6.1. Thus, the least educated were having two to three times the number of children of the most educated. It can be reasonably assumed that educational levels in these countries have been, to some degree, correlated with intelligence and hence that fertility in these countries was strongly dysgenic, like that in the United States, Britain, and other economically developed countries in the early stage of the demographic transition in the second half of the nineteenth century. This implies a genetic deterioration of the intelligence of the populations that is likely to last for two or three generations.

Table 10.1

Numbers of Children (Total Fertility Rates) of Women Aged 15–49 in Relation to Educational Level

Country	Educational Level			Dysgenic Ratio
	None	Primary	Secondary	
Brazil, 1996	5.0	3.3	1.8	2.8
Dominican Republic, 1996	5.0	2.9	2.2	2.3
Nicaragua, 1998	6.1	4.6	2.1	2.9
Sub-Saharan Africa, 1986–1992	6.6	6.0	4.3	1.5

Sources: For Brazil, *Studies in Family Planning*, 1998, 29, p. 88; For the Dominican Republic, *Studies in Family Planning*, 1998, 29, p. 428; For Nicaragua, *Studies in Family Planning*, 2000, 31, p. 178; For sub-Saharan Africa, Kirk and Pillet, 1998.

The figures in the table for sub-Saharan Africa are averages of surveys carried out in 21 countries over the years 1986 to 1992. These figures show that in sub-Saharan Africa the demographic transition was in a very early stage. Fertility was high among women of all levels of education, but it had begun to show a slight decline among women with secondary education. It can be anticipated that the demographic transition will continue in sub-Saharan Africa, developing first into a phase of strong dysgenic fertility and then into a second stage where dysgenic fertility slackens. This development is likely to take several generations.

The impact of dysgenic fertility in the economically developed nations has been around one to three IQ points per generation, depending on the size of the fertility differential in relation to intelligence. This effect can be illustrated for Brazil from the figures given in Table 10.1. If we assume that those with no education have an average IQ of 90, those with a primary education have an average IQ of 100, those with a secondary education an average IQ of 110, that there are equal numbers of the three educational classes, and that the average IQ of the children from each educational level is the same as that of their parents, then the parental generation will have an average IQ of 100, and the child generation an average IQ of 97.8, entailing a reduction of 2.2 IQ points in the intelligence level of the population for that generation. If this is repeated over four generations, there will be a loss of 8.8 IQ points. In the economically developed nations, dysgenic fertility has persisted for at least four generations, and it is likely to continue for an equally long period in the economically developing nations. This is likely to retard economic development in the economically developing nations during the course of the twenty-first century. The economically developed countries could help the economically developing countries in this regard by promoting an acceleration of the demographic transition through aid programs directed at the provision of contraception for the less educated.

PERSISTENCE OF NATIONAL DIFFERENCES IN MEAN IQs

In the previous sections, we consider several ways to increase the intelligence of the populations of poor nations. The quality of the nutrition of pregnant women and young children, the widespread malnutrition in underdeveloped countries, health, education, and dysgenic fertility all affect the intelligence of the populations. Thus, it would be possible to increase the level of intelligence in poor countries by providing healthy nutrition for pregnant women and young children. Rich countries could further such programs in poor countries by economic and educational aid. It is also probable that a number of diseases, which are more frequent in poor and especially tropical countries, impair intelligence. It would therefore be helpful for rich countries to increase their efforts to promote health care in poor countries.

Better health care would probably have some beneficial impact on the intelligence of the populations. Education as such may not improve intelligence in the sense of general learning and problem-solving ability, but it certainly helps to develop the available mental capabilities to carry out economic activities more effectively. It would be worthwhile to educate people at all levels of intelligence. Rich countries could further economic development in poor countries by supporting educational programs that are adapted to local conditions and needs. Finally, because dysgenic fertility is tending to reduce the intelligence of the populations of the poor countries, it would be advisable for the governments of poor countries as well as for rich countries to support programs designed to reduce dysgenic fertility.

These observations on various ways to increase intelligence in poor countries and by this means to promote economic development are consistent with many development aid programs already being carried out in developing countries. It would be advisable to continue these aid programs and to focus on programs that help to improve the intelligence of children in poor countries and to develop their available mental resources through education.

However, we must note that the probability of being able to increase significantly the intelligence of the populations of poor countries by any means of environmental and genetic interventions is quite limited for a number of reasons. The deficiencies in the nutrition of pregnant women reflect the poor quality of nutrition of the population in general. The same concerns the malnutrition of children in underdeveloped countries. Besides, population growth is so high in many poor countries that the large child populations and the widespread presence of hunger and disease retard economic growth. It is difficult to improve the quality of nutrition as long as the poor nations are unable to constrain their population growth. Rich countries could help to improve health care in poor countries and thus create better conditions for economic growth. However, if better health only increases population growth, it would not improve the quality of nutrition. Education, ultimately, may provide the best chances to solve the interrelated problems of population growth, poverty, and poor nutrition. Because the possibility of being able to increase the intelligence of the populations of poor countries by any of these means are quite limited, we have to accept the likely persistence of national differences in intelligence far into the future.

GENETIC BASIS OF NATIONAL DIFFERENCES IN INTELLIGENCE

We believe that national differences in intelligence have a substantial genetic basis. Differences in national IQs have evolved over many thousands of years as a result of adaptations of human populations to local geographical and climatic conditions. We do not know to what extent differences in national IQs are genetically determined, but it is quite probable that they are at least partly genetic. There are genetic differences between major geographical populations in many other characteristics including skin color, eye and hair color, body shape, teeth and eye shape, genetic diseases, and blood groups (see Cavalli-Sforza, Menozzi, and Piazza, 1996), so there is a presumption that the differences in average intelligence are also at least partly genetic. It is improbable that the genetic components of intelligence would have remained the same in all populations through tens of thousands of years, when so many other characteristics of the populations vary as a consequence of natural selection.

Detailed arguments for a genetic basis for national and racial differences in intelligence have been presented by Lynn (1991a, 1991b, 1997a), Jensen (1998), and Rushton (2000). The principal arguments are, first, that there are racial differences in the average size of the brain such that the Oriental populations of East Asia have the greatest brain size, European peoples have slightly smaller average brain size, and the peoples of sub-Saharan Africa have substantially smaller average brain size. There is a positive correlation between brain size and intelligence so the race difference in brain size suggests a genetic basis for the difference in intelligence. Second, black infants reared by white middle class adoptive parents in the United States show no improvement in intelligence, contrary to the prediction of environmental theory and consistent with a genetic explanation of the lower average IQ of Blacks. Third, Oriental infants reared by white Americans and Europeans have higher average IQs than whites.

The widely accepted explanation for the origin of these racial differences in intelligence is that humans evolved initially in tropical and semi-tropical Africa. Some groups migrated north into Eurasia where they encountered the problems of surviving during the cold winters, particularly the difficulties of keeping warm and hunting large animals to secure food during winter and spring when plant foods were unavailable. These problems exerted selection pressure for increased intelligence in the Oriental, Caucasian, and Native American peoples. This explains why peoples indigenous to temperate climates have higher average IQs than those indigenous to tropical and semi-tropical climates, and why they are more economically developed, which has frequently been observed (see Itzkoff, 2000).

The genetic factor in national IQs strengthens our thesis that national IQs are a causal factor responsible for the differences in economic development. The racial differences in intelligence that underlie the national differences in economic development and in the wealth and poverty of nations must have been present for thousands of years. The national differences in economic growth and development that have been quantified for the nineteenth and twentieth centuries are simply a continuation of the differences that first emerged some 5,000 years ago when the first civilizations were developed by the Oriental peoples in China and the Caucasian peoples in the Valleys of the Euphrates, Indus and Nile.

If differences in national IQs are genetically determined to a significant extent, as we believe, we have to conclude that it would not be possible to eradicate these differences by any environmental interventions or manipulations except possibly by massive eugenic measures that would not be practical. For this reason, it will be impossible to achieve economic equality between nations. It is more probable that, with further technological developments demanding high intelligence, international economic inequalities will increase even more in the future. Perhaps ultimately, with continued immigration of third world peoples into economically developed nations, there may be such a large amount of biological mixing of racial groups that national differences in intelligence may be reduced and or may even lead to the disappearance of the present differences in national IQs, but such a process would take a long time. Thus, our conclusion is that we must accept that the world is divided into rich and poor countries and that the gap between them is partly based on genetic differences in intelligence, which will make it impossible to equalize economic conditions in different parts of the world.

The prospects for rapid economic growth are best in countries with large negative residuals, because the negative residuals indicate that a country's level of per capita national income is much lower than expected on the basis of its population's average level of intelligence. Consequently, the human potential for economic growth is now greatest in the European and East Asian countries with large negative residuals, whereas the potential for growth is poorest in the countries of sub-Saharan Africa where intelligence levels are lowest.

Nevertheless, the results of our regression analyses, which showed that many countries deviate substantially from the regression of economic development on national intelligence, imply that there are several other important factors affecting economic development. Consequently, the actual level of economic development varies significantly around the regression line, especially at higher levels of national IQ. We found that approximately 50 to 60 percent of the variation in per capita income and economic growth rates seems to be due to those other factors, which may include systematic, local, and random factors. The major systematic factor affecting national rates of economic growth and development, apart from intelligence, appears to be the extent to which countries have market economies. It would be easier for poor countries to introduce market economies than to raise the intelligence levels of their populations. In practical terms, this would be the most promising way of accelerating the economic development of many poor nations without market economies. In addition, democratization would also be desirable because there is a strong relationship between democracy and market economies.

CONCLUSIONS: HOW SHOULD WE LIVE WITH PERSISTENT INEQUALITIES?

Hitherto theories of economic development have been based on the presumption that the present gaps between rich and poor countries are only temporary and that they are due to various environmental conditions and factors, which could be changed by aid from rich countries to poor countries and by the poor countries adopting appropriate institutions and policies. It has also been assumed that all human populations have equal mental abilities to adopt modern technologies and to achieve an equal level of economic development.

We have to conclude that this presumption is fundamentally mistaken. Because of the evidence we have assembled for a causal relationship between national IQs and economic disparities, it has to be accepted that there will inevitably be a continuation of economic inequalities between nations. Intelligence differences between nations will be impossible to eradicate because they have a genetic basis and have evolved over the course of tens of thousands of years. The results of our analyses show that the strong correlation between national IQs and per capita income has persisted at least since 1820. This gap between rich and poor countries will remain and may well become larger rather than decrease. Consequently, the problem is how to deal with this persistent gap and how to promote tolerable relations between cognitively and economically unequal nations.

Despite the conclusions that the gap between rich and poor nations will inevitably persist for the indefinite future, the results of our analyses also indicate that various other factors affect the wealth and poverty of nations and that some of these factors can be manipulated to improve the economic prospects of the poorer nations. Social, economic, and political engineering provide the means for reducing economic disparities. This will be accomplished most easily between countries for which the mean national IQs are approximately the same. The best chances for strong economic growth are for countries with large negative residuals, which indicate that the country has not fully utilized its population's mental abilities. Such is the case with the former and present socialist nations of eastern Europe and eastern Asia, which can be expected to catch up with the rich nations once they have adopted market economies and have achieved political stability. It will be more difficult for countries with national IQs below 90 and below the regression line to raise their per capita incomes significantly higher than expected on the basis of national IQ. Until now, this has been possible only with the help of large foreign investments.

The two most important implications of our study are these. First, the world needs a new international moral code based on the recognition of significant national differences in human mental abilities and consequent economic inequalities. The populations of the rich countries may have to accept that they have an ethical obligation to provide financial assistance to the peoples of the poor countries for the indefinite future, just as within countries the rich accept that they have an ethical obligation to pay taxes to support the poor. Second, the rich countries' economic aid programs for the poor countries should be continued and some of these should be directed at attempting to increase the intelligence levels of the populations of the poorer countries by improvements in nutrition and the like. The recognition that differences in intelligence are a major cause of national economic disparities should make it possible to reduce the differences in the wealth of nations.

Appendix 1

The Calculation of
National Intelligence Levels

Most intelligence tests have been constructed in Britain and the United States and have subsequently been administered to samples of the populations in many other countries throughout the world. From these studies, it is possible to calculate the mean IQs of the populations of 81 nations. In making these calculations, the mean IQ in Britain is set at 100 with a standard deviation of 15 and the mean IQs of other nations is calculated in relation to this yardstick. A factor that needs to be taken into account in making these calculations is that the mean IQs in economically developed nations have been increasing since the 1930s. An adjustment needs to be made for this increase when calculating the mean IQs obtained in countries from tests that were administered some years before or some years later than the British test with which it is being compared. In the case of the Standard Progressive Matrices test, which has been administered in many countries and which we use extensively for the calculation of national IQs, the British mean IQ increased at a rate of approximately 2 IQ points per decade from 1938, when the test was constructed, up to 1979, when the last British standardization on children was carried out (Lynn and Hampson, 1986; Flynn, 1987). Mean IQs on the Wechsler tests increased by approximately 3 IQ points per decade from the mid-1930s to the 1990s (Flynn, 1984, 1998). Where these tests have been used, adjustments for the secular rise of IQs have been made. There are a few studies that have employed tests for which the rate of secular increase in the means is not known. In these cases, we have assumed an increase of 2 IQ points per decade. When the date at which a standardization was carried out is not given, it is assumed to have taken place two years before the date of publication. A problem in estimating some national IQs is that the samples have scored below the first percentile in relation to British norms. The first percentile is equivalent to an IQ of 65. Where national samples have scored below the first percentile, they have been assigned an IQ of 64.

For a number of countries there is more than one study of the national IQ. In these cases, we have averaged the results giving equal weight to each study. These IQs have been calculated and averaged to the nearest whole number.

Argentina

The Progressive Matrices Test was standardized on a sample of 1,680 9- to 15-year-olds over the years of 1942–1946 by Rimoldi (1948). The mean IQ in relation to the British 1979 standardization sample was 86. Adjusting for the 35-year time interval between the two standardizations brings the Argentine IQ up to 93.

Norms for the Coloured Progressive Matrices were collected in 1993 for a sample of 420 5- to 11-year-olds. The data are given by Raven, Raven, and Court (1998). In relation to the 1979 standardization of the British Standard Progressive Matrices, the sample obtained a mean IQ of 101. Due to the 14-year interval between the two standardizations, this figure needs to be reduced to 98.

The average of the two results gives an IQ of 96 for Argentina.

Australia

Norms for the American Otis Test were collected about 1936 by McIntyre (1938) on a sample of 35,000 9- to 13-year-olds. The IQ was 95. Because the American Otis Test was standardized in the United States on whites, this needs to be raised to 97.

Norms for the Coloured Progressive Matrices were collected in 1980 for a sample of 5- to 10-year-olds. The data are given by Raven, Court, and Raven (1995). The mean IQ is 98.

Norms for the Standard Progressive Matrices for 8- to 17-year-olds for 1986 are given by Raven, Court, and Raven (1996). In relation to the 1979 British standardization sample, the mean IQ is 100.5. Because of the 7-year interval between the two standardizations, this needs to be reduced to 99.

The average of the three studies gives an IQ of 98 for Australia.

Austria

In 1981, the German psychologist, Vinko Buj (1981), published the results of a study in which Cattell's Culture Fair Test was given to representative samples of adults in 21 major European cities and also in Akkra, the capital of Ghana. In this study, the British IQ was 102. Hence the mean IQs in other countries have to be reduced by 2 IQ points to calibrate them to a British IQ of 100. In the case of Austria, the sample of 187 individuals obtained an IQ of 103. To calibrate this IQ against a British IQ of 100, this figure needs to be reduced to 101.

Data for the Standard Progressive Matrices for a sample of 67 13-year-old children tested around 1969 have been reported by Moyles and Wolins (1973). In relation to the 1979 British standardization sample, these children obtained an IQ of 101. Due to the 10-year interval between the two years of data collection, this needs to be raised to 103.

The average of the two results gives an IQ of 102 for Austria.

Barbados

Data for a sample of 108 9- to 15-year-olds were collected for the WISC-R by Geller, Ramsey, and Forde (1986) around the year of 1984. They obtained an IQ of 82. Because of the 12-year interval between the two years of data collection, this needs to be reduced to 78.

Belgium

The Coloured Progressive Matrices was standardized in Belgium by Goosens (1952a) on a sample of 944 7- to 13-year-olds. In relation to the 1979 British standardization of the Progressive Matrices, they obtained a mean IQ of 93. Because of the interval of approximately 30 years between the two standardizations, the Belgian IQ needs to be raised to 99.

The Cattell Culture Fair Test was standardized about 1950 on a sample of 920 10- to 16-year-olds by Goosens (1952b). The mean IQ was 104. To equate this IQ to a British IQ of 100, this needs to be reduced to 103.

Buj's sample of 247 obtained a mean IQ of 100. To calibrate this IQ against a British IQ of 100, this figure needs to be reduced to 98. The average of the three studies gives an IQ of 100 for Belgium.

Brazil

Around 1966, data for the Standard Progressive Matrices were collected for a sample of 160 14-year-olds by Natalicio (1968). In relation to the British 1979 standardization sample, the IQ was 85.5. To adjust for the 13-year interval between the two years of data collection, this needs to be raised to 88.

The Coloured Progressive Matrices was standardized on a sample of 505 7- to 11-year-olds in 1966, on a sample of 1,131 5- to 11-year-olds in 1982, and on a sample of 1,547 5- to 11-year-olds in 1988. The results of the three data sets are given by Angelini, Alves, Custodio, and Duarte (1988).

In relation to the British norms for the 1979 Standard Progressive Matrices and adjusting for the intervals between the standardizations, the Brazilian children obtained IQs of 84, 90, and 85.

The average of the four results gives an IQ of 87 for Brazil.

Bulgaria

Buj (1981) tested 215 adults with the Culture Fair Test and obtained a mean IQ of 96. This needs to be reduced to 94 to calibrate it against a British mean of 100.

A further standardization of the Cattell Culture Fair Test was carried out in Bulgaria in 1982 and the results were reported by Lynn, Paspalanova, Stetinsky, and Tzenova (1998). The sample consisted of 1,456 11- to 17-year-olds and the mean IQ was 95. This version of the Culture Fair Test was standardized in the United States in 1972, so for the 10-year interval between the two standardizations, the Bulgarian IQ needs to be reduced to 92. To equate this figure with a British IQ of 100, one IQ point needs to be subtracted, bringing the figure to 91. Averaging the two studies gives an IQ of 93 for Bulgaria.

Canada

In 1979, norms for the Standard Progressive Matrices were collected in Canada for a sample of 313 7- to 12-year-olds. The data are given by Raven, Court, and Raven (1996). The mean IQ of the sample is 97.

China

In 1986, norms for the Standard Progressive Matrices were collected in China for a sample of 5,108 5- to 16-year-olds and 18- to 80-year-olds by Zhang. The data are given by Raven, Court, and Raven (1996). For the 5- to 16-year-olds, the mean IQ in relation to the 1979 British standardization sample is 101. Because of the 7-year interval between the two standardizations, this needs to be reduced to 100. For the 18- to 70-year-olds, there are no detailed British norms with which the sample can be compared. Detailed adult American norms are provided by Raven, Court, and Raven (1996) for the year of 1993. These results can be used because the American IQ is 99 in relation to a British IQ of 100. In relation to the American norms, the Chinese sample obtained a mean IQ of 91.5 and in relation to British norms the sample obtained an IQ of 90.5. Because of the 9-year time interval between the two standardizations, this needs to be raised to 92.5. The average of the two data sets is 97.

In 1984, the WISC-R was standardized in China on a sample of 660 6- to 16-year-olds in Shanghai by Li, Jin, Vandenberg, Zhu, and Tang (1990). In relation to the American norms, the Chinese obtained an IQ of 112.4.

Because of the 10-year interval between the two standardizations, this needs to be reduced to 109.4. To equate this to a British IQ of 100, this figure needs to be reduced further to 107.4. This sample drawn from Shanghai almost certainly had a higher IQ than that in China as a whole. To adjust for this, we have arbitrarily reduced it by 6 IQ points to give a figure of 103.4.

A study by Li, Sano, and Merwin (1996) compared samples of 297 Chinese and 318 American 14- to 15-year-olds. The Chinese were at schools in and around Beijing and the Americans were at schools in Minneapolis and St. Paul. Six tests were given consisting of verbal and non-verbal reasoning, spatial visualization and spatial rotation, perceptual speed, and arithmetic. On the two reasoning tests combined, the Chinese children obtained an IQ of 103 in relation to an American mean of 100. As noted in our comments on the Stevenson *et al.* study in Japan, the IQ in Minneapolis is 5 IQ points higher than in the United States as a whole. However, the Chinese sample drawn from the Beijing schools probably had a higher IQ than that in China as a whole, so we have not made any adjustment for this.

The average of the three studies from China gives an IQ of 100.

Colombia

Results for a sample of 50 13- to 16-year-old white boys attending public schools in the city of Medellin were tested with the Spanish WISC-R around 1998 by Ardila, Pineda, and Rosselli (2000). Their IQ was found to be 98. The Spanish IQ was standardized in Spain in 1991, so to adjust for the 7-year interval between the two data collections, the Colombian IQ needs to be reduced to 96. In relation to a British IQ of 100, the Spanish IQ is 99 (see under Spain). Hence, in relation to a British IQ of 100, the IQ of whites in Colombia is estimated to be 95.

The population of Colombia is 20 percent white, 75 percent Native American and Mestizo, and 5 percent black (*Philip's World Atlas*, 1996). IQs assigned to these groups are 95 for whites, 89 for Native American and Mestizo (as found in Peru, see also under Mexico), and 72 for blacks (as found in Jamaica; see also under Africa). Weighting these IQs by the percentages in the population gives an IQ of 89 for Colombia.

Congo (Brazzaville)

Around 1950, normative data for the Standard Progressive Matrices was collected for a sample of 320 17- to 29-year-olds by Ombredane, Robaye, and Robaye (1952). The mean score was well below the first percentile of the detailed American norms for 1993 given by Raven, Court, and Raven (1996). This sample is therefore assigned an IQ of 64. Because of the 43-year interval between the two years of the data collection, this figure is raised to 73.

Data for a sample of 88 13-year-olds at school in Brazzaville tested with the Standard Progressive Matrices around 1992 have been reported by Nkaya, Huteau, and Bonnet (1994). In relation to the 1979 British standardization, their mean IQ is 75. Allowing for the 13-year interval between the two standardizations reduces this figure to 72. The average of the two results gives an IQ of 73 for the Congo (Brazzaville).

Congo (Zaire)

Data for the Progressive Matrices for a sample of 222 10- to 15-year-olds in Katanga have been reported by Laroche (1959). Their scores were below the 1st percentile of the British 1979 standardization sample, and they have been assigned an IQ of 64. Because of the 20 years between the two years of data collection, this figure has been raised to 68.

Boivin and his colleagues have reported three studies in which the Kaufman Assessment Battery for Children (K-ABC) was administered to children. In the first study, 47 children aged 8 took the test around 1991 and obtained a mean IQ of 65 (Boivin and Giordani, 1993). The K-ABC was standardised in the United States in 1982. This test is similar to the Wechsler tests, and we assume a similar rate of secular increase of 3 IQ points per decade. To adjust for the 9-year interval between the standardization of the K-ABC and the administration of the test in Zaire, the mean of the Zaire sample needs to be reduced by 3 IQ points to 62. In the second study, a sample of 95 7- to 12-year-old children were tested around 1993 and obtained a mean IQ of 71 (Boivin, Giordani, and Bornefeld, 1995). Because of the 10-year interval between the two sets of data, this needs to be reduced to 68. In the third study, a sample of 130 7- to 9-year-olds were tested around 1994 and obtained an IQ of 68 (Giordani, Boivin, Opel, Nseyila, and Lauer, 1996). The 12-year interval between the two data sets requires the reduction of this figure to 65.

The average of the three results is an average IQ for Congo (Zaire) of 65.

Croatia

Around 1952, norms for the Standard Progressive Matrices were collected for a sample of 299 13- to 16-year-olds by Sorokin (1954). In relation to the 1979 British standardization sample, their IQ was 84.5. Because of the 27-year interval between the two standardizations, this needs to be raised to 90.

Cuba

Around 1971, norms for the Standard Progressive Matrices were collected for a sample of 1,144 12- to 18-year-olds by Alonso (1974). In relation to the 1979 British standardization sample, their IQ was 83. To adjust for the 8-year interval between the two standardizations, this needs to be raised to 85.

Czech Republic

Buj's (1981) study of 363 adults tested with the Cattell Culture Fair Test and obtained an IQ of 100. To calibrate this figure against a British IQ of 100, it needs to be reduced to 98.

In 1983, the Coloured Progressive Matrices Test was standardized on a sample of 832 5- to 11-year-olds and the data is provided by Raven, Court, and Raven (1995). In relation to the 1979 British standardization of the Progressive Matrices, the mean IQ is 97. Adjusting for the 4-year time interval between the two standardizations brings the Czech IQ to 96.

The average of the two results gives an IQ of 97 for the Czech Republic.

Denmark

Around 1966, norms for the Standard Progressive Matrices were obtained on a sample of 628 12-year-old children by Vejleskov (1968). In relation to the British 1979 standardization sample, these children obtained a mean IQ of 94. Because of the 13-year interval between the two standardizations, this needs to be raised to 97.

In Buj's (1981) study on 122 adults tested with the Cattell Culture Fair Test, the IQ was 101. To calibrate this figure to a British IQ of 100, it needs to be reduced to 99. The average of the two studies gives an IQ of 98 for Denmark.

Ecuador

Normative data have been collected for the Matrix Analogies Test for a sample of 104 5- to 17-year-olds by Proctor, Kranzler, Rosenbloom, Martinez, and Guevara-Aguire (2000). Their IQ in relation to American Norms was 85. To adjust for the 15-year time period between the two years of data collection, this figure must be reduced to 82. To equate this figure to a British IQ of 100, it needs to be reduced to 80.

Egypt

Data for the Standard Progressive Matrices for a sample of 129 6- to 12-year-olds have been reported by Ahmed (1989). In relation to the 1979 British standardization sample, their IQ was 85. Because of the 12-year interval between the two dates of data collection, this needs to be reduced to 83.

Equatorial Guinea

Around 1984, data for 48 10- to 14-year-olds were collected on the WISC-R (Fernandez-Ballesteros, Juan-Espinoza, Colom, and Calero (1997)). Their IQ was 63. Because of the 12-year interval between the two data collections, this needs to be reduced to 59.

Ethiopia

Around 1989, data for a sample of 250 15-year-old Ethiopian immigrants to Israel tested with the Standard Progressive Matrices have been reported by Kaniel and Fisherman (1991). In relation to the 1979 British standardization sample, their mean IQ was 65. Because of the 10-year interval between the two collections of data, this needs to be reduced to 63.

Fiji

The population of Fiji is comprised of native Fijians and Indians in approximately equal numbers. Normative data for a sample of 12-year-olds for 76 Fijians and 140 Indians who were tested with the Australian Queensland Test have been published by Chandra (1975). In relation to white Australian children, both ethnic groups in Fiji obtained an IQ of 85. In 1968, the Queensland Test was standardized and the data from Fiji were collected about 1973. To adjust for the 5-year interval between the two years of data collection, the Fijian IQ needs to be reduced to 84.

Finland

In 1970, norms for the Coloured Progressive Matrices were collected by Kyöstiö (1972) for a sample of 755 7-year-olds drawn from various locations. In relation to the 1979 British standardization, their IQ was 96. Because of the 10-year interval between the two data collections, this needs to be raised to 98.

In Buj's (1981) study in Finland, 120 adults were tested with the Cattell Culture Fair Test and their IQ was 98. To calibrate this figure to a British IQ of 100, this needs to be reduced to 96. The average of the two results gives an IQ of 97 for Finland.

France

Around 1962, the Coloured Progressive Matrices Test was standardized in France by Bourdier (1964) on a sample of 618 6- to 9-year-olds. Their mean IQ was 93.5 in relation to the 1979 British standardization of the Standard Progressive Matrices. Because of the 15-year time interval between the two standardizations, this needs to be increased to 96.5.

Around 1962, the Columbia Mental Maturity Scale was standardized in France on a sample of 328 6- to 11-year-olds by Dague, Garelli, and Lebettre (1964). In relation to the American IQ of 100, the IQ of the French children was 103.5. To adjust for the 3-year interval between the two standardizations, the French IQ needs to be reduced to 102.5

Buj's sample of 1,320 adults obtained a mean IQ of 96 on the Culture Fair Test. Calibration against a British mean IQ of 100 requires the reduction of this figure to 94. The average of the three results gives an IQ of 98 for France.

Germany

Buj's (1981) sample of 1,572 adults in West Germany (the Federal Republic, as it was called at that time) were tested with the Cattell Culture Fair test and obtained a mean IQ of 109. To calibrate this figure against a British mean of 100, it needs to be reduced to 107.

Around 1970, the Coloured Progressive Matrices Test was standardized in West Germany by Winkelman (1972) on a sample of 563 5- to 7-year-olds. The mean IQ in relation to the British standardization sample of the Standard Progressive Matrices is 97. Because of the 9-year interval between the two standardizations, this figure needs to be raised to 99.

In 1978, the Coloured Progressive Matrices Test was standardized again in West Germany on a sample of 3,607 6- to 10-year-olds. The norms are given by Raven, Court, and Raven (1995). In relation to the 1979 British standardization sample of the Standard Progressive Matrices, the IQ of the German sample is 101.

In 1978, norms for the Standard Progressive Matrices were collected for a sample of 2,068 11- to 15-year-olds in West Germany. The data are given by Raven (1981). In relation to the 1979 British standardization sample, the IQ was 105.

Three studies have been made of intelligence in East Germany. In 1967, the Coloured Progressive Matrices Test was standardized in the city of Rostock by Kurth (1969) on a sample of 454 7- to 11-year-olds. Their mean IQ in relation to the 1979 British standardization sample of the Progressive Matrices is 87. Because of the 12-year interval between the two standardizations, this figure needs to be raised to 90.

In 1984, further norms for East Germany were obtained by Guthke and the data are given by Raven, Court, and Raven (1995). The mean IQ of the sample in relation to the 1979 British standardization of the Standard Progressive Matrices is 98. To adjust for the 5-year interval between the two standardizations, this figure needs to be reduced to 97.

Around 1978, norms for the Standard Progressive Matrices were obtained for approximately 1,000 11- to 15-year-olds by Mehlhorn. The data are given by Raven (1981). In relation to the 1979 British standardization sample, their IQ is 99.

The average of the results for West Germany is an IQ of 103 and for East Germany an IQ of 95. For united Germany, weighting these figures by the numbers of the populations of West and East (59.5 million and 16.6 million, respectively), the IQ of united Germany is 102.

Ghana

In the study by Buj (1981), 225 adults in Akkra were tested with the Cattell Culture Fair Test and obtained an IQ of 82. Calibrating this against a British IQ of 100 reduces this figure to 80.

Around 1990, normative data for the Coloured Progressive Matrices was collected for a representative sample of 1,639 adolescents with an average age of 15 by Glewwe and Jacoby (1992). Their mean score corresponded to the zero percentile on the 1979 British standardization sample of the Standard Progressive Matrices and they had an IQ of 64. Because of the 11-year interval between the two standardizations, this needs to be reduced to 62. The average of the two results gives an IQ of 71 for Ghana.

Greece

Around 1961, norms for the Wechsler Intelligence Scale for Children (WISC) were collected for a sample of 400 9- to 14-year-olds by Fatouros (1972). The mean IQ was 91. Because the WISC was standardized on white children, this figure needs to be raised to 93. Adjusting for the interval between the two data collections, this has to be reduced to 88.

The sample of 220 adults tested on the Cattell Culture Fair Test by Buj (1981) obtained an IQ of 97. To calibrate this figure against a British IQ of 100, this needs to be reduced to 95. The average of the two results gives an IQ of 92 for Greece.

Guatemala

Norms have been reported by Johnson, Johnson, and Price-Williams (1967) for the Draw-a-Man Test for a sample of 256 children who were tested around 1965. Their mean IQ was 85. The mean IQ for white American children obtained by Sundberg and Ballinger (1968) at this time was 105. To equate the result to a British IQ of 100, the IQ for Guatemala becomes 79.

Guinea

Around 1933, a sample of 50 village children aged 5- to 14 years was tested with the American Army Performance Scale by Nissen, Machover, and Kinder (1935). Their IQ in relation to the American norms was 61.

A sample of 1,144 young men at technical training centers were tested with the Standard Progressive Matrices in 1951–1955 by Latouche and Dormeau. The results are given by Faverge and Falmagne (1962). The average scores were well below the first percentile of the 15-year-olds in the 1979 British standardization sample and of 18- to 22-year-olds on the 1993 American standardization sample. The sample is assigned an IQ of 64. To adjust for the 40 years between the two data collections, the IQ is raised to 70 in relation to a British IQ of 100.

The average of the two results gives an IQ of 66 for Guinea.

Hong Kong

In 1968, data for a sample of 13,822 6- to 13-year-olds who were tested with the Standard Progressive Matrices in 1968 were published by Lynn, Pagliari, and Chan (1988). In relation to the 1979 British standardization sample, their mean IQ was 101.3. In order to adjust for the 11-year interval between the two standardizations, this figure has to be raised to 103.4.

In 1982, a further sample of 4,500 6- to 15-year-olds was tested with the Standard Progressive Matrices. In relation to the 1979 British standardization sample, their mean IQ was 110.4. In order to adjust for the 3-year interval between the two standardizations, this figure needs to be reduced to 110.

Data for a sample of 4,858 6-year-olds who were tested with the Coloured Progressive Matrices during 1981–1984 have been published by Chan and Lynn (1989). In relation to the British 1979 standardization sample, their IQ was 110. Because of the 4-year interval between the two data collections, this needs to be reduced to 109.

A small sample of 197 10-year-olds was tested with the Progressive Matrices in 1986 (Lynn, Pagliari, and Chan, 1988). In relation to the 1979 British standardization sample, their IQ was 108. Because of the 7-year interval between the two years of data collection, this needs to be reduced to 107.

In 1986, a sample of 376 9-year-olds was tested with the Cattell Culture Fair Test (Lynn, Hampson, and Lee, 1988). Their IQ was 113. This version of the Culture Fair Test was standardized in the United States in 1972, so to adjust for the 14-year interval between the two standardizations, the IQ for Hong Kong needs to be reduced to 107.

The average of the five studies gives an IQ of 107 for Hong Kong.

Hungary

The sample of 260 adults tested with the Cattell Culture Fair Test by Buj (1981) obtained an IQ of 101. To calibrate this figure against a British IQ of 100, this needs to be reduced to 99.

India

Sinha (1968) summarizes the results of nine studies providing normative data for the Coloured Progressive Matrices for India for a total of 5,607 9- to 15-year-olds. The Indian samples were drawn from Ahmedabad, Trivandrum, Patna, Allahabad, Uttar Pradesh, Cuttack, and Tiru. In relation to the 1979 British standardization sample of the Progressive Matrices, the children of India obtained a mean IQ of 77. There is a time interval of approximately 20 years between the collection of the data in India and Britain, which requires raising the Indian IQ to 81.

A further standardization of the Coloured Progressive Matrices in India was carried out by Rao and Reddy (1968) on a sample of 1,050 5- to 10-year-olds in urban and rural locations in Andhra Pradesh. The mean IQ in relation to the 1979 British standardization of the Progressive Matrices was 80. Adjusting for the 11 years between the two standardizations raises the Indian IQ to 82.

In 1992, norms were collected for the Standard Progressive Matrices for a sample of 569 11- to 15-year-olds in Delhi. The data are given by Raven, Court, and Raven (1996). In relation to the 1979 British standardization sample, the mean IQ is 84. To adjust for the 13-year interval between the two standardizations, this needs to be reduced to 82.

Data for 748 children aged 9 to 12 years old who were tested with the WISC-R have been reported by Afzal (1988). Their mean IQ was 82. Because of the 14-year interval between the standardization of the test and the collection of the data, this needs to be reduced to 78.

The average of the four data sets gives an IQ of 81 for India.

Indonesia

Data for the Draw-a-Man test were collected by Thomas and Sjah (1961) from school children in the city of Bandung. In relation to the 1926 American norms, their IQ was 96. To adjust for the 33 years between the two years of data collection, this figure has been reduced to 89.

Iran

Around 1957, norms for the Standard Progressive Matrices were collected by Valentine (1959) for 627 adolescents aged approximately 15 years old. Their mean IQ in relation to the British 1979 standardization sample is 80. Due to the interval of 22 years between the two standardization samples, this needs to be raised to 84.

Iraq

Around 1968, the Progressive Matrices was standardized in Iraq by Abul-Hubb (1972) on a sample of 204 14- to 17-year-olds and 1,185 adults aged 18- to 35. The mean IQ of the 14- to 17-year-olds in relation to the British 1979 standardization sample is 85. Due to the 10-year interval between the two standardization samples, this needs to be raised to 87. There are no detailed percentile British norms for adults for the Progressive Matrices, but they are given for the United States for the year of 1993 by Raven, Court, and Raven (1996). In relation to these, the mean IQ of the Iraq sample of adults is 85. Because of the 25-year interval between the two standardizations, this needs to be raised to 89. In relation to a British IQ of 100, this needs to be reduced to 87. Averaging the two results gives a mean IQ of 87 for Iraq.

Ireland

In 1972, norms for the Standard Progressive Matrices were obtained for a sample of 3,466 6- to 13-year-olds. The data are given by Raven (1981). In relation to the 1979 British standardization sample, the Irish children obtained a mean IQ of 86. Because the Irish data were collected seven years earlier, this needs to be raised to 87.

In Buj's (1981) study, 75 Adults obtained an IQ of 100 on the Cattell Culture Fair Test. To calibrate this figure against a British IQ of 100, this needs to be reduced to 98. The average of the two studies gives an IQ of 93 for Ireland.

Israel

Around 1975, norms for the American Lorge-Thorndike Test were collected for 180 10- to 12-year-olds by Miron (1977). The mean IQ was 100. In order to adjust for the 11-year interval between the two standardizations, this needs to be reduced to 98. In relation to a British IQ of 100, this needs to be reduced by one further point to 97.

Around 1989, data for the Standard Progressive Matrices for 1,740 9- to 15-year-olds were collected by Kaniel and Fisherman (1991). In relation to the British 1979 standardization sample, their IQ was 92. To adjust for the 10-year interval between the two years of data collection, this needs to be reduced to 90.

The average of the results gives an IQ of 94 for Israel.

Italy

Around 1960, norms for the Standard Progressive Matrices were obtained on a sample of 2,432 11- to 16-year-olds by Tesi and Boutourline Young (1962). In relation to the 1979 British standardization norms, the sample obtained an IQ of 99. Because of the 19-year interval between the two standardizations, this needs to be raised to 103.

The sample of 1,380 adults tested with the Culture Fair Test by Buj (1981) obtained an IQ of 103. To calibrate this figure against a British IQ of 100, this needs to be reduced to 101. The average of the two results gives an IQ of 102 for Italy.

Jamaica

In 1961, data for a sample of 1,730 11-year-olds tested with the British Moray House Test were published by Manley (1963). The IQ was 72, in relation to a British mean of 100.

Japan

The first calculation of the IQ in Japan appeared in Lynn (1977a). This paper presented a calculation of the Japanese IQ obtained from the Japanese standardization of the Wechsler Intelligence Scale for Children (WISC). The WISC was standardized in the United States in 1947 and in Japan in 1951. The verbal tests were altered in the Japanese standardization so they could not be used for a comparison, but the performance tests remained the same. On these tests, the Japanese standardization sample obtained an IQ of 103. Because the Japanese standardization was made four years after the American standardization, one IQ point has to be subtracted to give a Japanese IQ of 102. The American standardization was made on whites only, so in relation to the whole American population the Japanese IQ becomes 104. The American IQ in relation to the British IQ of 100 is 98 (see under United States). Thus, in relation to a British IQ of 100, the Japanese IQ becomes 102.

In 1980, a new method for calculating the Japanese IQ was devised (Lynn and Dziobon, 1980). This entailed the administration of the Japanese Kyoto NX test and the American Primary Mental Abilities to a sample of 213 9- to 10-year-olds in Northern Ireland and calibrating the Kyoto test against the American test. The result was that the average Japanese child, with an IQ of 100, obtained an IQ of 110 on the American test, and therefore that the Japanese had an average IQ of 110. Because the Japanese test was standardized in 1972 and the American test was standardized in 1962, adjustment for the 10-year interval between the two standardizations requires the reduction of the Japanese IQ to 108, and to calibrate the Japanese IQ against the British IQ of 100 requires a further reduction to 106.

The next study of the Japanese IQ was made by Misawa, Motegi, Fujita, and Hattori (1984), who analyzed the performance of Japanese children on the American test, the Columbia Mental Maturity Scale. This is a non-verbal reasoning test for 4- to 9-year-olds that was first published in 1954. A revised version and standardization appeared in 1972 and this version was standardized in Japan on a sample of 780 around 1980. The calculation of the Japanese IQ on the test in relation to the American norms shows that the Japanese attained an IQ of 113. Because of the 8-year interval between the two standardizations, this needs to be reduced to 111. To calibrate this IQ against a British IQ of 100, it needs to be reduced further to 109.

In 1985, Stevenson, Stigler, Lee, Lucker, Kitanawa, and Hsu (1985) published a study comparing the IQs of 240 6-year-olds and 240 10-year-olds in the American city of Minneapolis and the Japanese city of Sendai. They constructed their own test consisting of a number of subtests of various abilities. These tests did not include a test of non-verbal reasoning ability such as the Progressive Matrices. It did include a vocabulary test and a spatial test. The results were that in relation to the American children, the Japanese 6-year-olds obtained IQs of 89 on vocabulary and 105 on the spatial test, which can be averaged to 97 for a measure of general intelligence, and the Japanese 11-year-olds obtained IQs of 98 on vocabulary and 107 on the spatial test, which can be averaged to 102. Combining the two results gives a Japanese IQ of 100. This result led Stevenson and his colleagues to conclude that there is no difference between the IQ in Japan and the United States. This study is defective because Minneapolis is not representative for intelligence of American cities. A series of studies have shown that intelligence in the state of Minnesota, in which Minneapolis is situated, is higher than in the United States as a whole. In the military draft in World War I, whites from Minnesota obtained the highest score on the Army Beta Test out of all American states (Ashley Montagu, 1945) (the scores of blacks are not given). In the draft for the Vietnam war, the percentage of draftees (blacks and whites) who failed the pre-induction mental assessments was the second lowest in Minnesota among the American states (Office of the Surgeon General, 1968, p. 45). On the basis of these data, Flynn (1980) has calculated that the average IQ in Minnesota is 105. Thus, in order to equate the Japanese IQ to that of the United States, five IQ points need to be added to the mean of 100 found by Stevenson *et al.*, bringing the IQ to 105. To equate this to a British IQ of 100, one IQ point needs to be subtracted, giving an IQ of approximately 104.

An analysis of the Japanese IQ in terms of the American WISC-R has been made by Lynn and Hampson (1986a). On the Japanese standardization of this test on 1,100 6- to 16-year-olds, the Japanese obtained an IQ of 105. The American test was standardized in 1972 and the Japanese test in 1975, requiring the subtraction of one IQ point from the Japanese mean. To calibrate this figure against a British mean of 100 requires the subtraction of a further 1 point, bringing the Japanese mean to 102.

An analysis of the Japanese IQ in terms of the McCarthy Test has been made by Lynn and Hampson (1986b). The McCarthy Test is for children between the ages of 2.5 to 8.5 years. It was standardized in the United States in 1971 and in Japan in 1975 on a sample of 550 children. In relation to the American standardization sample, the Japanese obtained a mean IQ of 101.7. To adjust for the 4-year interval between the two standardizations, the Japanese mean needs to be reduced to approximately 101. To equate this figure to a British mean of 100, two IQ points need to be subtracted to give a Japanese IQ of 99. This figure is probably lower than the other calculations because half of the test is for young children aged 2.5 to 5.5 years, during which the Japanese children perform poorly when compared with the older age group, suggesting that Japanese children are slow developers during early childhood.

An analysis of the Japanese standardization sample of 600 on the American Wechsler Preschool and Primary Scale, an intelligence test designed for 4- to 6-year-olds, has been made by Lynn and Hampson (1987). Their mean IQ was 107.8. The American test was standardized in 1964 and the Japanese test in 1967. To adjust for the 3-year interval between the two standardizations, the Japanese mean needs to be reduced to 107. To equate this figure to a British mean of 100, two points need to be subtracted, giving a Japanese IQ of 105.

Data for the Standard Progressive Matrices of 444 Japanese 9-year-olds were collected in 1989 by Shigehisa and Lynn (1991). In relation to the 1979 British standardization, their IQ was 112. To adjust for the ten-year interval between the two data collections, this needs to be reduced to 110.

A study by Takeuchi and Scott (1992) reported the performance of a sample of 454 5- to 7-year-old Japanese children in the city of Nagoya on the Canadian Cognitive Abilities Test. The Japanese IQ on the abstract reasoning subtest was 106.9. The Canadian test was standardized around 1989. Because we have estimated the Canadian IQ at 97, three IQ points need to be deducted from the Japanese IQ to calibrate it against a British IQ of 100, bringing the Japanese IQ to 104.

A further study of intelligence in Japan compared with that in the United States has been published by Li, Sano, and Merwin (1996). The samples consisted of 239 14- to 15-year-olds in the Japanese city of Toyama and 318 adolescents of the same age in Minneapolis and St. Paul. Six tests were given including verbal and non-verbal reasoning tests. In relation to an American IQ of 100, the Japanese obtained an IQ of 103. Because the IQ in Minnesota, in which Minneapolis and St. Paul are situated, is 105 (Flynn, 1980), five IQ points need to be added to the Japanese mean to bring it to 108. To equate this figure to a British mean of 100, this needs to be reduced to 106.

The average of the ten calculations of Japanese intelligence gives an IQ of 105.

Kenya

Around 1983, data for the Coloured Progressive Matrices for 205 adults were collected by Boissiere, Knight, and Sabot (1985). In relation to the American 1993 norms for adults, their IQ is 69. Because of the 10-year interval between the two data collections, this needs to be raised to 71. In order to adjust to a British IQ of 100, this needs to be reduced to 69.

Around 1998, norms for the Coloured Progressive Matrices were collected in Kenya on a sample of 1,222 6- to 10-year-olds by Costenbader and Ngari (2000). Their mean IQ in relation to the 1979 British standardization sample of the Progressive Matrices is 79. Adjusting for the 19-year interval between the two standardizations reduces the Kenyan IQ to 75. The average of the two results gives an IQ of 72 for Kenya.

Lebanon

In 1955, data for the Draw-a-Man Test were collected for a sample of 416 5- to 10-year-old children by Dennis (1957). In relation to the 1926 American norms, their IQ was 89. To adjust for the 30-period between the two years of data collection, this has been reduced to 86.

Malaysia

Around 1992, norms for the Standard Progressive Matrices were collected for a sample of 5,412 7- to 12-year-olds by Chaim (1994). In relation to the 1979 British standardization sample, their IQ was 94.5. To adjust for the 13-year interval between the two standardizations, this needs to be reduced to 92.

Marshall Islands

Around 1961, norms were collected for the Cattell Culture Fair Test for a sample of 407 12- to 18-year-olds by Jordheim and Olsen (1963). Their IQ was 87.5. To adjust for the 14-year interval between the year of data collection and the American standardization of the test, this needs to be reduced to 84.5. In order to calibrate this figure against a British IQ of 100, this needs to be reduced to 83.5.

Mexico

Around 1961, a study of a sample of 520 6- to 13-year-old Native American and Mestizo children in southern Mexico were tested with the Draw-a-Man test by Modiano (1962). Their mean IQ in relation to American norms of 100 was 86.5. The population of Mexico is 90 percent Native American and Mestizo and 9 percent White (*Philip's World Atlas*, 1996). We assume that the whites have an IQ of 96, as in Argentina. Combining this estimate with the Modiano study, we obtain an IQ for Mexico of 87.

This result is corroborated by three studies of the IQs of Mexican immigrant children in the United States. Results for a sample of 597 6- to 11-year-old Mexican children in California and described as a representative sample were tested with the Coloured Progressive Matrices in 1972 and the results are given by Raven (1986). In relation to the 1979 British standardization sample, the Mexican children obtained an IQ of 82. Because of the 7-year interval between the two years of data collection, this needs to be raised to 84.

In 1972, data for the Coloured Progressive Matrices were collected for a sample of 434 6- to 11-year-old Mexican American children in Texas and the results are given by Raven (1986). In relation to the 1979 British standardization of the Standard Progressive Matrices, they obtained an IQ of 94. Because of the 7-year interval between the two data collections, this needs to be raised to 95.

Data for the Standard Progressive Matrices were collected for a sample of 404 9- to 12-year-olds in Texas (Raven, 1986). In relation to the British 1979 standardization sample, their IQ was 84.

The average of the three results gives an IQ of 88 for Mexican American children, corroborating the IQ of 87 obtained in the first study from Mexico.

Morocco

A sample of 167 Moroccan immigrants in the Netherlands has been tested with the Dutch General Intelligence Test Battery (Te Nijenhuis and van der Flier, 1997). This test consists of eight subtests measuring verbal, reasoning, numerical, spatial, and perceptual abilities. The Moroccans performed particularly poorly on the vocabulary test, on which they obtained a mean IQ of 69. This low score can be attributed to their poor knowledge of Dutch and has been excluded from the calculation. The mean IQ of the sample on the remaining seven tests in relation to a Dutch mean IQ of 100 is 84.

A further study of the intelligence of Moroccans in the Netherlands has been reported by Hamers, Hessels, and Pennings (1996). This study used a Learning Potential Test, which consists of classification, number series, immediate memory span, figural analogies and the like, and is in effect an intelligence test. The sample consisted of 200 5- to 7-year-olds and obtained an IQ of 85 in relation to a mean of 100 for Dutch children. The average of the two studies gives an IQ of 85 for Morocco.

Nepal

In 1958, normative data were collected for the Draw-a Man Test on a sample of 807 4- to 16-year-olds by Sundberg and Ballinger (1968). They also collected norms for American children. In relation to the American sample, the Nepalese children obtained a mean IQ of 78.

The Netherlands

In Buj's (1981) study of 333 adults tested with the Culture Fair Test, the mean IQ was 109. to calibrate this against a British mean IQ of 100, this needs to be reduced to 107.

In 1984, norms for the Coloured Progressive Matrices were collected by Van Bon and the data are given by Raven, Court, and Raven (1995). The mean IQ in relation to the British 1979 standardization of the standard Progressive Matrices is 99.5. In order to adjust for the 3-year interval between the two standardizations, this figure needs to be reduced to 99.

In 1992, norms for the Standard Progressive Matrices were collected for a sample of 4,032 6- to 12-year-olds. The data are given by Raven, Court, and Raven (1996). In relation to the 1979 British standardization sample, the IQ is 104. Because of the 13-year interval between the two standardizations, this needs to be reduced to 101.

The average of the three results gives an IQ of 102 for the Netherlands.

New Zealand

Around 1938, norms for the American Otis Test were collected by Redmond and Davies (1940) on a sample of 26,000 9- to 15-year-olds. Their IQ was 99.

In 1984, norms for the Standard Progressive Matrices were collected for a sample of 3,108 8- to 17-year-olds by Reid and Gilmore (1989). In relation to the 1979 British standardization, the mean IQ is 102. Because of the 5-year interval between the two standardizations, this needs to be reduced to 101.

The average of the two results gives an IQ of 100 for New Zealand.

Nigeria

In 1965, norms for the Standard Progressive Matrices were collected by Wober (1969) for a sample of 86 adult men. Their mean score was 15.9. This score is well below the bottom of the norm table for British 15-year-olds in the 1979 standardization and for adults in the detailed American norms. In terms of the British 1979 standardization, the score of the Nigerian sample is at the level of the average British 6.5-year-old. This sample is assigned an IQ of 64.

Around 1973, data for the Coloured Progressive Matrices for a sample of 375 6- to 13-year-olds were collected by Fahrmeier (1975). In relation to the 1979 British standardization of the Standard Progressive Matrices, the mean IQ is 70. Because of the 6-year interval between the two data collections, this needs to be reduced to 69.

The average of the two results gives an IQ of 67 for Nigeria.

Norway

In Buj's (1981) study, a sample of 100 adults tested with the Cattell Culture Fair test obtained an IQ of 100. To calibrate this to a British IQ of 100, this needs to be reduced to 98.

Peru

In 1993, norms were collected for the Coloured Progressive Matrices on a sample of 4,382 8- to 11-year-old Native American and Mestizo children (Raven, Court, and Raven, 1995). The mean IQ is 90 and is calculated in relation to the 1979 British standardization sample. Adjusting for the 4-year time interval between the two years of data collection brings the Peruvian IQ down to 89. The population of Peru is 88 percent Native American and Mestizo and 12 percent white (*Philip's World Atlas*, 1996). It is assumed that the whites have an IQ of 95, similar to that of whites in Argentina and Colombia. Weighting by the proportions in the population, the IQ for Peru is estimated at 90.

Philippines

Data have been collected by Flores and Evans (1972) for the Standard Progressive Matrices for 203 children aged 12–13. In relation to the British 1979 standardization sample, their IQ is 86.

Poland

Norms for the Standard Progressive Matrices for a sample of 4,006 6- to 15-year-olds were collected by Jaworowska and Szustrowa (1991). In relation to the British 1979 standardization sample, their mean IQ is 94. Because of the 10-year interval between the two standardizations, this needs to be reduced to 92.

Buj's (1981) sample of 835 adults tested with Cattell's Culture Fair Test obtained an IQ of 108. To calibrate this figure against a British IQ of 100, it needs to be reduced to 106.

The average of the two studies gives an IQ of 99 for Poland.

Portugal

Buj's sample of 242 adults tested with Cattell's Culture Fair Test obtained an IQ of 103. To calibrate this figure against a British IQ of 100, it needs to be reduced to 101.

Around 1987, norms for the Coloured Progressive Matrices were obtained by Simoes (1989) for a sample of 807 6- to 12-year-olds. In relation to the 1979 British standardization of the Standard Progressive Matrices, their IQ was 90. Because of the 12-year interval between the two standardizations, this needs to be reduced to 88.

The average of the two results gives an IQ of 95 for Portugal.

Puerto Rico

Around 1975, norms were collected for the Coloured Progressive Matrices for a representative sample of 2,400 5- to 11-year-olds. The data are given by Raven, Court, and Raven (1995). In relation to the 1979 standardization of the British Progressive Matrices, their mean IQ is 83.

In 1977, norms for the Standard Progressive Matrices were collected on a representative sample of 2,911 8- to 15-year-olds. The data are given by Raven and Court (1989). In relation to the 1979 British standardization sample, the Puerto Rican IQ was 84. The average of the two results gives an IQ of 84 for Puerto Rico.

Qatar

Norms for the Standard Progressive Matrices were collected for 273 12-year-olds by Bart, Kamal, and Lane (1987). In relation to 1979 British IQ of 100, their IQ is 78.

Romania

Around 1972, norms for the Coloured Progressive Matrices were collected for a sample of 300 6- to 10-year-olds by Zahirnic *et al.* (1974). In relation to the British 1979 standardization data, the Romanian sample obtained an IQ of 95. Because of the 7-year interval between the two standardizations, this needs to be reduced to 94.

Russia

In 1997, norms for the Standard Progressive Matrices were obtained for a representative sample of 14- to 15-year-olds from Briansk, a city in European Russia about 200 miles southwest of Moscow (Raven, 1998). Their mean IQ in relation to the British standardization sample was 100. Because of the 18-year interval between the two standardizations, this needs to be reduced to 96.

Sierra Leone

Around 1965, data for the Coloured Progressive Matrices for 22 skilled workers aged 23 years old were collected by Binnie-Dawson (1984). The average score of the sample was well below the first percentile of the American 1993 standardization sample. The Sierre Leone sample is assigned an IQ of 64.

Around 1964, data for 60 adults for the Coloured Progressive Matrices were collected by Berry (1966). In relation to the British 1979 standardization sample, their mean IQ was 64.

Both studies give the same result of an IQ of 64 for Sierra Leone.

Singapore

In 1974, data for a representative sample of 147 ethnic Chinese and 190 ethnic Malay 13-year-olds for the Standard Progressive Matrices were collected (Lynn, 1977b). In relation to the British 1979 standardization sample, the Chinese obtained a mean IQ of 106 and the Malays a mean IQ of 90.5. Because of the 5-year interval between the two years of data collection, the IQ of the Chinese needs to be increased to 107.5 and the IQ of the Malays needs to be increased to 92. The population of Singapore is 76 percent Chinese, 14 percent Malay, and 7 percent Indian, with the remaining 3 percent being unspecified (*Philip's World Atlas*, 1996). It is assumed that the IQ of the ethnic Indians is 81, the same as that in India. Weighting the IQs of the three ethnic groups by their percentages in the population, we arrive at an IQ of 103 for Singapore.

Slovakia

In 1983, the Coloured Progressive Matrices Test was standardized on a sample of 832 5- to 11-year-olds and the data are given by Raven, Court, and Raven (1995). In relation to the 1979 British standardization of the Progressive Matrices, the mean IQ of the Slovakian children is 97. Adjusting for the 4-year time interval between the two standardizations brings the Slovakian IQ down to 96.

Slovenia

In 1998, the Standard Progressive Matrices was standardized in Slovenia on a sample of 1,556 8- to 18-year-olds. In relation to the British 1979 standardization sample, their mean IQ was 99. To adjust for the 19 years between the two standardizations, this needs to be reduced to 95.

South Africa

In the 1920s, intelligence test data were collected in South Africa by Fick (1929) who gave the American Army Beta Test—a non-verbal test that was the model for the performance scale of the later Wechsler tests—to samples of 293 10- to 14-year-old Blacks, 762 Indians, and 4,921 Coloreds (who are largely of mixed black-white ancestry). In relation to the American norms collected a few years previously, the Blacks obtained an IQ of 65, the Indians of 77, and the Coloreds of 84.

In 1948, norms for Blacks for the Standard Progressive Matrices were collected by Notcutt (1950) for samples of 1,008 8- to 16-year-olds and 703 adults. In relation to the 1979 British standardization sample, the children obtained a mean IQ of 69. Because of the 31-year interval between the two standardizations, this needs to be raised to 75. The mean score of the adults is well below the bottom of the American norm table for adults provided by Raven, Court, and Raven (1996) and of 15-year-olds in the 1979 standardization sample. In relation to the 1979 British standardization, the mean score of the sample is at the level of the average 7.5-year-old. This sample is assigned an IQ of 64.

Around 1990, further normative data for the Standard Progressive Matrices were collected by Owen (1992) for 16-year-olds of the four major racial and ethnic groups of Whites, Blacks, Indians and Coloreds. In relation to the 1979 British standardization norms, the Whites (N = 1,056) obtained a mean IQ of 96. Because of the 11-year interval between the two standardizations, this needs to be reduced to 94. The mean IQ of the Blacks (N = 1,096) was 69, which needs to be reduced to 67. The mean IQ of the Coloreds (N = 778) was 82, which needs to be reduced to 80. The mean IQ of the Indians (N = 1,063) was 90, which needs to be reduced to 88.

In 1988, further data for the Standard Progressive Matrices were obtained for a sample of 350 Black 9-year-olds by Lynn and Holmshaw (1990). In relation to the 1979 British standardization sample, they obtained an IQ of 65. Because of the 9-year interval between the two data collections, this needs to be reduced to 63.

The averages of these results give the following IQs for the four racial groups—Whites: 94; Blacks: 66; Coloreds: 82; and Indians: 83. The percentages of the four groups in the population are Whites: 14; Blacks: 75; Coloreds: 9; and Indians: 2 (Ramsay, 2000). Weighting the IQs of the four groups by their percentages in the population gives an IQ of 72 for South Africa.

South Korea

In 1986, the Kaufman Assessment Battery for Children (K-ABC) was standardized by Moon (1988) on a sample of 440 2- to 12-year-olds. The K-ABC contains a test of "simultaneous processing," which is a measure of non-verbal reasoning. The Korean children obtained an IQ of 107.2. The Korean standardization was made five years after the American standardization, for which 1.5 points need to be deducted from the Korean IQ. To equate the Korean IQ to a British IQ of 100, one more IQ point needs to be deducted, bringing the Korean IQ down to 105.

In 1992, a study of a sample of 107 9-year-olds was tested with the Standard Progressive Matrices (Lynn and Song, 1994). In relation to the 1979 British standardization sample, their IQ was 109. To adjust for the 13 years between the two data collections, this needs to be reduced to 106.4.

The average of the two studies gives an IQ of 106 for South Korea.

Spain

Buj (1981) gives data for 848 adults tested with the Culture Fair Test. Their mean IQ was 100. To calibrate this figure against a British mean of 100, this needs to be reduced to 98.

Around 1992, normative data for the Coloured Progressive Matrices were collected and are given by Raven, Court, and Raven (1995). In relation to the 1979 British standardization of the Standard Progressive Matrices, their mean IQ is 99. To adjust for the 14-year interval between the two standardizations, this needs to be reduced to 96.

Data for the Standard Progressive Matrices for 113,749 military conscripts were reported by Nieto-Alegre, Navarro, Cruz, and Dominguez (1967). The mean IQ was equivalent to 90 on the 1979 British standardization. However, the Spanish conscripts were of a low educational level and were unrepresentative of the population (Colom, Andres-Pueyo, and Juan-Espinosa, 1998) and cannot be used.

The average of the two valid studies gives an IQ of 97 for Spain.

Sudan

Data for the Standard Progressive Matrices for a sample of 148 8- to 12-year-olds have been reported by Ahmed (1989). In relation to the 1979 British standardization sample, their mean IQ was 74. To adjust for the 12-year interval between the two years of data collection, this needs to be reduced to 72.

In 1954, a study of the intelligence of 291 children was made by Fahmy (1964). The sample was taken from the west bank of the white Nile, which is "inhabited by the Shilluk, one of the primitive Nilotic Negro tribes" (p.164). The children were given four American tests—the Goddard Formboard, the Porteus Maze, the Alexander Passalong, and the Draw-a-Man Test. Their average IQ was 73.5. The dates of the standardization of the first three of these tests in the United States are not known. This result has therefore not been used, but it provides some confirmation for the Progressive Matrices result, which indicates that the IQ in Sudan is around 72.

Suriname

There are a number of immigrants from this former Dutch colony in the Netherlands. A sample of 535 individuals with a mean age of 30 years has been tested with the Dutch General Aptitude Test Battery by Te Nijenhuis and van der Flier (1997). In relation to a Dutch IQ of 100, their mean IQ was 89.

Sweden

In a standardization of the WISC in Sweden in 1968 on a sample of 1,106 6- to 15-year-olds, the Swedish children obtained an IQ of 104 on the performance scale (Skandinaviska Testforlaget, 1970). Because the WISC was standardized on Whites, this figure needs to be raised to 106. To adjust for the 21-year interval between this and the American standardization, this needs to be reduced to 99. To equate this figure to an IQ of 100 for Britain, this needs to be reduced to 97.

Buj's (1981) sample of 205 adults tested with the Cattell Culture Fair Test obtained an IQ of 106. To calibrate this figure against a British IQ of 100, this needs to be reduced to 104. The average of the two results gives an IQ of 101 for Sweden.

Switzerland

Buj (1981) obtained a mean IQ of 103 on a sample of 163 adults tested with the Cattell Culture Fair Test. To calibrate this figure against a British IQ of 100, this needs to be reduced to 101.

The Coloured Progressive Matrices Test has been standardized twice, in 1970 and again in 1989. The data are given by Raven, Court, and Raven (1995). For the 1970 standardization on 6- to 10-year-olds (for which the sample size is not given), the equivalent British IQ derived from the 1979 standardization of the Progressive Matrices is 97. Adjusting for the nine years between the two standardizations brings the Swiss IQ up to 99.

On the 1989 Swiss standardization of the Standard Progressive Matrices based on a sample of 167 6- to 10-year-olds, the equivalent British IQ derived from the 1979 standardization sample of the Progressive Matrices is 104. Adjusting for the 10-year time interval between the two standardizations brings the Swiss IQ down to 102.

The average of the three studies gives an IQ of 101 for Switzerland.

Taiwan

Around 1956, data for a sample of 1,290 16-year-olds tested with the Cattell Culture Fair Test were collected by Rodd (1959). In relation to the American norms, their IQ was 105. The test was standardized in the United States in 1947. To adjust for the 9-year interval between the two years of data collection, the Taiwan IQ needs to be reduced to 103. In relation to a British IQ of 100, this figure needs to be reduced to 101.

In 1975, norms for the Coloured Progressive Matrices were collected by Hsu (1976) for all first grade children in Taipei, numbering 43,825 and with an average age of 6.8 years. In relation to the 1979 British standardization sample, their IQ was 102.7. Because of the 4-year interval between the two standardizations, this needs to be raised to 103.5.

A study by Stevenson *et al.* (1985) of intelligence in the United States and Japan has been previously described above under Japan. This study also included the collection of data on a sample of 480 6- and 10-year-olds in Taipei. The authors state that the mean IQ of the Taiwanese children was the same as that of the American. As noted in the summary of this study in our section on Japan, the American sample was drawn from the city of Minneapolis where the IQ is five points higher than that in the United States as a whole. This means that five points need to be added to the Taiwan figure, bringing it to 105.

Norms for the Standard Progressive Matrices were collected in 1989 for a sample of 2,496 9- to 12-year-olds and have been published by Lynn (1997b). The data are given by Raven, Court, and Raven (1996) and have been analyzed by Lynn (1997). In relation to the British 1979 standardization sample, the IQ was 106.6. Because of the 10-year interval between the two standardizations, this needs to be reduced to 105.

The average of the four studies gives an IQ of 104 for Taiwan.

Tanzania

Around 1965, data for the Standard Progressive Matrices were obtained for a sample of 2,959 secondary school adolescents with an average age of 17 (Klingelhofer, 1967). In relation to the British 1979 standardization sample, their IQ was 75. To adjust for the 14-year interval between the two years of data collection, this needs to be raised to 78.

Around 1983, data for the Coloured Progressive Matrices were obtained for a sample of 179 adults by Boissiere, Knight, and Sabot (1985). Their mean IQ in relation to the 1993 American norms for adults is 65. Because of the 10-year interval between the two data collections, this needs to be raised to 67. In relation to a British IQ of 100, this needs to be reduced to 65.

The average of the two studies gives an IQ of 72 for Tanzania.

Thailand

Data have been collected for the Colored Progressive Matrices for a sample of 8- to 10-year-olds by Pollitt *et al.* (1989). In relation to the British 1979 standardization sample, their mean IQ is 91.

Tonga

Data for the Progressive Achievement Test, a test of verbal intelligence measuring reading comprehension and vocabulary, have been reported for 80 8- to 9-year-old ethnically Polynesian children at schools in Auckland, New Zealand. The children's parents came from Tonga and Western Samoa. Their IQ in relation to New Zealand Whites was 86 (Beck and St. George, 1983).

In 1984, the Standard Progressive Matrices was normalized in New Zealand on a sample of 3,108 8- to 17-year-olds by Reid and Gilmore (1989). The sample included 65 ethnic Pacific Islanders. Their IQ in relation to the 1979 British standardization sample was 88.5. Because of the 5-year interval between the two standardizations, this needs to be reduced to 87.5.

The average of the two studies gives an IQ of 87 for Tonga.

Turkey

Around 1992, the Standard Progressive Matrices was standardized on a sample of 2,277 6- to 15-year-olds by Sahin and Duzen (1994). In relation to the 1979 British standardization sample, their IQ was 93. Because of the 13-year interval between the two standardizations, this needs to be reduced to 90. We adopt this as the best estimate of the IQ in Turkey.

Two corroboration studies are available for samples of Turkish immigrants in the Netherlands. In the first, a sample with a mean age of 24 has been tested with the Dutch General Aptitude Test Battery by Te Nijenhuis and van der Flier (1997). This test consists of eight subtests measuring a range of verbal, reasoning, spatial, and perceptual abilities. The Turkish sample performed exceptionally poorly on the vocabulary subtest. This is attributable to their imperfect knowledge of Dutch and has been discounted. On the remaining seven subtests, they obtained a mean IQ of 88 in relation to a Dutch mean of 100. A further sample of 200 5- to 7-year-old Turkish children in the Netherlands has been tested on the Learning Potential Test by Hamers, Hessels, and Pennings (1996). Their mean IQ in relation to 100 for Dutch children was 85.

Uganda

In 1972, data for the Coloured Progressive Matrices were collected for a representative sample of 2,019 11-year-olds and have been published by Heyneman and Jamison (1980). In relation to the 1979 British standardization of the Standard Progressive Matrices, their IQ was 72. Because of the 7-year interval between the two years of data collection, this needs to be raised to 73.

United States

It first became possible to compare the IQs in the United States and Britain in 1933. In this year, the Scottish Council for Research in Education (1933) published the results of its survey of the intelligence of Scottish children in which a representative sample of 1,000 11-year-olds were tested with the American Stanford Binet. The IQ of the Scottish children was 100. Three adjustments need to be made to this figure. First, the Stanford Binet was standardized in the United States in 1914. To allow for the 18-year interval between the two standardizations, the Scottish IQ must be reduced by five IQ points to 95. Second, the Scottish IQ is 97 in relation to a British IQ of 100 (Lynn, 1979), so 3 IQ points need to be added to this figure to compare the United States with Britain, bringing the British IQ to 98. Third, the American Stanford Binet was normalized on whites only. In the United States, the mean IQ of whites is 102.2 in relation to that of the total population (Jensen and Reynolds, 1982). Hence, two IQ points need to be added to the British IQ to calibrate it to an IQ of 100 for the American population that is inclusive of blacks. This brings the IQ in Britain to 100.

In 1949, the publication of the second survey of the intelligence of Scottish children made it possible to make a further comparison of the IQs in the United States and Britain. The second Scottish survey was carried out in 1947, and it included the testing of a representative sample of 1,215 11-year-olds with the American Terman Merrill Test. The mean IQ of the Scottish children was 102.5 (Scottish Council for Research in Education, 1949). As with the first Scottish survey, three adjustments are required. First, the Terman Merrill was standardized in the United States in 1932. Thus, to adjust for the 15-year interval between the two standardizations, 4.5 IQ points need to be subtracted from the Scottish mean, bringing it down to 98. Second, the Scottish IQ is three points below the British IQ, so three points need to be added bringing the IQ for Britain up to 101. Third, the American IQ is for whites only. The IQ for the total population is two points lower. This requires adding two points to the British IQ, bringing it up to 103.

The Differential Aptitude Test (DAT) was developed in the United States in 1947 for adolescents aged 13–18. In 1972, it was restandardized on a sample of approximately 64,000. In 1978, the test was standardized in Britain on a sample of approximately 10,000 adolescents (Hodgkiss, 1978). The DAT contains an abstract reasoning test which is taken as the best measure of general intelligence. On this test, the British sample obtained an IQ of 103. Because of the 5-year interval between the two standardizations, the British IQ needs to be reduced to 102.

Norms for the Standard Progressive Matrices for United States for adults aged 18–70 for 1993 are given by Raven, Court, and Raven (1996). In relation to the British 1992 standardization of the test on adults, the American IQ is 98. The average for the four results gives the United States an IQ of 98 in relation to a British IQ of 100.

Uruguay

Around 1957, norms for the Standard Progressive Matrices were collected by Risso (1961) for a sample of 1,634 adolescents and adults. The adolescents obtained an IQ of 89 in relation to the 1979 British standardization sample. Because of the 22-year interval between the two standardizations, this needs to be raised to 93. The adults obtained an IQ of 93 in relation to the 1993 American norms. Because of the 36-year interval between the two standardizations, this needs to be raised to 100. In relation to a British IQ of 100, this needs to be reduced to 98.

The average of the two results gives an IQ of 96 for Uruguay.

Western Samoa

Data for the Progressive Achievement Test, a test of verbal intelligence measuring reading comprehension and vocabulary, have been reported for 80 8- to 9-year-old ethnically Polynesian children at schools in Auckland, New Zealand. The children's parents came from Western Samoa and Tonga. Their mean IQ was 86 (Beck and St. George, 1983).

In 1984, data for 65 Pacific Islander children were obtained in the standardization of the Standard Progressive Matrices in New Zealand by Reid and Gilmore (1989). In relation to the 1979 British standardization sample, their IQ was 88.5. Because of the 5-year interval between the two standardizations, this needs to be reduced to 87.5.

The average of the two results gives an IQ of 87 for Western Samoa.

Zambia

In 1962, data for the Standard Progressive Matrices were collected for a representative sample of 759 13-year-olds at school by MacArthur, Irvine, and Brimble (1964). In relation to the 1979 British standardization sample, their IQ was 74. Because of the 17-year interval between the two standardizations, this needs to be raised to 77.

Zimbabwe

Intelligence data for 12- to 14-year-olds taking the WISC-R and the Progressive Matrices have been reported by Zindi (1994). On the WISC-R, the mean IQ of the sample was 67.1. This test was standardized in the United States in 1972. To adjust for the 20-year interval between the two data collections, six IQ points need to be subtracted from the Zimbabwe sample to give an IQ of 61. Zindi states that the sample obtained a mean IQ of 72.4 on the Progressive Matrices, although he does not describe how this figure was calculated or whether the test was the Standard or Coloured version of the test. Because there are no norms for the Coloured Progressive Matrices for 12- to 14-year-olds, it is assumed that the test was the Standard Progressive Matrices. Adjusting for the 13-year interval between the two data collections entails the reduction of the IQ to 70. The average of the two results gives an IQ of 66 for Zimbabwe.

Appendix 2

Data on Per Capita Income and Economic Growth in 185 Countries

Data on (1) GDP per capita (Maddison), (2) GNP per capita, (3) GNP per capita measured at PPP, (4) real GDP per capita (PPP $), and (5) GDP per capita at current prices for countries in U.S. dollars and in economic growth percentages.

Symbols used: — = Data are missing
( ) = estimated by the authors

Table 1

		(1) GDP per capita (1990 Geary-Khamis Dollars)							
	Country	1820	1850	1870	1880	1890	1900	1910	1920
1	Afghanistan	—	—	—	—	—	—	—	—
2	Albania	—	—	—	—	—	—	—	—
3	Algeria	—	—	—	—	—	—	—	—
4	Angola	—	—	—	—	—	—	—	—
5	Antigua and Barbuda	—	—	—	—	—	—	—	—
6	Argentina	—	—	1,311	—	2,152	2,756	3,822	3,473
7	Armenia	—	—	—	—	—	—	—	—

continues

Table 1   continued

	Country	1820	1850	1870	1880	1890	1900	1910	1920
8	Australia	1,528	3,070	3,801	4,590	4,775	4,299	5,581	5,047
9	Austria	1,295	1,661	1,801	2,093	2,460	2,901	3,312	2,428
10	Azerbaijan	—	—	—	—	—	—	—	—
11	Bahamas	—	—	—	—	—	—	—	—
12	Bahrain	—	—	—	—	—	—	—	—
13	Bangladesh	531	—	—	—	—	581	617	—
14	Barbados	—	—	—	—	—	—	—	—
15	Belarus	—	—	—	—	—	—	—	—
16	Belgium	1,291	1,808	2,640	3,000	3,355	3,652	3,978	3,878
17	Belize	—	—	—	—	—	—	—	—
18	Benin	—	—	—	—	—	—	—	—
19	Bhutan	—	—	—	—	—	—	—	—
20	Bolivia	—	—	—	—	—	—	—	—
21	Botswana	—	—	—	—	—	—	—	—
22	Brazil	670	711	740	—	772	704	795	937
23	Brunei	—	—	—	—	—	—	—	—
24	Bulgaria	—	—	—	—	—	—	1,498	909
25	Burkina Faso	—	—	—	—	—	—	—	—
26	Burma	—	—	—	—	—	647	562	658
27	Burundi	—	—	—	—	—	—	—	—
28	Cambodia	—	—	—	—	—	—	—	—
29	Cameroon	—	—	—	—	—	—	—	—
30	Canada	893	1,280	1,620	1,721	2,254	2,758	3,852	3,659
31	Cape Verde	—	—	—	—	—	—	—	—
32	Central African Republic	—	—	—	—	—	—	—	—
33	Chad	—	—	—	—	—	—	—	—
34	Chile	—	—	—	—	—	1,949	2,472	2,430

	Country	1820	1850	1870	1880	1890	1900	1910	1920
35	China	523	—	523	—	615	652	688	—
36	Colombia	—	—	—	—	—	973	1,236	—
37	Comoros	—	—	—	—	—	—	—	—
38	Congo (Brazzaville)	—	—	—	—	—	—	—	—
39	Congo (Zaire)	—	—	—	—	—	—	—	—
40	Costa Rica	—	—	—	—	—	—	—	—
41	Côte d'Ivoire	—	—	—	—	—	—	—	—
42	Croatia	—	—	—	—	—	—	—	—
43	Cuba	—	—	—	—	—	—	—	—
44	Cyprus	—	—	—	—	—	—	—	—
45	Czech. Republic	849	1,069	1,164	—	1,505	1,729	2,096	1,933
46	Denmark	1,225	1,700	1,927	2,099	2,427	2,902	3,564	3,840
47	Djibouti	—	—	—	—	—	—	—	—
48	Dominica	—	—	—	—	—	—	—	—
49	Dominican Republic	—	—	—	—	—	—	—	—
50	Ecuador	—	—	—	—	—	—	—	—
51	Egypt	—	—	—	—	—	509	508	—
52	El Salvador	—	—	—	—	—	—	—	—
53	Equatorial Guinea	—	—	—	—	—	—	—	—
54	Eritrea	—	—	—	—	—	—	—	—
55	Estonia	—	—	—	—	—	—	—	—
56	Ethiopia	—	—	—	—	—	—	—	—
57	Fiji	—	—	—	—	—	—	—	—
58	Finland	759	—	1,107	1,122	1,341	1,620	1,852	1,792
59	France	1,218	1,669	1,858	2,100	2,354	2,849	2,937	3,196
60	Gabon	—	—	—	—	—	—	—	—

continues

Table 1 continued

	Country	1820	1850	1870	1880	1890	1900	1910	1920
61	Gambia	—	—	—	—	—	—	—	—
62	Georgia	—	—	—	—	—	—	—	—
63	Germany	1,112	1,476	1,913	2,078	2,539	3,134	3,527	2,986
64	Ghana	—	—	—	—	—	462	648	—
65	Greece	—	—	—	—	—	—	1,621	—
66	Grenada	—	—	—	—	—	—	—	—
67	Guatemala	—	—	—	—	—	—	—	—
68	Guinea	—	—	—	—	—	—	—	—
69	Guinea—Bissau	—	—	—	—	—	—	—	—
70	Guyana	—	—	—	—	—	—	—	—
71	Haiti	—	—	—	—	—	—	—	—
72	Honduras	—	—	—	—	—	—	—	—
73	Hong Kong	—	—	—	—	—	—	—	—
74	Hungary	—	—	1,269	—	—	1,682	2,098	1,709
75	Iceland	—	—	—	—	—	—	—	—
76	India	531	547	558	—	608	625	688	629
77	Indonesia	614	657	657	—	663	745	844	973
78	Iran	—	—	—	—	—	—	—	—
79	Iraq	—	—	—	—	—	—	—	—
80	Ireland	954	—	1,773	—	2,225	2,495	2,733	—
81	Israel	—	—	—	—	—	—	—	—
82	Italy	1,092	—	1,467	1,546	1,631	1,746	2,281	2,531
83	Jamaica	—	—	—	—	—	—	—	—
84	Japan	702	—	741	—	974	1,135	1,254	1,631
85	Jordan	—	—	—	—	—	—	—	—
86	Kazakhstan	—	—	—	—	—	—	—	—
87	Kenya	—	—	—	—	—	—	—	—
88	Kiribati	—	—	—	—	—	—	—	—

	Country	1820	1850	1870	1880	1890	1900	1910	1920
89	Korea, N.	—	—	—	—	—	—	—	—
90	Korea, S.	—	—	—	—	—	850	898	1,167
91	Kuwait	—	—	—	—	—	—	—	—
92	Kyrgyzstan	—	—	—	—	—	—	—	—
93	Laos	—	—	—	—	—	—	—	—
94	Latvia	—	—	—	—	—	—	—	—
95	Lebanon	—	—	—	—	—	—	—	—
96	Lesotho	—	—	—	—	—	—	—	—
97	Liberia	—	—	—	—	—	—	—	—
98	Libya	—	—	—	—	—	—	—	—
99	Lithuania	—	—	—	—	—	—	—	—
100	Luxembourg	—	—	—	—	—	—	—	—
101	Macedonia	—	—	—	—	—	—	—	—
102	Madagascar	—	—	—	—	—	—	—	—
103	Malawi	—	—	—	—	—	—	—	—
104	Malaysia	—	—	—	—	—	—	—	—
105	Maldives	—	—	—	—	—	—	—	—
106	Mali	—	—	—	—	—	—	—	—
107	Malta	—	—	—	—	—	—	—	—
108	Marshall Islands	—	—	—	—	—	—	—	—
109	Mauritania	—	—	—	—	—	—	—	—
110	Mauritius	—	—	—	—	—	—	—	—
111	Mexico	760	668	710	—	990	1,157	1,435	1,555
112	Micronesia	—	—	—	—	—	—	—	—
113	Moldova	—	—	—	—	—	—	—	—
114	Mongolia	—	—	—	—	—	—	—	—
115	Morocco	—	—	—	—	—	—	—	—
116	Mozambique	—	—	—	—	—	—	—	—

continues

Table 1   continued

	Country	1820	1850	1870	1880	1890	1900	1910	1920
117	Namibia	—	—	—	—	—	—	—	—
118	Nepal	—	—	—	—	—	—	—	—
119	Netherlands	1,561	1,888	2,640	3,120	3,113	3,533	3,684	4,117
120	New Zealand	—	—	3,115	3,765	3,774	4,320	5,343	5,670
121	Nicaragua	—	—	—	—	—	—	—	—
122	Niger	—	—	—	—	—	—	—	—
123	Nigeria	—	—	—	—	—	—	—	—
124	Norway	1,004	1,080	1,303	1,444	1,617	1,762	2,052	2,529
125	Oman	—	—	—	—	—	—	—	—
126	Pakistan	531	—	—	—	—	687	729	—
127	Panama	—	—	—	—	—	—	—	—
128	Papua New Guinea	—	—	—	—	—	—	—	—
129	Paraguay	—	—	—	—	—	—	—	—
130	Peru	—	—	—	—	—	817	1,037	1,331
131	Philippines	—	—	—	—	—	1,033	1,418	—
132	Poland	—	—	—	—	—	—	—	—
133	Portugal	—	1,100	1,085	—	1,227	1,408	1,354	—
134	Puerto Rico	—	—	—	—	—	—	—	—
135	Qatar	—	—	—	—	—	—	—	—
136	Romania	—	—	—	—	—	—	—	—
137	Russia	751	—	1,023	—	925	1,218	1,488	—
138	Rwanda	—	—	—	—	—	—	—	—
139	Samoa (Western)	—	—	—	—	—	—	—	—
140	Sao Tome & Principe	—	—	—	—	—	—	—	—
141	Saudi Arabia	—	—	—	—	—	—	—	—
142	Senegal	—	—	—	—	—	—	—	—

	Country	1820	1850	1870	1880	1890	1900	1910	1920
143	Seychelles	—	—	—	—	—	—	—	—
144	Sierra Leone	—	—	—	—	—	—	—	—
145	Singapore	—	—	—	—	—	—	—	—
146	Slovakia	—	—	—	—	—	—	—	—
147	Slovenia	—	—	—	—	—	—	—	—
148	Solomon Islands	—	—	—	—	—	—	—	—
149	Somalia	—	—	—	—	—	—	—	—
150	South Africa	—	—	—	—	—	—	1,451	—
151	Spain	1,063	1,147	1,376	—	1,847	2,040	2,096	2,309
152	Sri Lanka	—	—	—	—	—	—	—	—
153	St. Kitts and Nevis	—	—	—	—	—	—	—	—
154	St. Lucia	—	—	—	—	—	—	—	—
155	St. Vincent and Grenadines	—	—	—	—	—	—	—	—
156	Sudan	—	—	—	—	—	—	—	—
157	Suriname	—	—	—	—	—	—	—	—
158	Swaziland	—	—	—	—	—	—	—	—
159	Sweden	1,198	1,289	1,664	1,846	2,086	2,561	2,980	2,802
160	Switzerland	—	—	2,172	—	—	3,531	4,068	4,255
161	Syria	—	—	—	—	—	—	—	—
162	Taiwan	—	—	—	—	—	759	958	921
163	Tajikistan	—	—	—	—	—	—	—	—
164	Tanzania	—	—	—	—	—	—	—	—
165	Thailand	—	—	717	—	789	812	846	—
166	Togo	—	—	—	—	—	—	—	—
167	Tonga	—	—	—	—	—	—	—	—
168	Trinidad and Tobago	—	—	—	—	—	—	—	—

continues

Table 1   continued

	Country	1820	1850	1870	1880	1890	1900	1910	1920
169	Tunisia	—	—	—	—	—	—	—	—
170	Turkey	—	—	—	—	—	—	979	561
171	Turkmenistan	—	—	—	—	—	—	—	—
172	Uganda	—	—	—	—	—	—	—	—
173	Ukraine	—	—	—	—	—	—	—	—
174	United Arab Emirates	—	—	—	—	—	—	—	—
175	United Kingdom	1,756	2,362	3,263	3,556	4,099	4,593	4,715	4,651
176	United States	1,287	1,819	2,457	3,193	3,396	4,096	4,970	5,559
177	Uruguay	—	—	—	—	—	—	—	—
178	Uzbekistan	—	—	—	—	—	—	—	—
179	Vanuatu	—	—	—	—	—	—	—	—
180	Venezuela	—	—	—	—	—	821	886	1,173
181	Vietnam	—	—	—	—	—	—	—	—
182	Yemen	—	—	—	—	—	—	—	—
183	Yugoslavia	—	—	—	—	—	—	1,029	1,054
184	Zambia	—	—	—	—	—	—	—	—
185	Zimbabwe	—	—	—	—	—	—	—	—

		(1) GDP per capita (Maddison)							
	Country	1930	1940	1950	1960	1970	1980	1990	1992
1	Afghanistan	—	—	1,365	—	—	—	1,000	—
2	Albania	—	—	1,007	—	—	—	2,500	—
3	Algeria	—	—	1,383	—	—	—	2,815	—
4	Angola	—	—	986	—	—	—	654	—
5	Antigua & Barbuda	—	—	1,828	—	—	—	5,159	—

	Country	1930	1940	1950	1960	1970	1980	1990	1992
6	Argentina	4,080	4,161	4,987	5,559	7,302	8,245	6,581	7,616
7	Armenia	—	—	—	—	—	—	—	—
8	Australia	4,792	5,940	7,218	8,539	11,637	13,805	16,417	16,237
9	Austria	3,610	3,985	3,731	6,561	9,813	13,881	16,792	17,165
10	Azerbaijan	—	—	—	—	—	—	—	—
11	Bahamas	—	—	9,451	—	—	—	15,177	—
12	Bahrain	—	—	5,424	—	—	—	10,418	—
13	Bangladesh	619	572	551	536	613	557	698	720
14	Barbados	—	—	2,276	—	—	—	8,223	—
15	Belarus	—	—	—	—	—	—	—	—
16	Belgium	4,873	4,465	5,346	6,779	10,410	14,022	16,807	17,165
17	Belize	—	—	1,689	—	—	—	3,868	—
18	Benin	—	—	1,087	—	—	—	1,107	—
19	Bhutan	—	—	492	—	—	—	926	—
20	Bolivia	—	—	1,884	—	—	—	1,744	—
21	Botswana	—	—	390	—	—	—	4,215	—
22	Brazil	1,061	1,302	1,673	2,335	3,067	5,246	4,812	4,637
23	Brunei	—	—	1,712	—	—	—	2,259	—
24	Bulgaria	1,284	1,548	1,651	2,912	4,773	6,031	5,764	4,054
25	Burkina Faso	—	—	503	—	—	—	616	—
26	Burma	836	685	393	549	602	756	687	748
27	Burundi	—	—	320	—	—	—	599	—
28	Cambodia	—	—	591	—	—	—	1,000	—
29	Cameroon	—	—	803	—	—	—	1,447	—
30	Canada	4,558	5,086	7,047	8,459	11,758	16,280	19,599	18,159
31	Cape Verde	—	—	580	—	—	—	1,465	—
32	Central African Republic	—	—	729	—	—	—	644	—

continues

Table 1   continued

	Country	1930	1940	1950	1960	1970	1980	1990	1992
33	Chad	—	—	449	—	—	—	418	—
34	Chile	3,143	3,259	3,827	4,304	5,217	5,711	6,380	7,238
35	China	786	778	614	878	1,092	1,462	2,700	3,098
36	Colombia	1,474	1,895	2,089	2,499	3,104	4,274	4,917	5,025
37	Comoros	—	—	528	—	—	—	535	—
38	Congo (Brazzaville)	—	—	1,330	—	—	—	2,631	—
39	Congo (Zaire)	—	—	636	808	711	538	458	353
40	Costa Rica	—	—	1,968	—	—	—	3,923	—
41	Côte d'Ivoire	—	—	859	1,051	1,633	1,909	1,224	1,134
42	Croatia	—	—	—	—	—	—	—	—
43	Cuba	—	—	3,651	—	—	—	3,000	—
44	Cyprus	—	—	2,067	—	—	—	9,501	—
45	Czech Republic	2,926	2,882	3,501	5,108	6,460	7,978	8,464	6,845
46	Denmark	5,138	4,922	6,683	8,477	12,204	14,645	17,953	18,293
47	Djibouti	—	—	523	—	—	—	1,210	—
48	Dominica	—	—	1,615	—	—	—	3,488	—
49	Dominican Republic	—	—	1,212	—	—	—	2,342	—
50	Ecuador	—	—	1,329	—	—	—	3,037	—
51	Egypt	—	—	517	712	941	1,483	2,030	1,927
52	El Salvador	—	—	1,522	—	—	—	1,961	—
53	Equatorial Guinea	—	—	578	—	—	—	1,382	—
54	Eritrea	—	—	—	—	—	—	—	—
55	Estonia	—	—	—	—	—	—	—	—
56	Ethiopia	—	—	277	302	393	401	350	300
57	Fiji	—	—	2,895	—	—	—	4,712	—
58	Finland	2,589	3,128	4,131	6,051	9,302	12,693	16,604	14,646

	Country	1930	1940	1950	1960	1970	1980	1990	1992
59	France	4,489	4,004	5,221	7,472	11,558	14,979	17,777	17,959
60	Gabon	—	—	866	—	—	—	2,859	—
61	Gambia	—	—	459	—	—	—	862	—
62	Georgia	—	—	—	—	—	—	—	—
63	Germany	4,049	5,545	4,281	8,463	11,933	15,370	18,685	19,351
64	Ghana	—	—	1,193	1,232	1,275	1,041	966	1,007
65	Greece	2,300	2,687	1,951	3,204	6,327	9,139	10,051	10,314
66	Grenada	—	—	906	—	—	—	2,793	—
67	Guatemala	—	—	1,677	—	—	—	2,461	—
68	Guinea	—	—	260	—	—	—	448	—
69	Guinea—Bissau	—	—	280	—	—	—	782	—
70	Guyana	—	—	1,092	—	—	—	1,123	—
71	Haiti	—	—	984	—	—	—	1,037	—
72	Honduras	—	—	1,036	—	—	—	1,510	—
73	Hong Kong	—	—	1,962	—	—	—	17,120	—
74	Hungary	2,404	2,626	2,480	3,649	5,028	6,307	6,348	5,638
75	Iceland	—	—	5,014	—	—	—	17,380	—
76	India	654	650	597	735	878	938	1,316	1,348
77	Indonesia	1,198	1,187	874	1,131	1,239	1,870	2,525	2,749
78	Iran	—	—	1,892	—	—	—	3,662	—
79	Iraq	—	—	1,046	—	—	—	1,882	—
80	Ireland	3,034	3,116	3,518	4,368	6,250	8,256	11,123	11,711
81	Israel	—	—	2,452	—	—	—	10,096	—
82	Italy	2,854	3,429	3,425	5,789	9,508	13,092	15,951	16,229
83	Jamaica	—	—	1,103	—	—	—	3,079	—
84	Japan	1,780	2,765	1,873	3,879	9,448	13,113	18,548	19,425
85	Jordan	—	—	824	—	—	—	3,147	—
86	Kazakhstan	—	—	—	—	—	—	—	—

continues

Table 1   continued

	Country	1930	1940	1950	1960	1970	1980	1990	1992
87	Kenya	—	—	609	717	894	1,031	1,079	1,055
88	Kiribati	—	—	3,820	—	—	—	2,084	—
89	Korea, North	—	—	643	—	—	—	2,259	—
90	Korea, South	1,173	1,618	876	1,302	2,208	4,103	8,977	10,010
91	Kuwait	—	—	26,097	—	—	—	5,736	—
92	Kyrgyzstan	—	—	—	—	—	—	—	—
93	Laos	—	—	1,151	—	—	—	2,367	—
94	Latvia	—	—	—	—	—	—	—	—
95	Lebanon	—	—	2,296	—	—	—	2,259	—
96	Lesotho	—	—	324	—	—	—	1,027	—
97	Liberia	—	—	1,126	—	—	—	864	—
98	Libya	—	—	801	—	—	—	2,815	—
99	Lithuania	—	—	—	—	—	—	—	—
100	Luxembourg	—	—	7,919	—	—	—	20,145	—
101	Macedonia	—	—	—	—	—	—	—	—
102	Madagascar	—	—	961	—	—	—	760	—
103	Malawi	—	—	306	—	—	—	584	—
104	Malaysia	—	—	1,696	—	—	—	5,638	—
105	Maldives	—	—	528	—	—	—	2,259	—
106	Mali	—	—	410	—	—	—	538	—
107	Malta	—	—	943	—	—	—	8,534	—
108	Marshall Islands	—	—	1,251	—	—	—	2,084	—
109	Maurtania	—	—	615	—	—	—	927	—
110	Mauritius	—	—	2,428	—	—	—	6,868	—
111	Mexico	1,371	1,556	2,085	2,781	3,774	5,254	4,997	5,112
112	Micronesia	—	—	1,251	—	—	—	2,084	—
113	Moldova	—	—	—	—	—	—	—	—
114	Mongolia	—	—	643	—	—	—	2,259	—

continued

ry	1930	1940	1950	1960	1970	1980	1990	1992
Arabia	—	—	2,190	—	—	—	10,222	—
al	—	—	1,110	—	—	—	1,269	—
elles	—	—	1,471	—	—	—	4,400	—
Leone	—	—	706	—	—	—	1,007	—
pore	—	—	2,038	—	—	—	14,663	—
kia	—	—	—	—	—	—	—	—
nia	—	—	—	—	—	—	—	—
non Islands	—	—	1,360	—	—	—	2,094	—
alia	—	—	950	—	—	—	857	—
h Africa	—	—	2,251	2,624	3,709	4,114	3,719	3,451
n	2,802	2,288	2,397	3,437	7,291	9,539	12,170	12,498
anka	—	—	969	—	—	—	2,752	—
itts Nevis	—	—	1,546	—	—	—	5,159	—
ucia	—	—	815	—	—	—	2,993	—
incent and Grenadines	—	—	1,404	—	—	—	3,267	—
an	—	—	1,014	—	—	—	1,123	—
name	—	—	1,094	—	—	—	2,605	—
ziland	—	—	566	—	—	—	2,052	—
eden	3,937	4,858	6,738	8,688	12,717	14,935	17,695	16,927
tzerland	6,160	6,309	8,939	12,286	16,671	18,520	21,661	21,036
ia	—	—	2,012	—	—	—	4,837	—
iwan	1,112	1,365	922	1,399	2,692	5,634	10,324	11,590
ikistan	—	—	—	—	—	—	—	—
nzania	—	—	427	498	615	657	599	601
ailand	799	832	848	1,029	1,596	2,384	4,173	4,694
go	—	—	547	—	—	—	761	—
nga	—	—	872	—	—	—	2,333	—

	Country	1930	1940	1950	1960
115	Morocco	—	—	1,611	1,511
116	Mozambique	—	—	1,001	—
117	Namibia	—	—	1,528	—
118	Nepal	—	—	729	—
119	Netherlands	5,467	4,714	5,850	8,085
120	New Zealand	4,985	6,332	8,495	9,491
121	Nicaragua	—	—	1,772	—
122	Niger	—	—	743	—
123	Nigeria	—	—	547	645
124	Norway	3,377	3,718	4,969	6,549
125	Oman	—	—	716	—
126	Pakistan	735	680	650	661
127	Panama	—	—	1,636	—
128	Papua New Guinea	—	—	919	—
129	Paraguay	—	—	1,340	—
130	Peru	1,417	1,823	2,263	3,023
131	Philippines	1,564	1,497	1,293	1,488
132	Poland	1,994	—	2,447	3,218
133	Portugal	1,536	1,707	2,132	3,095
134	Puerto Rico	—	—	1,952	—
135	Qatar	—	—	29,257	—
136	Romania	1,219	1,242	1,182	1,844
137	Russia	1,448	2,144	2,834	3,935
138	Rwanda	—	—	606	—
139	Samoa (Western)	—	—	1,349	—
140	Sao Tome and Principe	—	—	868	—

Tabl

141
142
143
144
145
146
147
148
149
150
151
152
153
154
155
156
157
158
159
160
161
162
163
164
165
166
167

	Country	1930	1940	1950	1960	1970	1980	1990	1992
168	Trinidad and Tobago	—	—	4,537	—	—	—	9,310	—
169	Tunisia	—	—	1,134	—	—	—	3,234	—
170	Turkey	985	1,321	1,299	1,801	2,437	3,192	4,263	4,422
171	Turkmenistan	—	—	—	—	—	—	—	—
172	Uganda	—	—	1,149	—	—	—	944	—
173	Ukraine	—	—	—	—	—	—	—	—
174	United Arab Emirates	—	—	10,594	—	—	—	14,134	—
175	United Kingdom	5,195	6,546	6,847	8,571	10,694	12,777	16,302	15,738
176	United States	6,220	7,018	9,573	11,193	14,854	18,270	21,866	21,558
177	Uruguay	—	—	3,926	—	—	—	5,153	—
178	Uzbekistan	—	—	—	—	—	—	—	—
179	Vanuatu	—	—	1,429	—	—	—	1,667	—
180	Venezuela	3,444	4,045	7,424	9,726	10,827	9,966	8,139	9,163
181	Vietnam	—	—	357	—	—	—	1,000	—
182	Yemen	—	—	783	—	—	—	2,000	—
183	Yugoslavia	1,325	1,412	1,546	2,401	3,520	5,876	5,458	3,887
184	Zambia	—	—	733	—	—	—	818	—
185	Zimbabwe	—	—	1,023	—	—	—	1,592	—

Sources: Maddison 1995, pp. 194–206, 217–221.

Table 2

		(2) GNP per capita in US dollars					
	Country	1976	1980	1985	1990	1995	1998
1	Afghanistan	160	—	—	—	—	(350)
2	Albania	540	—	—	—	670	810

continues

Table 2   continued

	Country	1976	1980	1985	1990	1995	1998
3	Algeria	990	1,870	2,550	2,060	1,600	1,550
4	Angola	330	470	—	—	410	340
5	Antigua and Barbuda	—	—	2,020	4,600	—	8,300
6	Argentina	1,550	2,390	2,130	2,370	8,030	8,970
7	Armenia	—	—	—	—	730	480
8	Australia	6,100	9,820	10,830	17,000	18,720	20,300
9	Austria	5,330	10,230	9,120	19,060	26,890	26,850
10	Azerbaijan	—	—	—	—	480	490
11	Bahamas	3,310	4,380	7,070	11,420	11,940	12,400[1]
12	Bahrain	2,140	5,560	9,420	—	7,840	7,660
13	Bangladesh	110	130	150	210	240	350
14	Barbados	1,550	3,040	4,630	6,540	6,560	7,890
15	Belarus	—	—	—	—	2,070	2,200
16	Belgium	6,780	12,180	8,280	15,540	24,710	25,380
17	Belize	—	—	1,190	1,990	2,630	2,610
18	Benin (Dahomey)	130	310	260	360	370	380
19	Bhutan	70	80	160	190	420	470[1]
20	Bolivia	390	570	470	630	800	1,000
21	Botswana	410	910	840	2,040	3,020	3,600
22	Brazil	1,140	2,050	1,640	2,680	3,640	4,570
23	Brunei	—	—	17,570	—	—	24,630[1]
24	Bulgaria	2,310	4,150	—	2,250	1,330	1,230
25	Burkina Faso (Upper Volta)	110	210	150	330	230	240
26	Burma	120	170	190	—	—	(400)
27	Burundi	120	200	230	210	160	140
28	Cambodia	—	—	—	—	270	280
29	Cameroon	290	670	810	960	650	610

	Country	1976	1980	1985	1990	1995	1998
30	Canada	7,510	10,130	13,680	20,470	19,380	20,020
31	Cape Verde	270	300	430	890	960	1,060
32	Central African Republic	230	300	260	390	340	300
33	Chad	120	120	—	190	180	230
34	Chile	1,050	2,150	1,430	1,940	4,160	4,810
35	China	410	290	310	370	620	750
36	Colombia	630	1,180	1,320	1,260	1,910	2,600
37	Comoros	180	300	240	480	470	370
38	Congo (Braz)	520	900	1,110	1,010	680	690
39	Congo (Zaire)	140	220	170	220	120	110
40	Costa Rica	1,040	1,730	1,300	1,900	2,610	2,780
41	Côte d'Ivoire	610	1,150	660	750	660	700
42	Croatia	—	—	—	—	3,250	4,520
43	Cuba	860	—	—	—	—	(2,000)
44	Cyprus	1,480	3,560	3,790	8,020	—	11,920[1]
45	Czech Republic	3,840	5,820	—	3,140	3,870	5,040
46	Denmark	7,450	12,950	11,200	22,080	29,890	33,260
47	Djibouti	580*	580	—	—	—	(600)
48	Dominica	—	620	1,150	2,210	2,990	3,010
49	Dominican Republic	780	1,160	790	830	1,460	1,770
50	Ecuador	640	1,270	1,160	980	1,390	1,530
51	Egypt	280	580	610	600	790	1,290
52	El Salvador	490	660	820	1,110	1,620	1,850
53	Equatorial Guinea	330	—	—	330	380	1,500
54	Eritrea	—	—	—	—	—	200
55	Estonia	—	—	—	—	2,860	3,390

continues

Table 2   continued

	Country	1976	1980	1985	1990	1995	1998
56	Ethiopia	100	140	110	120	100	100
57	Fiji	1,150	1,850	1,710	1,780	2,440	2,110
58	Finland	5,620	9,720	10,890	26,040	20,580	24,110
59	France	6,550	11,730	9,540	19,490	24,990	24,940
60	Gabon	2,590	4,440	3,670	3,330	3,490	3,950
61	Gambia	180	250	230	260	320	340
62	Georgia	—	—	—	—	440	930
63	Germany	7,380	13,590	10,940	22,320	27,510	25,850
64	Ghana	580	420	380	390	390	390
65	Greece	2,590	4,380	3,550	5,990	8,210	11,650
66	Grenada	420	690	970	2,190	2,980	3,170
67	Guatemala	630	1,080	1,250	900	1,340	1,650
68	Guinea	150	290	320	440	550	540
69	Guinea-Bissau	140	160	180	180	250	160
70	Guyana	540	690	500	330	590	770
71	Haiti	200	270	310	370	250	410
72	Honduras	390	560	720	590	600	730
73	Hong Kong	2,110	4,240	6,230	11,490	22,990	23,670
74	Hungary	2,280	4,180	1,970	2,780	4,120	4,510
75	Iceland	6,100	11,330	10,710	21,400	24,950	28,010
76	India	150	240	270	350	340	430
77	Indonesia	240	—	530	570	980	680
78	Iran	1,930	—	—	2,490	—	1,770
79	Iraq	1,390	3,020	—	—	—	(1,500)
80	Ireland	2,560	4,880	4,850	9,550	14,710	18,340
81	Israel	3,920	4,500	4,990	10,920	15,920	15,940
82	Italy	3,050	6,480	6,520	16,830	19,020	20,250
83	Jamaica	1,070	1,040	940	1,500	1,510	1,680

	Country	1976	1980	1985	1990	1995	1998
84	Japan	4,910	9,890	11,300	25,430	39,640	32,380
85	Jordan	610	1,420	1,560	1,240	1,510	1,520
86	Kazakhstan	—	—	—	—	1,330	1,310
87	Kenya	240	420	290	370	280	330
88	Kiribati	—	—	—	760	920	1,180
89	Korea, North	470	—	—	—	—	741*
90	Korea, South	670	1,520	2,150	5,400	9,700	7,970
91	Kuwait	15,480	19,830	14,480	—	17,390	20,200[1]
92	Kyrgyzstan	—	—	—	—	700	350
93	Laos	90	—	—	200	350	330
94	Latvia	—	—	—	—	2,270	2,430
95	Lebanon	—	—	—	—	2,660	3,560
96	Lesotho	170	420	470	530	770	570
97	Liberia	450	530	470	—	—	(350)
98	Libya	6,310	8,640	7,170	—	—	(4,000)
99	Lithuania	—	—	—	—	1,900	2,440
100	Luxembourg	6,460	14,510	14,260	28,730	41,210	43,570
101	Macedonia	—	—	—	—	860	1,290
102	Madagascar	200	350	240	230	230	260
103	Malawi	140	230	170	200	170	200
104	Malaysia	860	1,620	2,000	2,320	3,890	3,600
105	Maldives	120	260	290	450	990	1,230
106	Mali	100	190	150	270	250	250
107	Malta	1,780	3,470	3,310	6,610	—	9,440
108	Marshall Islands	—	—	—	—	—	1,540
109	Mauritania	340	440	420	500	460	410
110	Mauritius	680	1,060	1,090	2,250	3,380	3,700
111	Mexico	1,090	2,090	2,080	2,490	3,320	3,970

continues

Table 2   continued

Country	1976	1980	1985	1990	1995	1998
112 Micronesia	—	—	—	—	—	1,800
113 Moldova	—	—	—	—	920	410
114 Mongolia	860	—	—	—	310	400
115 Morocco	540	900	560	950	1,110	1,250
116 Mozambique	170	230	160	80	80	210
117 Namibia	—	—	—	—	2,000	1,940
118 Nepal	120	140	160	170	200	210
119 Netherlands	6,200	11,470	9,290	17,320	24,000	24,760
120 New Zealand	4,250	7,090	7,010	12,680	14,480	14,700
121 Nicaragua	750	740	770	—	380	370[1]
122 Niger	160	330	250	310	220	190
123 Nigeria	380	1,010	800	290	260	300
124 Norway	7,420	12,650	14,370	23,120	31,250	34,330
125 Oman	2,680	4,380	6,730	—	4,820	(6,000)
126 Pakistan	170	300	380	320	460	480
127 Panama	1,310	1,730	2,100	1,830	2,750	3,080
128 Papua New Guinea	490	780	680	860	1,160	890
129 Paraguay	640	1,300	860	1,110	1,690	1,760
130 Peru	800	930	1,010	1,160	2,310	2,460
131 Philippines	410	690	580	730	1,050	1,050
132 Poland	2,860	3,900	2,050	1,690	2,790	3,900
133 Portugal	1,690	2,370	1,970	4,900	9,740	10,690
134 Puerto Rico	—	3,486*	5,530*	—	—	7,010*
135 Qatar	11,400	26,080	16,270	15,860	11,600	12,000[1]
136 Romania	1,450	2,340	—	1,640	1,480	1,390
137 Russia	2,760	4,550	—	—	2,240	2,300
138 Rwanda	110	200	280	310	180	230

	Country	1976	1980	1985	1990	1995	1998
139	Samoa (Western)	350	—	660	730	1,120	1,020
140	Sao Tome and Principe	490	490	320	400	350	280
141	Saudi Arabia	4,480	11,260	8,850	7,050	7,040	6,910[1]
142	Senegal	390	450	370	710	600	530
143	Seychelles	610	1,770	—	4,670	6,620	6,450
144	Sierra Leone	200	280	350	—	180	140
145	Singapore	2,700	4,430	7,420	11,160	26,730	30,060
146	Slovakia	—	—	—	—	2,950	3,700
147	Slovenia	—	—	—	—	8,200	9,760
148	Solomon Islands	—	460	510	590	910	750
149	Somalia	110	—	280	120	—	(150)
150	South Africa	1,340	2,300	2,010	2,530	3,160	2,880
151	Spain	2,920	5,400	4,290	11,020	13,580	14,080
152	Sri Lanka	200	270	380	470	700	810
153	St. Kitts and Nevis	—	—	1,550	3,330	5,170	6,130
154	St. Lucia	—	900	1,240	1,900	3,370	3,410
155	St. Vincent and Grenadines	—	520	850	1,720	2,280	2,420
156	Sudan	290	410	300	—	—	290
157	Suriname	1,370	2,840	2,580	3,050	880	1,660
158	Swaziland	470	680	670	810	1,170	1,400
159	Sweden	8,670	13,520	11,890	23,660	23,750	25,620
160	Switzerland	8,880	16,440	16,370	32,680	40,630	40,080
161	Syria	780	1,340	1,570	1,000	1,120	1,020
162	Taiwan	1,070	2,344*	—	8,111*	11,597*	13,233*
163	Tajikistan	—	—	—	—	340	350
164	Tanzania	180	280	290	110	120	210

continues

Table 2   continued

	Country	1976	1980	1985	1990	1995	1998
165	Thailand	380	670	800	1,420	2,740	2,200
166	Togo	260	410	230	410	310	330
167	Tonga	—	—	730	1,010	1,630	1,690
168	Trinidad and Tobago	2,240	4,370	6,020	3,610	3,770	4,430
169	Tunisia	840	1,310	1,190	1,440	1,820	2,050
170	Turkey	990	1,470	1,080	1,630	2,730	3,160
171	Turkmenistan	—	—	—	—	920	650[1]
172	Uganda	240	300	—	220	240	320
173	Ukraine	—	—	—	—	1,630	850
174	United Arab Emirates	13,990	26,850	19,270	19,860	17,400	18,220
175	United Kingdom	4,020	7,920	8,460	16,100	18,700	21,400
176	United States	7,890	11,360	16,690	21,790	26,980	29,340
177	Uruguay	1,390	2,810	1,650	2,560	5,170	6,180
178	Uzbekistan	—	—	—	—	970	870
179	Vanuatu	—	530	880	1,100	1,200	1,270
180	Venezuela	2,570	3,630	3,080	2,560	3,020	3,500
181	Vietnam	—	—	—	—	240	330
182	Yemen	250	430	550	—	260	300
183	Yugoslavia	1,680	2,620	2,070	3,060	—	(1,500)
184	Zambia	440	560	390	420	400	330
185	Zimbabwe	550	630	680	640	540	610

Sources: 1976: *World Development Report,* 1978, Table 1 and p. 114, if not otherwise noted.

    * Djibouti for 1977. World Development Report 1979, p. 176.

    1980: *World Development Report,* 1982, Table 1 and p. 163.

    * Puerto Rico. Banks and Overstreet, 1982, p. 529.

    * Taiwan. *The Far East and Australasia 1999,* p. 322.

1985: *World Development Report*, 1987, Table 1 and p. 269.

* Puerto Rico for 1987. *World Development Report*, 1989, Box A.1. and p. 230.

1990: *World Development Report*, 1992: Table 1 and p. 285.

* Taiwan. *The Far East and Australasia 1999*, p. 322.

1995: *World Development Report*, 1997, Table 1 and Table 1a.

* Taiwan for 1994. *Europa World Year Book*, 1996, p. 867.

1998: *World Development Report*, 1999/2000: Table 1 and Table 1a if not otherwise noted.

[1] *Human Development Report*, 2000, Table 13.

* North Korea for 1997. *The Far East and Australasia*, 1998/99, p. 539.

* Puerto Rico for 1997. World Development Report 1998/99, Table 1a.

* Taiwan for 1997. *The Far East and Australasia*, 1999, p. 322.

Tables 3 and 4

		(3) GNP per capita (PPP $)		(4) Real GDP per capita (PPP $)			
	Country	1995	1998	1987	1990	1995	1998
1	Afghanistan	—	—	1,000	714	—	(1,200)
2	Albania	—	—	2,000	3,000	2,853	2,804
3	Algeria	5,300	4,380	2,633	3,011	5,618	4,792
4	Angola	1,300	840	1,000	814	1,839	1,821
5	Antigua and Barbuda	—	9,440	—	4,000	9,131	9,277
6	Argentina	8,310	10,200	4,647	4,295	8,498	12,013
7	Armenia	2,260	—	—	—	2,208	2,072
8	Australia	18,940	20,130	11,782	16,051	19,632	22,452
9	Austria	21,250	22,740	12,386	16,504	21,322	23,166
10	Azerbaijan	1,460	1,820	—	—	1,463	2,175
11	Bahamas	14,710	10,460	—	11,235	15,738	14,614
12	Bahrain	13,400	13,700	—	10,706	16,751	13,111
13	Bangladesh	1,380	1,100	883	872	1,382	1,361
14	Barbados	10,620	12,260	—	8,304	11,306	12,001

continues

Tables 3 and 4   continued

Country	1995	1998	1987	1990	1995	1998
15 Belarus	4,220	—	—	—	4,398	6,319
16 Belgium	20,985	23,480	13,140	16,381	21,548	23,223
17 Belize	5,590	3,940	—	3,000	5,623	4,566
18 Benin	1,760	1,250	665	1,043	1,800	867
19 Bhutan	1,260	—	700	800	1,382	1,536
20 Bolivia	2,540	2,820	1,380	1,572	2,617	2,269
21 Botswana	5,580	8,310	2,496	3,419	5,611	6,103
22 Brazil	5,400	6,160	4,307	4,718	5,928	6,625
23 Brunei	—	—	—	14,000	31,165	16,765
24 Bulgaria	4,480	—	4,750	4,700	4,604	4,809
25 Burkina Faso	780	1,020	500	618	784	870
26 Burma	—	—	752	659	1,130	1,199
27 Burundi	630	620	450	625	637	570
28 Cambodia	—	1,240	1,000	1,100	1,110	1,257
29 Cameroon	2,120	1,810	1,381	1,646	2,355	1,474
30 Canada	21,130	24,050	16,375	19,232	21,916	23,582
31 Cape Verde	1,870	2,950	—	1,769	2,612	3,233
32 Central African Republic	1,070	1,290	591	768	1,092	1,118
33 Chad	700	—	400	559	1,172	856
34 Chile	9,520	12,890	4,862	5,099	9,930	8,787
35 China	2,920	3,220	2,124	1,990	2,935	3,105
36 Colombia	6,130	7,500	3,524	4,237	6,347	6,006
37 Comoros	1,320	1,480	—	721	1,317	1,398
38 Congo (Brazzaville)	2,050	1,430	756	2,362	2,554	995
39 Congo (Zaire)	490	750	220	367	355	822
40 Costa Rica	5,850	6,620	3,760	4,542	5,969	5,987
41 Côte d'Ivoire	1,580	1,730	1,123	1,324	1,731	1,598

Country	1995	1998	1987	1990	1995	1998
42 Croatia	—	—	—	—	—	6,749
43 Cuba	—	—	2,500	2,200	3,100	3,967
44 Cyprus	—	—	—	9,953	13,379	17,482
45 Czech Republic	9,770	11,380*	7,750	7,300	9,775	12,362
46 Denmark	21,230	23,830	15,119	16,781	21,983	24,218
47 Djibouti	—	—	—	1,000	1,300	1,266
48 Dominica	—	3,940	—	3,910	6,424	5,102
49 Dominican Republic	3,870	4,700	1,750	2,404	3,923	4,598
50 Ecuador	4,220	4,630	2,687	3,074	4,602	3,003
51 Egypt	3,820	3,130	1,357	1,988	3,829	3,041
52 El Salvador	2,610	2,850	1,733	1,950	2,610	4,036
53 Equatorial Guinea	—	4,400	—	700	1,712	1,817
54 Eritrea	—	950	—	—	983	833
55 Estonia	4,220	—	—	—	4,062	7,682
56 Ethiopia	450	500	454	369	455	574
57 Fiji	5,780	3,580	—	4,427	6,159	4,231
58 Finland	17,417	20,270	12,795	16,446	18,547	20,847
59 France	21,510	22,320	13,961	17,405	21,176	21,175
60 Gabon	—	6,660	2,068	4,147	3,766	6,353
61 Gambia	930	1,430	—	913	948	1,453
62 Georgia	1,470	—	—	—	1,389	3,353
63 Germany	20,070	20,810	14,730	18,213	20,370	22,169
64 Ghana	1,990	1,610	481	1,016	2,032	1,735
65 Greece	11,710	13,010	5,500	7,336	11,636	13,943
66 Grenada	—	4,720	—	4,081	5,425	5,838
67 Guatemala	3,340	4,070	1,957	2,576	3,682	3,505
68 Guinea	—	1,760	500	501	1,139	1,782

continues

Tables 3 and 4   continued

	Country	1995	1998	1987	1990	1995	1998
69	Guinea—Bissau	790	750	—	841	811	616
70	Guyana	2,420	2,680	—	1,464	3,205	3,403
71	Haiti	910	1,250	775	933	917	1,383
72	Honduras	1,900	2,140	1,119	1,470	1,977	2,433
73	Hong Kong	22,950	22,000	13,906	15,595	22,950	20,763
74	Hungary	6,410	—	4,500	6,116	6,793	10,232
75	Iceland	20,460	22,830	—	16,496	21,064	25,110
76	India	1,400	1,700	1,053	1,072	1,422	2,077
77	Indonesia	3,800	2,790	1,660	2,181	3,971	2,651
78	Iran	—	—	3,300	3,523	5,480	5,121
79	Iraq	—	—	2,400	3,508	3,170	3,197
80	Ireland	15,680	18,340	8,566	10,589	17,590	21,482
81	Israel	16,490	17,310	9,182	10,840	16,699	17,301
82	Italy	19,870	20,200	10,682	15,890	20,174	20,585
83	Jamaica	3,540	3,210	2,506	2,979	3,801	3,389
84	Japan	22,110	23,180	13,135	17,616	21,930	23,257
85	Jordan	4,060	3,230	3,161	2,345	4,187	3,347
86	Kazakhstan	3,010	3,400	—	—	3,037	4,378
87	Kenya	1,380	1,130	794	1,058	1,438	980
88	Kiribati	—	3,480	—	—	—	(3,000)
89	Korea, North	—	—	2,000	2,000	4,058	(3,000)
90	Korea, South	11,450	12,270	4,832	6,733	11,594	13,478
91	Kuwait	23,790	—	13,843	15,178	23,848	25,314
92	Kyrgyzstan	1,800	2,200	—	—	1,927	2,317
93	Laos	—	1,300	1,000	1,100	2,571	1,734
94	Latvia	3,370	—	—	—	3,273	5,728
95	Lebanon	—	6,150	2,250	2,300	4,977	4,326
96	Lesotho	1,780	2,320	1,585	1,743	1,290	1,626

Country	1995	1998	1987	1990	1995	1998
97 Liberia	—	—	696	857	—	(1,200)
98 Libya	—	—	7,250	7,000	6,309	6,697
99 Lithuania	4,120	4,310	—	—	3,843	6,436
100 Luxembourg	37,930	37,420	—	19,244	34,004	33,505
101 Macedonia	—	3,660	—	—	4,058	4,254
102 Madagascar	640	900	634	704	673	756
103 Malawi	750	730	476	640	773	523
104 Malaysia	9,020	6,990	3,849	6,140	9,572	8,137
105 Maldives	3,080	—	—	1,200	3,540	4,083
106 Mali	550	720	543	572	565	681
107 Malta	—	13,610	—	8,732	13,316	16,448
108 Marshall Islands	—	—	—	—	—	(3,000)
109 Mauritania	1,540	1,660	840	1,057	1,622	1,563
110 Mauritius	13,210	9,400	2,617	5,750	13,294	8,312
111 Mexico	6,400	8,190	4,624	5,918	6,769	7,704
112 Micronesia	—	—	—	—	—	(3,000)
113 Moldova	—	—	—	—	1,547	1,947
114 Mongolia	1,950	1,520	2,000	2,100	3,916	1,541
115 Morocco	3,340	3,120	1,761	2,348	3,477	3,305
116 Mozambique	810	850	500	1,072	959	782
117 Namibia	4,150	4,950	—	1,400	4,054	5,176
118 Nepal	1,170	1,090	722	920	1,145	1,157
119 Netherlands	19,950	21,620	12,661	15,695	19,876	22,176
120 New Zealand	16,360	15,840	10,541	13,481	17,267	17,288
121 Nicaragua	2,000	1,790	2,209	1,497	1,837	2,142
122 Niger	750	830	452	645	765	739
123 Nigeria	1,220	820	668	1,215	1,270	795

continues

Tables 3 and 4   continued

Country	1995	1998	1987	1990	1995	1998
124 Norway	21,940	24,290	15,940	16,028	22,427	26,342
125 Oman	8,140	—	7,750	9,972	9,383	9,960
126 Pakistan	2,230	1,560	1,585	1,862	2,209	1,715
127 Panama	5,980	6,940	4,009	3,317	6,258	5,249
128 Papua New Guinea	2,420	2,700	1,843	1,786	2,500	2,359
129 Paraguay	3,650	3,650	2,603	2,790	3,583	4,288
130 Peru	3,770	—	3,129	2,622	3,940	4,282
131 Philippines	2,850	3,540	1,878	2,303	2,762	3,555
132 Poland	5,400	6,740	4,000	4,237	5,442	7,619
133 Portugal	12,670	14,380	5,597	8,770	12,674	14,701
134 Puerto Rico	—	—	—	—	—	(8,000)
135 Qatar	17,690	—	—	11,400	19,772	20,987
136 Romania	4,360	3,970	3,000	2,800	4,431	5,648
137 Russia	4,480	3,950	6,000	7,968	4,531	6,460
138 Rwanda	540	690	571	657	—	660
139 Samoa (Western)	2,030	3,440	—	1,900	2,948	3,832
140 Sao Tome and Principe	—	1,350	—	600	1,744	1,469
141 Saudi Arabia	—	—	8,320	10,989	8,516	10,158
142 Senegal	1,780	1,710	1,068	1,248	1,815	1,307
143 Seychelles	—	10,530	—	4,191	7,697	10,600
144 Sierra Leone	580	390	480	1,086	625	458
145 Singapore	22,770	28,620	12,790	15,880	22,604	24,210
146 Slovakia	3,610	—	—	—	7,320	9,699
147 Slovenia	—	—	—	—	10,594	14,293
148 Solomon Islands	2,190	2,080	—	2,689	2,266	1,940
149 Somalia	—	—	1,000	836	—	(1,000)
150 South Africa	5,030	6,990	4,981	4,865	4,334	8,488
151 Spain	14,520	16,060	8,989	11,723	14,789	16,212

Country	1995	1998	1987	1990	1995	1998
152 Sri Lanka	3,250	—	2,053	2,405	3,408	2,979
153 St. Kitts and Nevis	9,410	7,940	—	3,300	10,150	10,672
154 St. Lucia	—	4,610	—	3,470	6,530	5,183
155 St. Vincent and Grenadines	—	4,090	—	3,647	5,969	4,692
156 Sudan	—	1,360	750	949	1,110	1,394
157 Suriname	2,250	—	—	3,927	4,862	5,161
158 Swaziland	2,880	3,580	—	2,384	2,954	3,816
159 Sweden	18,540	19,480	13,780	17,014	19,297	20,659
160 Switzerland	25,860	26,620	15,403	20,874	24,881	25,512
161 Syria	5,320	3,000	3,250	4,756	5,374	2,892
162 Taiwan	—	—	—	—	—	(13,000)
163 Tajikistan	920	—	—	—	943	1,041
164 Tanzania	630	490	405	572	636	480
165 Thailand	7,540	5,840	2,576	3,986	7,742	5,456
166 Togo	1,130	1,390	670	734	1,167	1,372
167 Tonga	8,610	3,860	—	—	—	(3,000)
168 Trinidad and Tobago	—	6,720	3,664	6,604	9,437	7,485
169 Tunisia	5,000	5,160	2,741	3,579	5,261	5,404
170 Turkey	5,580	—	3,781	4,652	5,516	6,422
171 Turkmenistan	—	—	—	—	2,345	2,550
172 Uganda	1,470	1,170	511	524	1,483	1,074
173 Ukraine	2,400	—	—	—	2,361	3,194
174 United Arab Emirates	16,470	19,720	12,191	16,753	18,008	17,719
175 United Kingdom	19,260	20,640	12,270	15,804	19,302	20,336
176 United States	26,980	29,340	17,615	21,449	26,977	29,605
177 Uruguay	6,630	9,480	5,063	5,916	6,854	8,623
178 Uzbekistan	2,370	2,900	—	—	2,376	2,053

continues

Tables 3 and 4   continued

	Country	1995	1998	1987	1990	1995	1998
179	Vanuatu	2,290	3,160	—	2,005	2,507	3,120
180	Venezuela	7,900	8,190	4,306	6,169	8,090	5,808
181	Vietnam	—	1,690	1,000	1,100	1,236	1,689
182	Yemen	—	740	1,250	1,562	856	719
183	Yugoslavia	—	—	5,000	—	—	(4,000)
184	Zambia	930	860	717	744	986	719
185	Zimbabwe	2,030	2,150	1,184	1,484	2,135	2,669

Sources: *(3) GNP per capita measured at PPP*
    1995: World Development Report, 1997, Table 1 and Table 1a.
    1998: World Development Report, 1999/2000, Table 1 and Table 1a.
    * Czech. Republic for 1997. World Development Report, 1998/99, Table 1.

Sources: *(4) Real GDP per capita (PPP $)*
    1987: Human Development Report, 1990, Table 1.
    1990: Human Development Report, 1993, Table 1.
    1995: Human Development Report, 1998, Table 1.
    1998: Human Development Report, 2000, Table 1.

Table 5

	Country	*(5) GDP per capita in US dollars at current prices*			
		1983	1990	1993	1996
1	Afghanistan	—	1,286	2,337	70
2	Albania	2,388	660	265	490
3	Algeria	2,375	2,562	1,912	1,534
4	Angola	696	1,113	1,236	293
5	Antigua and Barbuda	2,473	6,166	7,023	8,485
6	Argentina	3,524	4,346	7,613	8,446
7	Armenia	9,507	4,261	130	438

Country	1983	1990	1993	1996
8 Australia	11,488	17,504	16,675	22,235
9 Austria	8,870	20,701	23,113	28,218
10 Azerbaijan	2,780	3,075	212	420
11 Bahamas	7,311	12,290	11,888	12,493
12 Bahrain	9,408	8,176	8,753	9,309
13 Bangladesh	150	220	227	279
14 Barbados	4,186	6,693	6,373	7,639
15 Belarus	3,639	6,278	136	1,121
16 Belgium	8,189	19,697	21,298	26,403
17 Belize	1,196	2,120	2,523	2,685
18 Benin	291	394	417	413
19 Bhutan	129	173	138	176
20 Bolivia	1,048	741	827	939
21 Botswana	1,051	2,762	2,727	2,966
22 Brazil	1,562	2,961	2,836	4,648
23 Brunei	16,512	13,972	14,607	18,167
24 Bulgaria	2,288	2,377	1,262	1,102
25 Burkina Faso	1,000	239	218	178
26 Burma	172	580	1,343	2,633
27 Burundi	247	209	161	166
28 Cambodia	96	99	94	143
29 Cameroon	730	1,094	901	672
30 Canada	13,203	20,441	19,000	19,515
31 Cape Verde	459	963	920	985
32 Central African Republic	329	510	509	393
33 Chad	147	220	172	171
34 Chile	1,563	2,321	3,315	4,986

continues

Table 5   continued

	Country	1983	1990	1993	1996
35	China	287	342	511	671
36	Colombia	1,369	1,236	1,456	2,325
37	Comoros	262	478	458	359
38	Congo (Braz)	1,156	1,286	1,406	1,262
39	Congo (Zaire)	155	299	212	90
40	Costa Rica	1,262	1,881	2,300	2,636
41	Côte d'Ivoire	743	924	805	763
42	Croatia	2,515	5,401	2,591	4,236
43	Cuba	1,835	1,848	1,391	2,071
44	Cyprus	3,325	8,162	9,093	11,500
45	Czech Republic	2,989	3,067	3,037	4,919
46	Denmark	10,936	25,122	25,989	33,387
47	Djibouti	1,141	899	889	868
48	Dominica	1,080	2,355	2,761	3,242
49	Dominican Republic	1,409	1,070	1,261	1,638
50	Ecuador	1,439	1,041	1,303	1,627
51	Egypt	833	779	780	1,065
52	El Salvador	873	903	1,294	1,791
53	Equatorial Guinea	247	463	478	601
54	Eritrea	—	—	174	174
55	Estonia	4,567	7,624	1,092	2,975
56	Ethiopia	126	173	98	101
57	Fiji	1,663	1,902	2,171	2,639
58	Finland	10,160	27,037	16,689	24,410
59	France	9,626	21,063	21,699	26,374
60	Gabon	3,711	5,871	5,624	4,305
61	Gambia	327	312	325	303
62	Georgia	3,513	4,115	402	595

	Country	1983	1990	1993	1996
63	Germany	16,521	24,485	23,255	28,727
64	Ghana	515	415	371	380
65	Greece	3,551	8,113	8,879	11,673
66	Grenada	1,052	2,202	2,319	2,738
67	Guatemala	1,203	832	1,137	1,446
68	Guinea	369	479	467	527
69	Guinea—Bissau	467	242	229	172
70	Guyana	622	498	550	820
71	Haiti	288	386	217	382
72	Honduras	739	625	657	699
73	Hong Kong	5,335	13,108	19,482	24,902
74	Hungary	2,008	3,452	3,778	4,463
75	Iceland	11,232	24,507	23,140	26,922
76	India	280	360	296	375
77	Indonesia	531	581	745	1,018
78	Iran	3,454	9,087	1,138	1,900
79	Iraq	2,971	4,146	6,650	13,880
80	Ireland	5,252	12,996	13,790	19,902
81	Israel	7,118	11,811	13,520	16,091
82	Italy	7,332	19,184	17,239	21,219
83	Jamaica	1,614	1,795	1,738	2,198
84	Japan	9,937	24,042	34,336	36,658
85	Jordan	1,490	944	1,121	1,301
86	Kazakhstan	2,507	4,122	281	1,251
87	Kenya	323	364	215	330
88	Kiribati	381	447	423	573
89	Korea, North	770	943	611	195

continues

Table 5   continued

	Country	1983	1990	1993	1996
90	Korea, South	2,071	5,917	7,549	10,698
91	Kuwait	13,357	8,619	12,858	16,893
92	Kyrgyzstan	2,180	2,918	223	409
93	Laos	392	207	292	371
94	Latvia	4,403	6,986	832	2,007
95	Lebanon	1,147	1,302	2,440	4,155
96	Lesotho	241	349	367	387
97	Liberia	526	511	848	1,200
98	Libya	8,546	6,643	4,382	3,741
99	Lithuania	3,919	5,182	682	1,510
100	Luxembourg	9,360	27,155	32,430	41,187
101	Macedonia	—	2,114	1,182	1,651
102	Madagascar	295	249	216	132
103	Malawi	180	185	216	222
104	Malaysia	2,027	2,394	3,335	4,824
105	Maldives	382	675	913	1,166
106	Mali	145	272	255	235
107	Malta	3,143	6,531	6,815	9,035
108	Marshall Islands	1,165	1,493	1,707	1,872
109	Mauritania	489	552	431	433
110	Mauritius	1,090	2,418	2,853	3,800
111	Mexico	2,064	2,932	4,114	3,554
112	Micronesia	1,288	1,787	1,812	2,311
113	Moldova	3,120	4,363	137	440
114	Mongolia	1,487	1,096	260	386
115	Morocco	668	1,074	1,052	1,395
116	Mozambique	173	104	78	88
117	Namibia	1,410	1,822	1,841	2,036

Country	1983	1990	1993	1996
118 Nepal	143	188	173	200
119 Netherlands	9,531	18,972	20,494	25,426
120 New Zealand	7,331	12,828	12,566	18,291
121 Nicaragua	730	621	506	482
122 Niger	292	324	264	212
123 Nigeria	916	337	302	856
124 Norway	13,367	27,223	27,021	36,293
125 Oman	6,789	6,546	6,157	6,398
126 Pakistan	340	395	433	504
127 Panama	2,120	2,216	2,858	3,029
128 Papua New Guinea	778	839	1,248	1,181
129 Paraguay	1,872	1,248	1,501	1,947
130 Peru	1,072	1,674	1,770	2,546
131 Philippines	631	729	837	1,206
132 Poland	2,029	1,633	2,238	3,486
133 Portugal	2,098	6,839	8,507	10,923
134 Puerto Rico	5,786	9,125	10,937	13,199
135 Qatar	21,123	15,176	13,554	14,528
136 Romania	1,985	1,648	1,148	1,567
137 Russia	4,382	6,523	1,161	2,974
138 Rwanda	268	336	255	241
139 Samoa (Western)	643	700	732	1,045
140 Sao Tome and Principe	356	428	151	40
141 Saudi Arabia	11,866	5,172	7,101	6,650
142 Senegal	411	793	697	592
143 Seychelles	2,249	5,266	6,485	7,294
144 Sierra Leone	320	159	201	243
145 Singapore	6,954	12,417	18,196	27,693

continues

Table 5   continued

Country	1983	1990	1993	1996
146 Slovakia	2,525	2,947	2,264	3,547
147 Slovenia	4,157	9,062	6,583	9,716
148 Solomon Islands	488	526	735	947
149 Somalia	298	124	112	83
150 South Africa	2,576	2,879	2,961	2,979
151 Spain	4,113	12,526	12,119	14,641
152 Sri Lanka	325	465	588	771
153 St. Kitts and Nevis	1,297	3,359	4,175	5,114
154 St. Lucia	1,173	2,996	3,508	3,999
155 St. Vincent and Grenadines	934	1,811	2,157	2,448
156 Sudan	344	1,017	110	40
157 Suriname	2,698	4,333	14,031	898
158 Swaziland	896	1,155	1,213	1,365
159 Sweden	11,123	26,844	21,342	28,546
160 Switzerland	15,197	33,422	33,637	40,746
161 Syria	1,936	1,930	2,734	3,779
162 Taiwan	—	—	—	13,000*
163 Tajikistan	1,722	2,080	120	177
164 Tanzania	309	148	123	167
165 Thailand	808	1,536	2,191	3,136
166 Togo	259	464	323	329
167 Tonga	706	1,289	1,482	1,819
168 Trinidad and Tobago	6,908	4,100	3,670	4,178
169 Tunisia	1,171	1,509	1,687	2,144
170 Turkey	1,304	2,686	3,059	2,788
171 Turkmenistan	2,381	3,111	1,269	237

	Country	1983	1990	1993	1996
172	Uganda	236	224	183	305
173	Ukraine	3,322	4,835	630	853
174	United Arab Emirates	22,680	17,585	16,898	19,738
175	United Kingdom	8,156	16,939	16,301	19,847
176	United States	14,492	21,857	24,182	27,420
177	Uruguay	1,709	2,700	4,321	5,832
178	Uzbekistan	2,093	2,374	251	332
179	Vanuatu	811	1,026	1,215	1,424
180	Venezuela	5,005	2,492	2,871	3,017
181	Vietnam	107	97	181	312
182	Yemen	529	1,089	1,353	443
183	Yugoslavia	1,819	3,141	1,443	1,018
184	Zambia	676	564	217	204
185	Zimbabwe	797	690	692	776

Sources: 1983: United Nations, Statistical Yearbook, 1992.

1990, 1993, 1996: United Nations, Statistical Yearbook, 1996, if not otherwise noted.

* Taiwan for 1997. The Far East and Australasia Yearbook, 1999, p. 322.

Table 6

		(6) Economic growth percentages					
	Country	Growth 1820–1992 GDP (M) %	Growth 1950–90 GDP (M) %	Growth 1976–98 GNP %	Growth 1995–98 GNP-PPP %	Growth 1987-98 Real GDP %	Growth 1983–96 GDP (UN) %
1	Afghanistan	—	–26.7	118.8	—	20.0	—
2	Albania	—	148.3	50.0	—	40.2	–79.5
3	Algeria	—	103.5	56.6	–17.4	82.0	–35.4

continues

Table 6   continued

	Growth 1820–1992 GDP (M) %	Growth 1950–90 GDP (M) %	Growth 1976–98 GNP %	Growth 1995–98 GNP-PPP %	Growth 1987-98 Real GDP %	Growth 1983–96 GDP (UN) %
4 Angola	—	–33.7	3.0	–35.4	82.1	–57.9
5 Antigua and Barbuda	—	182.2	—	—	—	243.1
6 Argentina	—	32.0	478.7	–22.7	158.5	139.7
7 Armenia	—	—	—	—	—	–95.4
8 Australia	962.6	127.4	232.8	6.3	90.6	93.5
9 Austria	1,225.5	350.1	403.8	7.0	87.0	218.1
10 Azerbaijan	—	—	—	24.7	—	–84.9
11 Bahamas	—	60.6	274.6	–28.9	—	70.9
12 Bahrain	—	92.1	257.9	2.2	—	–1.1
13 Bangladesh	35.6	26.7	218.2	–20.3	54.1	86.0
14 Barbados	—	261.3	409.0	15.4	—	82.5
15 Belarus	—	—	—	—	—	–69.2
16 Belgium	1,229.6	214.4	274.3	11.9	76.7	222.4
17 Belize	—	129.0	—	–29.5	—	124.5
18 Benin	—	1.8	192.3	–29.0	30.4	41.9
19 Bhutan	—	88.2	571.4	—	119.4	36.4
20 Bolivia	—	–7.4	156.4	11.0	64.4	–10.4
21 Botswana	—	980.8	778.0	48.9	144.5	182.2
22 Brazil	592.1	187.6	300.9	14.1	53.8	107.6
23 Brunei	—	32.0	—	—	—	10.0
24 Bulgaria	—	249.1	–46.8	—	1.2	–51.8
25 Burkina Faso	—	–22.5	118.2	30.8	74.0	–82.2
26 Burma	—	74.8	233.3	—	59.4	1,430.8
27 Burundi	—	87.2	16.7	–1.6	26.7	–32.8
28 Cambodia	—	69.2	—	—	25.7	49.0

	Country	Growth 1820–1992 GDP (M) %	Growth 1950–90 GDP (M) %	Growth 1976–98 GNP %	Growth 1995–98 GNP-PPP %	Growth 1987-98 Real GDP %	Growth 1983–96 GDP (UN) %
29	Cameroon	—	80.2	110.3	–14.6	6.7	–7.9
30	Canada	1,933.5	178.1	166.6	13.8	44.0	47.8
31	Cape Verde	—	152.3	292.6	57.8	—	114.6
32	Central African Republic	—	–11.7	30.4	20.6	89.2	19.5
33	Chad	—	–6.9	91.7	—	114.0	16.3
34	Chile	—	66.7	358.1	35.4	80.7	219.0
35	China	492.3	339.7	82.9	10.3	46.2	133.8
36	Colombia	—	135.4	312.7	23.3	70.4	69.8
37	Comoros	—	1.3	105.6	12.1	—	37.0
38	Congo (Braz)	—	97.8	32.7	–30.2	31.6	9.2
39	Congo (Zaire)	—	–28.0	–21.4	53.1	273.6	–41.9
40	Costa Rica	—	99.3	60.7	13.2	59.2	108.9
41	Côte d'Ivoire	—	42.5	14.8	9.5	42.3	2.7
42	Croatia	—	—	—	—	—	68.4
43	Cuba	—	–17.8	132.6	—	58.7	12.9
44	Cyprus	—	359.7	705.4	—	—	245.9
45	Czech Republic	706.2	141.8	31.3	16.5	59.5	64.6
46	Denmark	1,393.3	168.6	346.4	12.2	60.2	205.3
47	Djibouti	—	131.4	3.4	—	—	–23.9
48	Dominica	—	116.0	—	—	—	200.2
49	Dominican Republic	—	93.2	126.9	22.0	162.7	16.3
50	Ecuador	—	128.5	139.1	9.7	11.8	13.1
51	Egypt	—	292.6	360.7	–18.1	124.1	27.9
52	El Salvador	—	28.8	277.6	9.2	132.9	105.2

continues

Table 6   continued

Country	Growth 1820–1992 GDP (M) %	Growth 1950–90 GDP (M) %	Growth 1976–98 GNP %	Growth 1995–98 GNP-PPP %	Growth 1987-98 Real GDP %	Growth 1983–96 GDP (UN) %
53 Equatorial Guinea	—	139.1	354.5	—	—	143.3
54 Eritrea	—	—	—	—	—	—
55 Estonia	—	—	—	—	—	–34.9
56 Ethiopia	—	26.4	0.0	11.1	26.4	–19.8
57 Fiji	—	62.8	83.5	–38.1	—	58.7
58 Finland	1,829.6	301.9	329.0	16.4	62.9	140.3
59 France	1,374.5	240.5	280.8	3.8	51.7	174.0
60 Gabon	—	230.1	52.5	—	207.2	16.0
61 Gambia	—	87.8	88.9	53.8	—	–7.3
62 Georgia	—	—	—	—	—	–83.1
63 Germany	1,640.2	336.5	250.3	3.7	50.5	73.9
64 Ghana	—	–19.0	–32.8	–19.1	260.7	–26.2
65 Greece	—	415.2	349.8	11.1	153.5	228.7
66 Grenada	—	208.3	654.8	—	—	170.3
67 Guatemala	—	46.8	161.9	21.9	79.1	20.2
68 Guinea	—	72.3	260.0	—	256.4	42.8
69 Guinea-Bissau	—	179.3	14.3	–5.1	—	–63.2
70 Guyana	—	2.8	42.6	10.7	—	31.8
71 Haiti	—	5.4	105.0	37.4	78.5	32.6
72 Honduras	—	45.8	87.2	12.6	117.4	–5.4
73 Hong Kong	—	772.6	1,021.8	–4.1	49.3	366.8
74 Hungary	—	156.0	97.8	—	127.4	122.3
75 Iceland	—	246.6	359.2	11.6	—	139.7
76 India	153.9	120.4	186.7	21.4	97.2	33.9
77 Indonesia	347.2	188.9	183.3	–26.6	59.7	91.7

Country	Growth 1820–1992 GDP (M) %	Growth 1950–90 GDP (M) %	Growth 1976–98 GNP %	Growth 1995–98 GNP-PPP %	Growth 1987-98 Real GDP %	Growth 1983–96 GDP (UN) %
78 Iran	—	93.6	–8.3	—	55.2	–45.0
79 Iraq	—	79.9	7.9	—	32.2	367.2
80 Ireland	1,127.6	216.2	616.4	17.0	150.8	278.9
81 Israel	—	311.7	306.6	5.0	88.4	126.1
82 Italy	1,447.4	365.7	563.9	1.7	92.7	189.4
83 Jamaica	—	179.1	57.0	–9.3	35.2	36.2
84 Japan	2,667.1	890.3	559.5	–4.8	77.1	268.9
85 Jordan	—	281.9	149.2	–20.4	5.9	–12.9
86 Kazakhstan	—	—	—	13.0	—	–50.1
87 Kenya	—	–22.8	37.5	–18.1	23.4	2.2
88 Kiribati	—	–45.4	—	—	—	50.4
89 Korea, North	—	251.3	57.7	—	50.0	–74.7
90 Korea, South	—	924.8	1,089.6	7.2	178.9	416.0
91 Kuwait	—	–78.0	30.5	—	82.9	26.5
92 Kyrgyzstan	—	—	—	22.2	—	–81.2
93 Laos	—	105.6	266.7	—	73.4	–5.4
94 Latvia	—	—	—	—	—	–54.4
95 Lebanon	—	–1.6	—	—	92.3	262.2
96 Lesotho	—	217.0	235.3	30.3	2.6	60.6
97 Liberia	—	–23.3	–22.2	—	72.4	128.1
98 Libya	—	251.4	–36.6	—	–7.6	–56.2
99 Lithuania	—	—	—	4.6	—	–61.5
100 Luxembourg	—	154.4	574.5	–1.3	—	340.0
101 Macedonia	—	—	—	—	—	—
102 Madagascar	—	–20.9	30.0	40.6	19.2	–55.3

continues

Table 6   continued

Country	Growth 1820–1992 GDP (M) %	Growth 1950–90 GDP (M) %	Growth 1976–98 GNP %	Growth 1995–98 GNP-PPP %	Growth 1987-98 Real GDP %	Growth 1983–96 GDP (UN) %
103 Malawi	—	90.8	42.9	–2.7	9.9	23.2
104 Malaysia	—	232.4	318.6	–22.5	111.4	138.0
105 Maldives	—	327.8	925.0	—	—	205.2
106 Mali	—	31.2	150.0	30.9	25.4	62.1
107 Malta	—	805.0	430.3	—	—	187.5
108 Marshall Islands	—	66.6	—	—	—	60.7
109 Mauritania	—	50.7	20.6	7.8	86.1	–11.5
110 Mauritius	—	182.9	444.1	–28.8	217.6	248.6
111 Mexico	572.6	139.7	264.2	28.0	66.6	72.2
112 Micronesia	—	66.5	—	—	—	79.4
113 Moldova	—	—	—	—	—	–85.9
114 Mongolia	—	251.3	–53.5	—22.1	–23.0	–74.0
115 Morocco	—	48.9	131.5	–6.6	87.7	108.8
116 Mozambique	—	–14.2	23.5	4.9	56.4	–49.1
117 Namibia	—	40.1	—	19.3	—	44.4
118 Nepal	—	61.2	75.0	–6.8	60.2	39.9
119 Netherlands	982.5	183.2	299.4	8.4	75.2	166.8
120 New Zealand	—	64.7	245.9	–3.2	64.0	149.5
121 Nicaragua	—	–15.1	–50.7	–10.5	–3.0	–34.0
122 Niger	—	–26.8	18.8	10.7	63.5	–27.4
123 Nigeria	—	104.4	–21.1	–32.8	19.0	–6.6
124 Norway	1,647.3	240.0	362.7	10.7	65.3	171.5
125 Oman	—	909.2	123.9	—	28.5	–5.8
126 Pakistan	209.2	142.3	182.4	–30.0	8.2	48.2
127 Panama	—	112.8	135.1	16.1	30.9	42.9

	Country	Growth 1820–1992 GDP (M) %	Growth 1950–90 GDP (M) %	Growth 1976–98 GNP %	Growth 1995–98 GNP-PPP %	Growth 1987–98 Real GDP %	Growth 1983–96 GDP (UN) %
128	Papua New Guinea	—	72.5	81.6	11.6	28.0	51.8
129	Paraguay	—	99.3	175.0	0.0	64.7	4.0
130	Peru	—	32.6	207.5	—	36.8	137.5
131	Philippines	—	77.9	156.1	24.2	89.3	91.1
132	Poland	—	108.9	36.4	24.8	90.5	71.9
133	Portugal	—	401.2	532.5	13.5	162.7	420.6
134	Puerto Rico	—	462.2	—	—	—	128.1
135	Qatar	—	–46.2	5.3	—	—	–31.2
136	Romania	—	192.7	–4.1	–8.4	88.3	–21.1
137	Russia	522.0	142.4	–16.7	–11.8	7.7	–32.1
138	Rwanda	—	22.3	109.1	27.8	15.6	–10.1
139	Samoa (Western)	—	38.5	191.4	69.5	—	62.5
140	Sao Tome and Principe	—	59.2	–42.9	—	—	–88.8
141	Saudi Arabia	—	366.8	54.2	—	–22.1	–44.0
142	Senegal	—	14.3	35.9	–3.9	22.4	44.0
143	Seychelles	—	199.1	957.4	—	—	224.3
144	Sierra Leone	—	42.6	–30.0	–32.8	–4.6	–24.1
145	Singapore	—	619.5	1,013.3	25.7	89.3	298.2
146	Slovakia	—	—	—	—	—	40.5
147	Slovenia	—	—	—	—	—	133.7
148	Solomon Islands	—	54.0	—	–5.0	—	94.1
149	Somalia	—	–9.8	36.4	—	0.0	–72.1
150	South Africa	—	65.2	114.9	39.0	70.4	15.6
151	Spain	1,075.7	407.7	382.2	10.6	80.4	256.0

continues

Table 6   continued

	Country	Growth 1820–1992 GDP (M) %	Growth 1950–90 GDP (M) %	Growth 1976–98 GNP %	Growth 1995–98 GNP-PPP %	Growth 1987-98 Real GDP %	Growth 1983–96 GDP (UN) %
152	Sri Lanka	—	184.0	305.0	—	45.1	137.2
153	St. Kitts and Nevis	—	233.7	—	–15.6	—	294.3
154	St. Lucia	—	267.2	—	—	—	240.9
155	St. Vincent and Grenadines	—	132.7	—	—	—	162.1
156	Sudan	—	10.7	0.0	—	85.9	–88.4
157	Suriname	—	138.1	21.2	—	—	–66.7
158	Swaziland	—	262.5	197.9	24.3	—	52.3
159	Sweden	1,312.9	162.6	195.5	5.1	49.9	156.6
160	Switzerland	—	142.3	351.4	2.9	65.6	168.2
161	Syria	—	140.4	30.8	–43.6	–11.0	95.2
162	Taiwan	—	1,019.7	1,136.7	—	—	—
163	Tajikistan	—	—	—	—	—	–89.7
164	Tanzania	—	40.3	16.7	–22.2	18.5	–46.0
165	Thailand	—	401.6	478.9	–22.5	111.8	288.1
166	Togo	—	39.1	26.9	23.0	104.8	27.0
167	Tonga	—	167.5	—	–55.2	—	157.6
168	Trinidad and Tobago	—	105.2	97.8	—	104.3	–39.5
169	Tunisia	—	185.2	144.0	3.2	97.2	83.1
170	Turkey	—	228.2	219.2	—	69.8	113.8
171	Turkmenistan	—	—	—	—	—	–90.0
172	Uganda	—	–17.8	33.3	–20.4	110.2	29.2
173	Ukraine	—	—	—	—	—	–74.3
174	United Arab Emirates	—	33.4	30.2	19.7	45.3	–13.0

	Country	Growth 1820–1992 GDP (M) %	Growth 1950–90 GDP (M) %	Growth 1976–98 GNP %	Growth 1995–98 GNP-PPP %	Growth 1987-98 Real GDP %	Growth 1983–96 GDP (UN) %
175	United Kingdom	796.2	138.1	432.3	7.2	65.7	143.3
176	United States	1,575.1	128.4	271.9	8.7	68.1	89.2
177	Uruguay	—	31.3	344.6	43.0	70.3	241.3
178	Uzbekistan	—	—	—	22.4	—	–84.1
179	Vanuatu	—	–16.7	—	38.0	—	75.6
180	Venezuela	—	9.6	36.2	3.7	34.9	–39.7
181	Vietnam	—	180.1	—	—	68.9	191.6
182	Yemen	—	155.4	20.0	—	–42.5	–16.3
183	Yugoslavia	—	253.0	–10.7	—	–20.0	–44.0
184	Zambia	—	11.6	–25.0	–7.5	0.3	–69.8
185	Zimbabwe	—	55.6	10.9	5.9	125.4	–2.6

Data for the economic growth percentages are presented in the previous sections of this Appendix.

Bibliography

Abul-Hubb, D. 1972. "Application of progressive matrices in Iraq." In L. J. Cronbach and P. J. Drenth (Eds.), *Mental Tests and Cultural Adaptation*. The Hague: Mouton.

Africa South of the Sahara 2000. 2000. London: Europa Publications.

Afzal, M. 1988. Consequences of consanguinity on cognitive behavior. *Behavior Genetics,* 18: 583–594.

Ahmed, R. A. 1989. "The development of number, space, quantity and reasoning concepts in Sudanese schoolchildren." In L. L. Adler (Ed.), *Cross Cultural Research in Human Development.* Westport, CT: Praeger.

Alemayehu, M. 2000. *Industrializing Africa: Development Options and Challenges for the 21st Century.* Trenton, NJ: Africa World Press.

Alonso, O. S. 1974. Raven, g factor, age and school level. *Havana Hospital Psiquiatrico Revista,* 14: 60–77.

Amin, S. 1996. "On the origins of the economic catastrophe in Africa." In S. C. Chew and R. A. Denemark (Eds.), *The Underdevelopment of Development. Essays in Honor of Andrè Gunder Frank.* Thousands Oaks: Sage Publications.

Angelini, A. L., I. C. Alves, E. M. Custodio, and W. F. Duarte. 1988. *Manual Matrizes Progressivas Coloridas.* Sao Paulo: Casa do Psicologo.

Ardila, A., D. Pineda, and M. Rosselli. 2000. Correlation between intelligence test scores and executive function measures. *Archives of Clinical Neuropsychology,* 15: 31–36.

Ashley Montagu, F. M. 1945. Intelligence of northern Negroes and southern Whites in the first world war. *American Journal of Psychology,* 58: 161–188.

Auletta, K. 1982. *The Underclass.* New York: Random House.

Ayittey, G. B. N. 1999. *Africa in Chaos.* New York: St. Martin's Griffin.

Bajema, C. J. 1968. Relation of fertility to occupational status, IQ, educational attainments, and size of family of origin: A follow-up of the male Kalamazoo public school population. *Eugenics Quarterly,* 15: 198–203.

Baker, D. P., and D. P. Jones. 1993. Creating gender equality; cross national gender stratification and mathematical performance. *Sociology of Education,* 66: 91–103.

Balazs, E. 1968. *La Bureaucratie Celeste.* Paris: Gallimard.

Banks, A. S., A. J. Day, and T. C. Muller (Eds.). 1997. *Political Handbook of the World 1997.* Binghamton, New York: CSA Publications.

Banks, A. S., and W. Overstreet, (Eds.). 1982. *Political Handbook of the World 1982–1983.* New York: McGraw-Hill Book Company.

Baran, P. A. 1952. On the political economy of backwardness. *Manchester School of Economic and Social Studies,* 20: 66–84.

Baran, P. A. 1957. *The Political Economy of Growth.* New York: Monthly Review Press.

Baran, P. 1975. *The Political Economy of Neo-Colonialism.* London: Heinemann.

Barro, J. R. 1991. Economic growth in a cross section of countries. *Quarterly Journal of Economics,* 106: 407–433.

Bart, W., A. Kamal, and J. F. Lane. 1987. The development of proportional reasoning in Qatar. *Journal of Genetic Psychology,* 148: 95–103.

Bauer, P. T. 1981. *Equality, the Third World, and Economic Delusion.* Cambridge, MA: Harvard University Press.

Beaton, A. E., I. V. Mullis, M. O. Martin, E. J. Gonzalez, D. L. Kelly, and T. A. Smith. 1996a. *Mathematical Achievement in the Middle School Years.* Boston College, Chestnut Hill, MA: TIMSS.

Beaton, A. E., I. V. Mullis, M. O. Martin, E. J. Gonzalez, D. L. Kelly, and T. A. Smith. 1996b. *Science Achievement in the Middle School Years.* Boston College, Chestnut Hill, MA: TIMSS.

Beck, L. R., and R. St. George. 1983. The alleged cultural bias of PAT: Reading comprehension and reading vocabulary tests. *New Zealand Journal of Educational Studies,* 18: 32–47.

Benson, V. E. 1942. The intelligence and later scholastic success of sixth grade pupils. *School and Society,* 55: 163–167.

Berry, J. W. 1966. Temne and Eskimo perceptual skills. *International Journal of Psychology,* 1: 207–229.

Bhuleskar, A. K. (Ed.). 1972. *Towards Socialist Transformation of Indian Economy.* Bombay: Popular Prakashan.

Binnie-Dawson, J. L. 1984. Biosocial and endocrine bases of spatial ability. *Psychologia,* 27: 129–151.

Birch, H. G., C. Pineiro, E. Alcalde, T. Toca, and J. Cravioto. 1971. Kwashiorkor in early childhood and intelligence at school age. *Pediatric Research,* 5: 579–584.

Blank, D. E. 1973. *Politics in Venezuela.* Boston: Little, Brown and Company.

Blunden, C., and M. Elvin. 1983. *Cultural Atlas of China.* Oxford: Phaidon.

Boben, D. 1999. *Slovene Standardization of Raven's Progressive Matrices.* Ljubljana: Center za psihodiagnostica sredstva.

Boissiere, M., J. B. Knight, and R. H. Sabot. 1985. Earnings, schooling, ability and cognitive skills. *American Economic Review,* 75: 1016–1030.

Boivin, M. J., and B. Giordani. 1993. Improvements in cognitive performance for schoolchildren in Zaire following an iron supplement and treatment for intestinal parasites. *Journal of Pediatric Psychology*, 18: 249–264.

Boivin, M. J., B. Giordani, and B. Bornfeld. 1995. Use of the tactual performance test for cognitive ability testing with African children. *Neuropsychology*, 9: 409–417.

Bond, R., and P. Saunders. 1999. Routes of success: Influences on the occupational attainment of young British men. *British Journal of Sociology*, 50: 217–249.

Bouchard, T. J. 1993. "The genetic architecture of human intelligence." In P. A. Vernon (Ed.), *Biological Approaches to the Study of Human Intelligence*. Norwood, NJ: Ablex.

Bouchard, T. J. 1998. Genetic and environmental influences on adult intelligence and special mental abilities. *Human Biology*, 70: 257–279.

Bourdier, G. 1964. Utilisation et nouvel etalonnage du P.M. 47. *Bulletin de Psychologie*, 235: 39–41.

Brand, C. 1987. "The importance of general intelligence." In S. Modgil and C. Modgil (Eds.), *Arthur Jensen: Consensus and Controversy*. New York: Falmer.

Brown, W. W., and M. O. Reynolds. 1975. A model of IQ, occupation and earnings. *American Economic Review*, 65: 1002–1007.

Buj, V. 1981. Average IQ values in various European countries. *Personality and Individual Differences*, 2: 168–169.

Burt, C. L. 1937. *The Backward Child*. London: University of London Press.

Cahan, S., and N. Cohen. 1989. Age versus schooling effects on intelligence development. *Child Development*, 60: 1239–1249.

Cardoso, F. H. 1972. "Dependency and development in Latin America." In T. Roberts and A. Hite (Eds.), *From Modernization to Globalization*. 2000. Malden, MA: Blackwell Publishers.

Carroll, J. B. 1994. *Human Cognitive Abilities*. Cambridge, UK: Cambridge University Press.

Carroll, J. B. 1987. Psychometrics, intelligence and public perception. *Intelligence*, 24: 25–52.

Cavalli-Sforza, L., P. Menozzi, and A. Piazza. 1996. *The History and Geography of Human Genes*. Princeton, NJ: Princeton University Press.

Ceci, S. J. 1991. How much does schooling influence general intelligence and its components? A reassessment of the evidence. *Developmental Psychology*, 27: 703–722.

Ceci, S. J. 1992. Schooling and intelligence. *Psychological Science Agenda*, 5: 7–9.

Central Intelligence Agency. 2000. *The World Factbook 2000*. Washington, D. C.: Brassey's (United States).

Chan, J., and R. Lynn. 1989. The intelligence of six-year-olds in Hong Kong. *Journal of Biosocial Science*, 21: 461–464.

Chandra, S. 1975. Some patterns of response on the Queensland Test. *Australian Psychologist*, 10: 185–191.

Chai, J. C. H. 1998. *China: Transition to a Market Economy*. Oxford: Clarendon Press.

Chaim, H. H. 1994. "Is the Raven Progressive Matrices valid for Malaysians?" Unpublished.

Chew, S. C., and R. A. Denemark (Eds.). 1996. *The Underdevelopment of Development: Essays in Honor of Andrè Gunder Frank.* Thousand Oaks: Sage Publications.

Chilcote, R. H. 1984. *Theories of Development and Underdevelopment.* Boulder and London: Westview Press.

Chisholm, M. 1982. *Modern World Development: A geographical perspective.* London: Hutchinson.

Chorley, M. J., K. Chorley, N. Seese, M. J. Owen, J. Daniels, P. McGuffin, L. A. Thompson, D. K. Detterman, C. Benbow, D. Lubinski, T. Eley, and R. Plomin. 1998. A quantitative trait locus associated with cognitive ability in children. *Psychological Science,* 9: 159–166.

Clement, A. G., and R. H. Robertson. 1961. *Scotland's Scientific Heritage.* Edinburgh: Oliver and Boyd.

Collier, P., and J. W. Gunning. 1999. Explaining African economic performance. *Journal of Economic Literature,* 37: 64–111.

Collier, P., and J. W. Gunning. 1999. Why has Africa grown slowly? *Journal of Economic Perspectives,* 13, 3: 3–22.

Colom, R., A. Andres-Pueyo, and M. Juan-Espinosa. 1998. Generational IQ gains: Spanish data. *Personality and Individual Differences,* 25: 927–936.

Costenbader, V., and S. M. Ngari. 2000. "A Kenya standardisation of the Coloured Progressive Matrices." Unpublished Ms.

Cox, C. 1926. *The Early Mental Traits of Three Hundred Geniuses.* Stanford: University Press.

Crowther, W. 1997. "Moldova: Caught between nation and empire." In I. Bremmer and R. Taras (Eds.), *New States New Politics: Building the Post-Soviet Nations.* Cambridge, UK: University Press.

Dague, P., M. Garelli, and A. Lebettre. 1964. Recherches sur l'echelle de maturite mentale de Columbia. *Revue de Psychologie Applique,* 14: 71–96.

Datt, R., and K. P. M. Sundharam, 1979. *Indian Economy.* 16th Ed., rev. Ram Nagar, Delhi: S. Chand.

Davenport, K. S., and H. H. Remmers. 1950. Factors in state characteristics related to average A-12 V-12 scores. *Journal of Educational Psychology,* 41: 110–115.

De Groot, A. D. 1951. War and the intelligence of youth. *Journal of Abnormal and Social Psychology,* 46: 596–597.

De Long, J. B. 1988. Productivity growth, convergence and welfare: Comment. *American Economic Review,* 78: 1138–1154.

Deary, I. J. 2000. *Looking Down on Human Intelligence.* Oxford: Oxford University Press.

Deary, I. J., L. J. Whalley, H. Lemmon, J. R. Crawford, and J. M. Starr. 2000. The stability of individual differences in mental ability from childhood to old age: Follow-up of the 1932 Scottish Mental Ability Survey. *Intelligence,* 28: 49–56.

Dennis, W. 1957. Performance of near eastern children on the Draw-a-Man test. *Child Drevelopment,* 28: 427–430.

Diamond, J. 1998. *Guns, Germs and Steel: A Short History of Everybody for the Last 13,000 Years.* London: Vintage.

Doe, L. March 1997. The economic development of francophone Africa: A comparison with the Republic of Korea. *International Social Science Journal,* 151: 105–121.

Doorman, Frans. 1998. *Global Development: Problems, Solutions, Strategy.* Utrecht, The Netherlands: International Books.

Dudwick, Nora. 1997. "Armenia: Paradise Lost." In I. Bremmer and R. Taras (Eds.), *New States New Politics: Building the Post-Soviet Nations.* Cambridge, UK: Cambridge University Press.

Duncan, O. D. 1968. Ability and achievement. *Eugenics Quarterly,* 15: 1–11.

Duncan, O. D., D. L. Featherman, and B. Duncan. 1972. *Socioeconomic Background and Achievement.* New York: Seminar Press.

Easterly, W., and R. Levine. 1997. Africa's growth tragedy: Policies and ethnic divisions. *Quarterly Journal of Economics,* 112: 1203–1250.

Eastern Europe and the Commonwealth of Independent States 1999. 1999. London: Europa Publications.

Economic Freedom of the World: 2000 Annual Report. 2000. *See* Gwartney and Lawson.

Edgerton, R. B. 1993. *The Cloak of Competence.* Berkeley: University of California Press.

The Europa World Year Book. 1991–1999. London: Europa Publications.

Eysenck, H. J. 1979. *Intelligence: Structure and Measurement.* Berlin: Springer Verlag.

Eysenck, H. J. 1995. *Genius; The Natural History of Creativity.* Cambridge, UK: Cambridge University Press.

Eysenck, H. J. 1998. *Intelligence.* New Brunswick, NJ: Transaction.

Eysenck, H. J., and G. H. Gudjonsson. 1989. *The Causes and Cures of Criminality.* New York: Plenum.

Eysenck, H. J., and S. J. Schoenthaler. 1997. "Raising IQ level by vitamin and mineral supplementation." In R. J. Sternberg and E. Grigorenko (Eds.), *Intelligence, Heredity and Environment.* Cambridge, UK: Cambridge University Press.

Fahmy, M. 1964. Initial exploring of the intelligence of Shilluk children. *Vita Humana,* 7: 164–177.

Fahrmeier, E. D. 1975. The effect of school attendance on intellectual development in Northern Nigeria. *Child Development,* 46: 281–285.

Falconer, D. S. 1960. *Introduction to Quantitative Genetics.* London: Longman.

The Far East and Australiasia 1999. 1999. London: Europa Publications.

Fatouros, M. 1972. "The influence of maturation and education on the development of abilities." In L. J. Cronbach and P. J. Drenth (Eds.), *Mental Tests and Cultural Adaptation.* The Hague: Mouton.

Faverge, J. M., and J. C. Falmagne. 1962. On the interpretation of data in intercultural psychology. *Psychologia Africana,* 9: 22–96.

Fei, J. C. H., and G. Ranis. 1964. *Development of the Labor Surplus Economy: Theory and Policy.* Homewood, Illinois: Irvin.

Fernandez-Ballesteros, R., M. Juan-Espinoza, R. Colom, and M. D. Calero. 1997. "Contextual and personal sources of individual differences in intelligence." In J. S. Carlson, (Ed.), *Advances in Cognition and Educational Practice.* Greenwich, CT: JAI Press.

Fick, M. L. 1929. Intelligence test results of poor white, native (Zulu), coloured and Indian school children and the social and educational implications. *South Africa Journal of Science,* 26: 904–920.

Finison, L. J. 1986. The application of McClelland's national development model to recent data. *Journal of Social Psychology,* 98: 55–59.

Firebaugh, G. 1999. Empirics of World Income Inequality. *American Journal of Sociology* 104, 6: 1597–1630.

Fisher, H. A. 1936. *A History of Europe.* London: Arnold.

Flores, M. B., and G. T. Evans. 1972. Some differences in cognitive abilities between selected Canadian and Filipino students. *Multivariate Behavioral Research,* 7: 175–191.

Flynn, J. R. 1980. *Race, IQ and Jensen.* London: Routledge and Kegan Paul.

Flynn, J. R. 1984. The mean IQ of Americans: Massive gains 1932 to 1978. *Psychological Bulletin,* 95: 29–51.

Flynn, J. R. 1987. Massive IQ gains in 14 nations: What IQ tests really measure. *Psychological Bulletin,* 101: 171–191.

Flynn, J. R. 1998. WAIS-111 and WISC-111 IQ gains in the United States from 1992 to 1995: How to compensate for obsolete norms. *Perceptual and Motor Skills,* 86: 1231–1239.

Frank, A. G. 1967. *Capitalism and Underdevelopment in Latin America: Historical Studies of Chile and Brazil.* New York: Monthly Review Press.

Frank, A. G. 1996. "The underdevelopment of development." In S. C. Chew and R. A. Denemark (Eds.), *The Underdevlopment of Development. Essays in Honor of Andrè Gunder Frank.* Thousands Oaks: Sage Publications.

Frank, A. G. 1969. "The development of underdevelopment." In T. Roberts and A. Hite (Eds.), *From Modernization to Globalization.* 2000. Malden, Massachusetts: Blackwell Publishers.

Galbraith, J. K. 1951. Conditions for economic change in underdeveloped countries. *Journal of Farm Economics,* 33: 693–702.

Gardner, H. S. 1998. *Comparative Economic Systems.* 2d Ed. Philadelphia, PA: Dryden Press.

Geller, J. R., F. Ramsey., and V. Forde. 1986. A follow-up study in the influence of early malnutrition on subsequent development. *Nutrition and Behavior,* 3: 211–222.

Ghiselli, E. E. 1966. *The Validity of Occupational Aptitude Tests.* New York: Wiley.

Ghosh, A. 1979. *Indian Economy: Its Nature and Problems.* 22d Ed., rev. Calcutta: The World Press Private.

Giordani, B., M. J. Boivin, B. Opel, D. N. Nseyila, and R. E. Lauer. 1996. Use of the K-ABC with children in Zaire. *International Journal of Disability, Development and Education,* 43: 5–24.

Glewwe, P., and H. Jacoby. 1992. *Estimating the Determinants of Cognitive Achievement in Low Income Countries.* Washington, D.C.: World Bank.

Goosens, G. 1952a. Etalonnage du Matrix 1947 de J.C. Raven. *Revue Belge de Psychologie et de Pedagogie,* 14: 74–80.

Goosens, G. 1952b. Une application du test d'intelligence de R. B. Cattell. *Revue Belge de Psychologie et de Predagogie,* 14: 115–124.

Gordon, R. A. 1997. Everyday life as an intelligence test: Effects of intelligence and intelligence context. *Intelligence,* 24: 203–320.

Gottfredson, L. S. 1997a. Editorial: Mainstream science on intelligence. *Intelligence*, 24: 13–24.

Gottfredson, L. S. 1997b. Why g matters: The complexity of everyday life. *Intelligence*, 24: 79–132.

Gwartney, J., and R. Lawson, with D. Samida. 2000. *Economic Freedom of the World. 2000 Annual Report.* Canada: The Fraser Institute.

Hakstian, A. R., and S. G. Vandenberg. 1979. The cross-cultural generalisability of a higher order cognitive structure model. *Intelligence,* 3: 73-103.

Haller, A. O., and A. Portes. 1973. Status attainment process. *Sociology of Education,* 46: 51–91.

Hamers, J. H., M. G. Hessels, and A. H. Pennings. 1996. Learning potential in ethnic minority groups. *European Journal of Psychological Assessment,* 12: 183–192.

Hanson, R., J. A. Smith, and W. Hume. 1985. Achievements of infants on items of the Griffiths scales: 1980 compared to 1950. *Child: Care, Health and Development,* 11: 91–104.

Harnqvist, K. 1968. Relative changes in intelligence from 13–18. *Scandinavian Journal of Psychology,* 9: 50–64.

Harrel, R. F., E. Woodyard, and A. I. Gates. 1955. *The effects of mother's diet on the intelligence of offspring.* New York: Bureau of Publications, Teachers' College, Columbia University.

Harrison, L. E. 1985. "Underdevelopment is a state of mind." In M. A. Seligson and J. T. Passé-Smith (Eds.), *Development and Underdevelopment: The Political Economy of Global Inequality.* 1998. Boulder and London: Lynne Rienner Publishers.

Harrison, L. E. 2000. "Introduction: Why culture matters." In L. E. Harrison and S. P. Huntington (Eds.), *Culture Matters: How Values Shape Human Progress.* New York: Basic Books.

Hetzel, B. S., J. T. Dunn, and J. B. Stanbury. 1987. *The Prevention and Control of Iodine Deficiency Disorders.* Amsterdam: Elsevier.

Herrnstein, R. J., and C. Murray. 1994. *The Bell Curve: Intelligence and Class Structure in American Life.* New York: The Free Press.

Hertzig, M. E., H. G. Birch, S. A. Richardson, and J. Tizard. 1972. Intellectual levels of schoolchildren malnourished during the first two years of life. *Pediatrics,* 49: 814–824.

Hess, P., and C. Ross. 1997. *Economic Development. Theories, Evidence, and Policies.* Fort Worth: The Dryden Press.

Heyneman, S. P., and D. T. Jamison. 1980. Student learning in Uganda. *Comparative Education Review,* 24: 207–220.

Hirschi, T., and M. J. Hindelung. 1977. Intelligence and delinquency: A revisionist review. *American Sociological Review,* 42: 571–587.

Hodgkiss, J. 1978. *Differential Aptitude Test: British Manual.* Windsor: NFER.

Hossain, M., I. Islam, and R. Kibria. 1999. *South Asian Economic Development: Transformation, Opportunities and Challenges.* London and New York: Routledge.

Hoyos, C., and M. Littlejohn. April 4th, 2000. "Annan draws up a road map to guide UN." *Financial Times,* p. 16.

Human Development Report. See United Nations Development Program (UNDP).

Hunter, J. E., and R. F. Hunter. 1984. Validity and utility of alternative predictors of job performance. *Psychological Bulletin,* 96: 72–98.

Huntington, S. P. 2000. Foreword: "Cultures Count." In L. E. Harrison and S. P. Huntington (Eds.), *Culture Matters: How Values Shape Human Progress.* New York: Basic Books.

Hsu, C. 1976. The learning potential of first graders in Taipei city as measured by Raven's Coloured Progressive Matrices. *Acta Pediatrica Sinica,* 17: 262–274.

International Educational Achievement. 1998. *Science achievement in Seventeen Countries.* Oxford: Pergamon.

Inkeles, A., and D. H. Smith. 1974. "Becoming Modern." In M. A. Seligson and J. T. Passé-Smith (Eds.), *Development and Underdevelopment: The Political Economy of Global Inequality.* 1998. Boulder and London: Lynne Rienner Publishers.

International Labour Office. 1999. *Yearbook of Labour Statistics 1999.* No. 58. Geneva: International Labour Office.

Irvine, S. H., and J. W. Berry. 1988. "The abilities of mankind: A revaluation." In S. H. Irvine and J. W. Berry, (Eds.), *Human Abilities in Cultural Context.* Cambridge, UK: Cambridge University Press.

Itzkoff, S.W. (2000) *The Inevitable Domination of Man: An Evolutionary Detective Story.* Ashfield, MA: Paideia Publishers.

Jaworowska, A. and Szustrowa, T. (1991) *Podrecznik Do Testu Matryc Ravena.* Warsaw: Pracownia Testow Psychologicznych.

Jencks, S. 1972. *Inequality.* London: Penguin.

Jencks, C. 1979. *Who Gets Ahead? The Determinants of Economic Success in America.* New York: Basic Books.

Jensen, A. R. 1980. *Bias in Mental Testing.* London: Methuen.

Jensen, A. R. 1998. *The g Factor. The Science of Mental Ability.* Westport, CT: Praeger.

Jensen, A. R., and C. R. Reynolds. 1982. Race, social class and ability patterns on the WISC-R. *Personality and Individual Differences,* 3: 423–438.

Johnson, D. L., C. A. Johnson, and D. Price-Williams. 1967. The Draw-a-Man test and Raven Progressive Matrices performance of Guatemalan boys and Latino children. *Revista Interamericana de Psicologia,* 1: 143–157.

Johnson, D. M. 1948. Applications of the standard score IQ to social statistics. *Journal of Social Psychology,* 27: 217–227.

Jolly, R. December 1999. Global Inequality. *WIDER Angle,* 2: 6–7.

Jones, C. I. 1997. Convergence revisited. *Journal of Economic Growth,* 2: 131–153.

Jordheim, G. D., and I. A. Olsen. 1963. The use of a non-verbal test of intelligence in the trust territory of the Pacific. *American Anthropologist,* 65: 1122–1125.

Kagan, J. September 4th, 1971. The magical aura of the IQ. *Saturday Review,* pp. 92–93.

Kagitcibasi, C., and I. Savasir. 1988. "Human abilities in the Eastern Mediterranean." In S. H. Irvine and J. W. Berry (Eds.), *Human Abilities in Cultural Context.* Cambridge, UK: Cambridge University Press.

Kahn, H. 1979. "The Confucian Ethic and Economic Growth." In M. A. Seligson and J. T. Passè-Smith (Eds.), *Development and Underdevelopment: The*

Political Economy of Global Inequality. 1998. Boulder and London: Lynne Rienner Publishers.

Kamarck, A. M. 1976. *The Tropics and Economic Development: A Provocative Inquiry into the Poverty of Nations.* Published for the World Bank. Baltimore: The Johns Hopkins University Press.

Kaniel, S., and S. Fisherman. 1991. Level of performance and distribution or errors in the progressive matrices test: A comparison of Ethiopian and Israeli adolescents. *International Journal of Psychology,* 26: 25–33.

Kantor, H. 1969. *Patterns of Politics & Political Systems In Latin America.* Chicago: Rand McNally and Company.

Keesing's Record of World Events (1991–2000). Cambridge, MA: Keesing's Worldwide.

Kendall, I. M., M. A. Verster, and J. W. von Mollendorf. 1998. "Test performance of blacks in South Africa." In S. H. Irvine and J. W. Berry (Eds.), *Human Abilities in Cultural Context.* Cambridge, UK: Cambridge University Press.

Keynes, J. M. 1964. *Collected Works.* Vol. 10. Cambridge, UK: Cambridge University Press.

Kirk, D., and B. Pillet. 1998. Fertility in sub-Saharan Africa in the 1980's and 1990's. *Studies in Family Planning,* 29: 1–22.

Klingelhofer, E. L. 1967. Performance of Tanzanian secondary school pupils on the Raven Standard Progressive Matrices test. *Journal of Social Psychology,* 72: 205–215.

Kramer, M. S. 1987. Intrauterine growth and gestational duration determinants. *Pediatrics,* 80: 502–511.

Kurian, G. T. 1987. *Encyclopedia of the Third World.* 3rd Ed. New York: Facts On File.

Kurth, E. von. 1969. Erhohung der leistungsnormen bei den farbigen Progressiv Matrizen. *Zeitschrift fur Psychologie,* 177: 85–90.

Kyöstiö, O. K. 1972. "Divergence among school beginners caused by different cultural influences." In L. J. Cronbach and P. J. Drenth (Eds.), *Mental Tests and Cultural Adaptation.* The Hague: Mouton.

Landes, D. S. 1998. *The Wealth and Poverty of Nations: Why Some Are So Rich and Some So Poor.* New York: W.W. Norton and Company.

Laroche, J. L. 1959. Effets de repetition du Matrix 38 sur les resultats d'enfants Katangais. *Bulletin du Centre d'etudes et Recherches Psychotechniques,* 1: 85–99.

Lewis, A. W. 1954. Economic development with unlimited supplies of labor. *Machester School of Economic and Social Studies,* 22: 139–191.

Lewis, A. W. 1955. *The Theory of Economic Growth.* London: Allen and Unwin.

Li, C. C. 1975. *Path Ananysis—A Primer.* Pacific Grove, CA: Boxwood Press.

Li, D., Y. Jin, S. G. Vandenberg, Y. Zhu, and C. Tang. 1990. Report on Shanghai norms for the Chinese translation of the Wechsler Intelligence Scale for Children—Revised. *Psychological Reports,* 67: 531–541.

Li, X., H. Sano, and J. C. Merwin. 1996. Perception and reasoning abilities among American, Japanese and Chinese adolescents. *Journal of Adolescent Research,* 11: 173–193.

Lieblich, A., A. Ninio, and S. Kugelmass. 1972. Effects of ethnic origin and parental SES on WPPSI performance of pre-school children in Israel. *Journal of Cross-Cultural Psychology,* 3: 159–168.

Lipton, M. 1976. *Why Poor People Stay Poor: Urban Bias in World Development.* Reprint. London: Temple Smith.

Lipton, M. 1998. "Urban Bias and Inequality." In M. A. Seligson and J. T. Passé-Smith (Eds.), *Development and Underdevelopment: The Political Economy of Global Inequality.* Boulder and London: Lynne Rienner Publishers.

Loehlin, J. C., J. M. Horn, and L. Willerman. 1989. Modeling IQ change: Evidence from the Texas adoption project. *Child Development,* 60: 993–1004.

Lucas, A., R. Morely, T. J. Cole, G. Lister, and C. Leeson-Payne. 1992. Breast milk and subsequent intelligence quotient in children born preterm. *Lancet,* 339: 261–264.

Lykken, D. T. 1995. *The Antisocial Personalities.* Hillsdale, NJ: Erlbaum.

Lynn, R. 1977a. The intelligence of the Japanese. *Bulletin of the British Psychological Society,* 30: 69–72.

Lynn, R. 1977b. The intelligence of the Chinese and Malays in Singapore. *Mankind Quarterly,* 18: 125–128.

Lynn, R. 1977c. Selective migration and the decline of intelligence in Scotland. *Social Biology* 24, 1: 73–182.

Lynn, R. 1979. The social ecology of intelligence in the British Isles. *British Journal of Social and Clinical Psychology,* 18: 1–12.

Lynn, R. 1980. The social ecology of intelligence in France. *British Journal of Social and Clinical Psychology,* 19: 325–331.

Lynn, R. 1981. "The social ecology of intelligence in the British Isles, France and Spain." In M. P. Friedman, J. P. Das, and N. O'Connor (Eds.), *Intelligence and Learning.* New York: Plenum.

Lynn, R. 1990. The role of nutrition in secular increases of intelligence. *Personality and Individual Differences,* 11: 273–285.

Lynn, R. 1991a. Race differences in intelligence: A global perspective. *The Mankind Quarterly* 31, 3: 255–296.

Lynn, R. 1991b. The evolution of racial differences in intelligence. *The Mankind Quarterly,* 32: 1–2, 99–121.

Lynn, R. 1996a. *Dysgenics.* Westport, CT: Praeger.

Lynn, R. 1996. Racial and ethnic differences in intelligence in the United States on the Differential Ability Scale. *Personality and Individual Differences,* 20: 271–273.

Lynn, R. 1997a. "Geographical Variation in Intelligence." In H. Nyborg (Ed.), *The Scientific Study of Human Nature,* Oxford: Pergamon.

Lynn, R. 1997b. Intelligence in Taiwan. *Personality and Individual Differences,* 22: 585–586.

Lynn, R. 1998. "In support of nutrition theory." In U. Neisser (Ed.), *The Rising Curve.* Washington, D.C.: American Psychological Association.

Lynn, R., and J. Dziobon. 1980. On the intelligence of the Japanese and other Mongoloid peoples. *Personality and Individual Differences,* 1: 95–96.

Lynn, R., S. Hampson, and M. Magee. 1984. Home background, intelligence, personality and education as predictors of unemployment in young people. *Personality and Individual Differences,* 5: 549–547.

Lynn, R., and S. L. Hampson. 1986. The rise of national intelligence: Evidence from Britain, Japan and the USA. *Personality and Individual Differences,* 7: 23–332.

Lynn, R., and S. Hampson. 1986a. The structure of Japanese abilities: An analysis in terms of the hierarchical model of intelligence. *Current Psychological Research and Reviews,* 4: 309–322.

Lynn, R., and S. Hampson. 1986b. Intellectual abilities of Japanese children: An assessment of 2–8 year olds derived from the McCarthy Scales of Children's Abilities. *Intelligence,* 10: 41–58.

Lynn, R., and S. Hampson. 1987. Further evidence on the cognitive abilities of the Japanese: Data from the WPPSI. *International Journal of Behavioral Development,* 10: 23–36.

Lynn, R., S. Hampson, and M. Lee. 1988. The intelligence of Chinese children in Hong Kong. *School Psychology International,* 9: 29–32.

Lynn, R., and E. P. Harland, 1998. A positive effect of iron supplementation on the IQs of iron deficient children. *Personality and Individual Differences,* 24: 883–885.

Lynn, R., and M. Holmshaw. 1990. Black-white differences in reaction times and intelligence. *Social Behavior and Personality,* 18: 299–308.

Lynn, R., and M. J. Song. 1994. General intelligence, visuospatial and verbal abilities of Korean children. *Personality and Individual Differences,* 16: 363–364.

Lynn, R., C. Pagliari, and J. Chan. 1988. Intelligence in Hong Kong measured for Spearman's g and the visuospatial and verbal primaries. *Intelligence,* 12: 423–433.

Lynn, R., E. Paspalanova, D. Stetinsky, and B. Tzenova. 1998. Intelligence in Bulgaria. *Psychological Reports,* 82: 912–914.

MacArthur, R. S., S. H. Irvine, and A. R. Brimble. 1964. *The Northern Rhodesia Mental Ability Survey.* Lusaka: Rhodes Livingstone Institute.

MacDonald, K. 1994. *A People that Shall Dwell Alone.* Westport, CT: Praeger.

MacKay, D. I. 1969. *Geographical Mobility and the Brain Drain.* London: Allen and Unwin.

Mackintosh, N. J. 1998. *IQ and Human Intelligence.* Oxford, UK: Oxford University Press.

McCall, R. B. 1977. Childhood IQs as predictors of adult educational and occupational status. *Science,* 197: 482–483.

McClelland, D. C. 1963. *The Achieving Society.* Princeton, NJ: Van Nostrand.

McIntyre, G. A. 1938. *The Standardisation of Intelligence Tests in Australia.* Melbourne: University Press.

Maddison, A. 1983. A comparison of levels of GDP per capita in developed and developing countries, 1700–1980. *Journal of Economic History* 43, 1: 27–41.

Maddison, A. 1995. *Explaining the Economic Performance of Nations.* Brookfield, VT: Edward Elgar.

Maddison, A. 1995. *Monitoring the World Economy 1820–1992.* Paris: Development Centre of the Organisation for Economic Co-operation and Development.

Maddison, A. 1998. "Income Growth, Income Gaps, and the Ranking of Nations." In M. A. Seligson and J. T. Passè-Smith (Eds.), *Development and Underdevelopment: The Political Economy of Global Inequality.* Boulder and London: Lynne Rienner Publishers.

Maller, J. B. 1933a. Economic and social correlatives of school progress in New York City. *Teachers College Record,* 34: 655–670.

Maller, J. B. 1933b. Vital indices and their relation to psychological and social factors. *Human Biology,* 5: 94–121.

Manley, D. R. 1963. Mental ability in Jamaica. *Social and Economic Studies,* 12: 51–77.

Martin, M. O. 1997. *Science Achievement in the Primary School Years.* Boston College, Chestnut Hill, MA: TIMSS.

Martin, M. O., I. V. S. Mullis, E. J. Gonzalez, K. D. Gregory, T. A. Smith, S. J. Chrostowski, R. A. Garden, and K M. O'Connor. 2000. *TIMSS 1999 International Science Report.* Chestnut Hill, MA: International Study Center, Lynch School of Education, Boston College.

Martinussen, J. 1999. *Society, State & Market. A Guide to Competing Theories of Development.* London and New York: Zed Books.

Martorell, R. 1998. "Nutrition and the worldwide rise in IQ scores." In U. Neisser (Ed.), *The Rising Curve.* Washington, D.C.: American Psychological Association.

Matarazzo, J. D. 1972. *Wechsler's Appraisal and Measurement of Adult Intelligence.* Baltimore: Williams and Wilkins.

Maxwell, J. 1969. *The Level and Trend of Scottish Intelligence.* London: University of London Press.

The Middle East and North Africa 1998. 1998. London: Europa Publications.

Miron, M. 1977. A validation study of a transferred group intelligence test. *International Journal of Psychology,* 12: 193–205.

Misawa, G., M. Motegi, K. Fujita, and K. Hattori. 1984. A comparative study of intellectual abilities of Japanese and American children on the Columbia Mental Maturity Scale. *Personality and Individual Differences,* 5: 173–181.

Modiano, N. 1962. "Mental testing among Tzeltal and Tzotzil children." Proceedings of the 35th International Congress of Americanists. Mexico City, Mexico.

Moffitt, T. E. 1993. Adolescent limited and life course persistent antisocial behavior: A developmental taxonomy. *Psychological Review,* 100: 674–701.

Moffitt, T. E., W. F. Gabrielli, S. A. Mednick, and F. Schulsinger. 1981. Socioeconomic status, IQ and delinquency. *Journal of Abnormal Psychology,* 90: 152–156.

Montesquieu, 1748. "De l'Esprit des lois." Texte ètabli avec une introduction, des notes et des variantes par Gonzague Truc. 1961. Paris: Editions Garnier Fréres.

Moon, S. B. 1988. "A cross cultural study of the Kaufman Assessment Battery for children with Korean children." Ph.D thesis, University of Alabama.

Motyl, A., and B. Krawchenko. 1997. "Ukraine: From Empire to Statehood." In I. Bremmer and R. Taras (Eds.), *New States New Politics: Building the Post-Soviet Nations.* Cambridge, UK: Cambridge University Press.

Moyles, E. W., and M. Wolins. 1973. Group care and intellectual development. *Developmental Psychology,* 4: 370–380.

Mullis, I.V.S. (1997) *Mathematics Achievment in the Primary School Years.* Boston College, Chestnut Hill, MA: TIMSS.

Mullis, I. V. S., M. O. Martin, E. J. Gonzalez, K. D. Gregory, R. A. Garden, K. M. O'Connor, S. J. Chrostowski, and T. A. Smith. 2000. *TIMSS 1999 International Mathematics Report.* Chestnut Hill, MA: International Study Center, Lynch School of Education, Boston College.

Murray, C. 1998. *Income Inequality and IQ.* Washington, D.C.: AEI Press.

Myrdal, G. 1962. *Challenge to Affluence.* New York: Pantheon Books.

Nafziger, E. W. 1997. *The Economics of Developing Countries.* 3rd Ed. Upper Saddle River, NJ: Prentice Hall.

Natalicio, L. 1968. Aptidatao general, status social e sexo: um estudio de adolescentes Brasilieros e norte-Americanos. *Revista Interamericana de Psicologia,* 2: 25-34.

Neisser, U. 1996. *Intelligence: Knowns and Unknowns.* Washington, D.C.: American Psychological Association.

Nieto-Alegre, S., L. Navarro, G. Cruz, and A. Dominguez. 1967. Diferencices regionales en la medida de la inteligencia con el test M.P. *Revista de Psicologia General y Applicada,* 22: 699–707.

Nissen, H. W., S. Machover, and E. F. Kinder. 1935. A study of performance tests given to a group of native African Negro children. *British Journal of Psychology,* 25: 308–355.

Nkaya, H. N., M. Huteau, and J-P. Bonnet. 1994 Retest effect on cognitive performance on the Raven Matrices in France and in the Congo. *Perceptual and Motor Skills,* 78: 503–510.

Notcutt, B. 1950. The measurement of Zulu intelligence. *Journal of Social Research,* 1: 195–206.

Office of the Surgeon General. 1968. "Supplement to Health of the Army." Washington, D.C.: Department of the Army.

Olson, M. 1996. Big Bills Left on the Sidewalk: Why Some Nations are Rich, and Others Poor. Distinguished Lecture on Economics in Government. *Journal of Economic Perspectives* 10, 2: 3–24.

Olson, M. 2000. *Power and Prosperity: Outgrowing Communist and Capitalist Dictatorships.* New York: Basic Books.

Ombredane, A., F. Robaye, and E. Robaye. 1952. Analyse des resultats d'une application experimentale du matrix 38 a 485 noirs Baluba. *Bulletin Centre d'etudes et Researches Psychotechniques,* 7: 235–255.

Ord, L. C. 1948. *Politics and Poverty.* London: The Mayflower Publishing Company.

O'Toole, B. I., and L. Stankov. 1992. Ultimate validity of psychological tests. *Personality and Individual Differnces,* 13: 699–716.

Owen, K. 1992. The suitability of Raven's Progressive Matrices for various groups in South Africa. *Personality and Individual Differences,* 13: 149–159.

Philip's Encyclopedic World Atlas Country by Country. 1993. 2d Ed. London: George Philip Limited.

Philip's Science and Technology Encyclopedia. 1998. London: Philip.

Philip's World Atlas. 1996. London: Chancellor.

Plomin, R., J. C. DeFries, and G. E. McClearn. 1980. *Behavioral Genetics.* San Francisco: Freeman.

Pollitt, E., P. Hathirat, N. Kotchabhakdi, L. Missell, and A. Valyasevi. 1989. Iron deficiency and educational achievement in Thailand. *American Journal of Clinical Nutrition,* 50: 687–697.

The Polyarchy Dataset. 2000. Found at the following site: http://www.svt. ntnu.no/iss/data/Vanhanen/.

Prebisch, R. 1950. *The Economic Development of Latin America and Its Principal Problems.* New York: United Nations.

Proctor, B. E., J. H. Kranzler, A. L. Rosenbloom, V. Martinez, and J. Guevara-Aguire. 2000. An initial investigation of validation of the Matrix Analogies Test-Expanded Form in Ecuador. *Psychological Reports,* 86: 445–453.

Quah, D. T. 1996. Convergence empirics across economies with some capital mobility. *Journal of Economic Growth,* 1: 95–124.

Quay, H. C. 1987. "Intelligence." In H. C. Quay (Ed.), *Handbook of Juvenile Delinquency.* New York: Wiley.

Raine, A. 1993. *The Psychopathology of Crime.* New York: Academic Press.

Ramsay, F. J. 2000. *Global Studies: Africa.* Guilford, CT: Dushkin/McGraw-Hill.

Rao, S. N., and I. K. Reddy. 1968. Development of norms for Raven's Coloured Progressive Matrices on elementary school children. *Psychological Studies,* 13: 105–107.

Raven, J. 1981. *Irish and British Standardisations.* Oxford: Oxford Psychologists Press.

Raven, J. 1986. *Manual for Raven's Progressive Matrices and Vocabulary Scales.* London: Lewis.

Raven, J. 1998. *Manual for Raven's Progressive Matrices.* Oxford: Oxford Psychologists Press.

Raven, J., and J. H. Court. 1989. *Manual for Raven's Progressive Matrices and Vocabulary Scales.* London: Lewis.

Raven, J. C., J. H. Court, and J. Raven. 1995. *Coloured Progressive Matrices.* Oxford, UK: Oxford Psychologists Press.

Raven, J., J. H. Court, and J. C. Raven. 1996. *Standard Progressive Matrices.* Oxford, UK: Oxford Psychologists Press.

Raven, J., J. C. Raven, and J. H. Court. 1998. *Coloured Progressive Matrices.* Oxford, UK: Oxford Psychologists Press.

Ray, D. 1998. *Development Economics.* Princeton, New Jersey: Princeton University Press.

Redmond, M., and F. R. Davies. 1940. *The Standardisation of Two Intelligence Tests.* Wellington: New Zealand Council for Educational Research.

Ree, M. J., and J. A. Earles, 1994. "The ubiquitous predictiveness of g." In M. G. Rumsey, C. B. Walker and J. H. Harris (Eds.), *Personnel Selection and Classification.* Hillsdale, NJ: Erlbaum.

Reid, N., and A. Gilmore. 1989. The Raven's Standard Progressive Matrices in New Zealand. *Psychological Test Bulletin,* 2: 25–35.

Reuning, H. 1988. "Testing Bushmen in the Kalahari desert." In S. H. Irvine and J. W. Berry (Eds.), *Human Abilities in Cultural Context.* Cambridge, UK: Cambridge University Press.

Reynolds, C. R., R. L. Chastain, A. S. Kaufaman, and J. E. McClean. 1987. Demographic characteristics and IQ among adults. *Journal of School Psychology,* 25: 323–342.

Rimoldi, H. J. 1948. A note on Raven's Progressive Matrices Test. *Educational and Psychological Measurement,* 8: 347–352.

Risso, W. L. 1961. "El test de Matrice Progressivas y el test Domino." Proceedings of the 1961 Conference of the Psychological Society of Uruguay.

Roberts, J. T., and A. Hite (Eds.), 2000. *From Modernization to Globalization: Perspectives on Development and Social Change*. Malden, Massachusetts: Blackwell Publishers.

Rodd, W. G. 1959. A cross cultural study of Taiwan's schools. *Journal of Social Psychology,* 50: 30–36.

Roe, A. 1953. A psychological study of eminent psychologists and anthropologists, and a comparison with biological and physical scientists. *Psychological Monographs: General & Applied* 67, no. 352.

Rostow, W. W. 1961. *The Stages of Economic Growth. A Non-Communist Manifesto*. 5th Ed. Cambridge, UK: Cambridge University Press.

Rostow, W. W. 1971. *Politics and the Stages of Growth*. Cambridge, UK: Cambridge University Press.

Rostow, W. W. 1998. "The Five Stages of Growth." In Mitchell A. Seligson and John T. Passé-Smith (Eds.), *Development and Underdevelopment: The Political Economy of Global Inequality*. Boulder and London: Lynne Rienner Publishers.

Rostow, W. W. 1960. "The Stages of Economic Growth: A Non-Communist Manifesto." In T. Roberts and A. Hite (Eds.) *From Modernization to Globalization*. 2000. Malden, MA: Blackwell Publishers.

Rushton, J. P. 2000. *Race, Evolution and Behavior*. Port Huron, MI: Charles Darwin Research Institute.

Sachs, J. 2000. "Notes on a New Sociology of Economic Development." In L. E. Harrison and S. P. Huntington (Eds.), *Culture Matters: How Values Shape Human Progress*. New York: Basic Books.

Sachs, J. D., and A. M. Warner. 1999. Sources of slow growth in African economies. *Journal of African Economies,* 6: 335–376.

Sahin, N., and E. Duzen. 1994. "Turkish standardisation of Raven's SPM." Proceedings of the 23rd International Congress of Applied Psychology, Madrid, Spain.

Santos, T. dos. 1970. "The Structure of Dependence." In M. A. Seligson and J. T. Passé-Smith (Eds.), *Development & Underdevelopment: The Political Economy of Inequality*. Boulder and London: Lynne Rienner Publishers.

Saunders, P. 1996. *Unequal but Fair*. London: Institute of Economic Affairs.

Savage, S. W. January 1946. Intelligence and infant mortality in problem families. *British Medical Journal,* 19: 86–87.

Scarr, S., and R. A. Weinberg, 1978. The influence of family background on IQ. *American Sociological Review,* 43: 674–692.

Schmidt, F. L., and J. E. Hunter. 1998. The validity and utility of selection methods in psychology: Practical and theoretical implications of 85 years of research findings. *Psychological Bulletin,* 124: 262–274.

Scottish Council for Research in Education. 1933. *The Intelligence of Scottish Children*. London: University of London Press.

Scottish Council for Research in Education. 1949. *The Trend of Scottish Intelligence*. London: University of London Press.

Seligson, M. A. and J. T. Passé-Smith (Eds.). 1998. *Development and Underdevelopment: The Political Economy of Global Inequality*. Boulder and London: Lynne Rienner Publishers.

Shigehisa, T., and R. Lynn. 1991. Reaction times and intelligence in Japanese children. *International Journal of Psychology,* 26: 195–202.

Sigman, M. 1995. More food for thought. *Current Directions in Psychological Science,* 4: 52–55.

Sigman, M., and S. E. Whaley, 1998. "The role of nutrition in the development of intelligence." In U. Neisser (Ed.), *The Rising Curve.* Washington, D.C.: American Psychological Association.

Simoes, M. M. R. 1989. "Un estudo exploratorio com o teste das matrizes progressivas de Raven para criancas." Proceedings of the Congress of Psychology, Lisbon, Portugal.

Singer, H. W. 1950. The Distribution of gains between borrowing and investing countries, *American Economic Review* 40, 2: 473–485.

Singh, T. 1998a. Yesterday's men and ideas: All Nehru's apolitical Italian heir offers is lip service. *India Today,* 23, 38, p. 13.

Singh, T. 1998b. Set to stagnate: Beware the swadeshi brigade's economic fossils. *India Today*, 23, 40, p. 17.

Singh, T. 1999. Don't get left behind: Prosperity comes from sound policies, not political cleverness. *India Today,* 24, 37, p. 11.

Sinha, U. 1968. The use of Raven's Progressive Matrices in India. *Indian Educational Review,* 3: 75–88.

Skandinaviska Testforlaget. 1970. *Manual of the Swedish WISC.* Stockholm: Skandinaviska Testforlaget.

Smith, A. 1776. *An Inquiry into the Nature and Causes of The Wealth of Nations,* Ed. Edwin Cannan, 1976. Chicago: The University of Chicago Press.

Solow, R. M. 1956. A contribution to the theory of economic growth. *Quarterly Journal of Economics,* 70: 65–94.

Sommer, A., and K. P. West. 1996. *Vitamin A deficiency: Health, survival and vision.* New York: Oxford University Press.

Sorokin, B. 1954. "Standardisation of the Progressive Matrices test. Unpublished Report.

South America, Central America and the Caribbean 1999. London: Europa Publications.

Spearman, C. 1904. General intelligence, objectively determined and measured. *American Journal of Psychology,* 15: 201–293.

Stevenson, H. W., J. W. Stigler, S. Lee, G. W. Lucker, S. Kitanawa, and C. Hsu. 1985. Cognitive performance and academic achievement of Japanese, Chinese and American children. *Child Development,* 56: 718–734.

Streeten, P. 1971. "How poor are the poor countries?" In D. Seers and L. Joy (Eds.), *Development in a Divided World.* Harmondsworth, UK: Penguin.

Streeten, P. 1976. Foreword. In A. M. Kamarck (Ed.), *The Tropics and Economic Development.* Baltimore and London: The Johns Hopkins University Press.

Studies in Family Planning. 1998, 2000. New York: Population Council.

Sundberg, N., and T. Ballinger. 1968. Nepalese children's cognitive development as revealed by drawings of man, woman and self. *Child Development,* 39: 969–985.

Takeuchi, M., and R. Scott. 1992. Cognitive profiles of Japanese and Canadian kindergarten and first grade children. *Journal of Social Psychology,* 132: 505–512.

Te Nijenhuis, J., and H. van der Flier. 1997. Comparability of GATB scores for immigrant and majority group members: Some Dutch findings. *Journal of Applied Psychology,* 82: 675–685.

Temple, J. 1999. "A positive effect of human capital on growth," reprint from *Economics* letters, 65: 131–134).

Terman, L. M. 1925. "Genetic Studies of Genius." In vol. 1. of *Mental and Physical Traits of a Thousand Gifted Children.* Stanford, CA: Stanford University Press.

Terman, L. M., and M. H. Oden. 1959. "Genetic Studies of Genius." In vol.1 of *The Gifted Child Grows Up.* Stanford, CA: Stanford University Press.

Tesi, G., and H. Bourtourline Young. 1962. A standardisation of Raven's Progressive Matrices. *Archive de Psicologia Neurologia e Pscichologia,* 5: 455–464.

Thomas, H. 1981. *An Unfinished History of the World.* London: Pan.

Thomas, R. M., and A. Sjah. 1961. The Draw-a-Man test in Indonesia. *Journal of Educational Psychology,* 32: 232–235.

Thorndike, E. L. 1939. *Your City.* New York: Harcourt Brace.

Thorndike, E. L., and E. Woodyard. 1942. Differences within and between communities in the intelligence of the children. *Journal of Educational Psychology,* 33: 641–656.

Thorne, J. O., and T. C. Collocott. 1985. *Chambers Biographical Dictionary.* London: Chambers.

Todaro, M. P. 2000. *Economic Development.* 7th Ed. Reading, MA: Addison-Wesley.

Toppen, J. T. 1971. Unemployment: Economic or psychological? *Psychological Reports,* 28: 111–122.

Trevor Roper, H. 1967. *Religion, The Reformation and Other Essays.* London: Macmillan.

UNICEF. 1996. *The State of the World's Children.* New York: Oxford University Press.

United Nations. 1979–1999. *Statistical Yearbook.* New York: United Nations.

United Nations Development Program (UNDP). 1990-2000. *Human Development Report.* New York: Oxford University Press.

Valentine, M. 1959. Psychometric testing in Iran. *Journal of Mental Science,* 105: 93–107.

Vanhanen, T. 1997. *Prospects of Democracy: A Study of 172 Countries.* London and New York: Routledge.

Vanhanen, T. 1999a. Domestic ethnic conflict and ethnic nepotism: A comparative analysis. *Journal of Peace Research* 36, 1: 55–73.

Vanhanen, T. 1999b. *Ethnic Conflicts Explained by Ethnic Nepotism.* Research in Biopolitics. Vol. 7. Stamford, Connecticut: JAI Press.

Vanhanen, T. 2000. "The Economic Development and Poverty in South Asia in Comparative Perspective." Paper presented at the 16th European Conference on Modern South Asian Studies, Edinburgh, September 6-9, 2000.

Vejleskov, H. 1968. An analysis of Raven Matrix responses in fifth grade children. *Scandinavian Journal of Psychology,* 9: 177–186.

Vernon, P.A. 1987. *Speed of Information Processing and Intelligence.* Norwood, NJ: Ablex.

Vernon, P. E. 1969. *Intelligence and Cultural Environment.* London: Methuen.

Villar, J., and J. M. Belizan. 1982. The relative contribution of prematurity and fetal growth retardation to low birth weight in developing and developed societies. *American Journal of Obstetrics and Gynecology,* 143: 793–798.

Waller, J. H. 1971. Achievement and social mobility: Relationships among IQ score, education and occupation in two generations. *Social Biology,* 18: 252–259.

Wallerstein, I. 1975. "The Present State of the Debate on World Inequality." In M. A. Seligson and J. T. Passé-Smith (Eds.), *Development & Underdevelopment: The Political Economy of Inequality,* 1993. Boulder and London: Lynne Rienner Publishers.

Wallerstein, I. 1979. "The Rise and Future Demise of the World Capitalist System: Concepts for Comparative Analysis." 1979. In T. Roberts and A. Hite (Eds.), *From Modernization to Globalization.* 2000. Malden, MA: Blackwell Publishers.

Waterlow, J. C. 1992. *Protein-energy malnutrition.* London: Edward Arnold.

Weber, M. 1930. *The Protestant Ethic and the Spirit of Capitalism,* 1904. Translated by Talcott Parsons. 10th impression, 1970. London: Unwin University Books.

Weede, E. 1998. "Why People Stay Poor Elsewhere." In M. A. Seligson and J. T. Passé-Smith (Eds.), *Development and Underdevelopment: The Political Economy of Global Inequality.* Boulder and London: Lynne Rienner Publishers.

White, K. R. 1982. The relation between socioeconomic status and academic achievement. *Psychological Bulletin,* 91,: 461–481.

Wilson, J. Q., and R. J. Herrnstein. 1985. *Crime and Human Nature.* New York: Simon and Schuster.

Winkelmann, W. von. 1972. Normen fur den Mann-Zeichen-Test von Ziler und die Coloured Progressive Matrices von Raven fur 5-7 jahrige kinder. *Psychologische Beitrage,* 17: 80–94

Williams, W. M. 1998. "Are we raising smarter children today? School- and home-related influences on IQ." In U. Neisser (Ed.), *The Rising Curve.* Washington, D.C.: American Psychological Association.

Wober, M. 1969. The meaning and stability of Raven's matrices test among Africans. *International Journal of Psychology,* 4: 229–235.

World Bank. 1992. *Social Indicators of Development 1991–92.* Baltimore and London: The Johns Hopkins University Press.

World Bank. 1978–2001. *World Development Report.* New York: Oxford University Press.

World Development Report. See World Bank.

The World Guide 1999/2000: A View from the South. 1999. Oxford: New Internationalist Publications.

Yergin, D., and J. Stanislaw. 1999. *The Commanding Heights: The Battle Between Government and the Marketplace That Is Remaking the Modern World.* New York: Touchtone.

Yip, R., and P. R. Dallman, 1996. "Iron." In E. E. Zigler and L. J. Filer (Eds.), *Present Knowledge in Nutrition.* Washington, D.C.: ILSI press.

Yule, W., R. D. Gold, and C. Busch. 1982. Long-term predictive validity of the WPPSI: An 11 year follow-up study. *Personality and Individual Differences,* 3: 65–71.

Zahirnic, C., M. Girboveanu, A. Onofrei, A. Turcu, C. Voicu, M. Voicu, and O. M. Visan. 1974. Etolonarea matricelor progressive colorate Raven. *Revista de Psihologie,* 20: 313–321.

Zeidner, M. 1987. Test of the cultural bias hypothesis: some Israeli findings. *Journal of Applied Psychology,* 72: 38–48.

Zindi, F. 1994. Differences in psychometric performance. *The Psychologist,* 7: 549–552.

Index

ABOUT THE AUTHORS

RICHARD LYNN is Emeritus Professor of Psychology of the University of Ulster, Coleraine, Northern Ireland. He graduated in Psychology at the University of Cambridge and has held positions at the University of Exeter and the Economic and Social Research Institute, Dublin. Among his earlier books are *Dysgenics: Genetic Deterioration in Modern Populations* and *Eugenics: A Reassessment*.

TATU VANHANEN is Emeritus Professor of Political Science of the University of Tampere, Finland, and Emeritus Docent of Political Science of the University of Helsinki. He became Doctor of Social Sciences at the University of Tampere in 1968 and has held positions at the University of Jyväskylä, the University of Tampere and the University of Helsinki. Among his earlier books are *The Process of Democratization: A Comparative Study of 147 States, 1980–88* (1990), *On the Evolutionary Roots of Politics* (1992), *Prospects of Democracy: A Study of 172 Countries* (1997) and *Ethnic Conflicts Explained by Ethnic Nepotism* (1999).